Breaking Chains

Dennis Nickell & Diana Hershey-Nickell

authorHOUSE®

AuthorHouse™
1663 Liberty Drive
Bloomington, IN 47403
www.authorhouse.com
Phone: 1-800-839-8640

First published by AuthorHouse 2/22/2010

ISBN: 978-1-4140-5542-8 (e)
ISBN: 978-1-4140-5541-1 (sc)
ISBN: 978-1-4140-5540-4 (hc)

Library of Congress Control Number: 2004090198

Printed in the United States of America
Bloomington, Indiana

This book is printed on acid-free paper.

Dedication

WITH THANKS TO OUR Heavenly Father, His son Jesus Christ, the Messiah, and the gentle Holy Spirit , we dedicate Breaking Chains to our true earthly treasures, our children.

Isaac and Heather, you are a living revelation of the goodness of God. Seeing your children Evan, Micah and Natalie Joy, are a constant reminder of the kingdom's plan for families. It is a joy to have been given the privilege of being your earthly parents.

Isaiah and Heather and Brock , you all are the constant reminder of God's faithfulness to the third and fourth generation. To think that your Grandpa and Grandma Hershey's great-grandson, Brock was born in the home that I, your mother, grew up in, is overwhelming. To add to that sweetness, having Brock literally born on our thirtieth wedding anniversary, brings comfort and is a reminder constantly that there is no greater gift, than our children, and our childrens' children.

Israel and Jamael, you are the constant reminders of the true warrior's heart of God, and you both are a delight to our hearts. You challenge the spirit of religion with your example and life and we couldn't be prouder of both of you.

To Sarah, Mykayla, Jake, and Esther…and to all of our spiritual children, we couldn't love you more. The special place that you have in our hearts is eternal and second to none.

Micah, Isaac ,Heather, Natalie, Sarah, Dorothy, Diana,
Jamael, Israel, Dennis, Heather, and Esther

Evan, Denny, Mykayla *Brock, Isaiah, and Jake*

We also dedicate this book to
"Mamma Lori and our wonderful friend "Captain"

No earthly words would ever express our love and appreciation for your living example of what it means to be a follower of Jesus. We love you!

Contents

Foreword

"I read the entire book in one long night.
Great- Powerful- Wonderful."

"I can't see how anyone would not be deeply moved.
Thanks for impacting my life."

"One's walk in life with God is not the absence of struggle.
It's not where everything works out as we may desire.
Just look at the life of such people as Abraham, Isaac, Jacob,
Joseph, Moses, Gideon, Elijah, Job, David, Isaiah, Daniel, Peter
Mary, Paul, John and etc.…even Dennis and Diana Nickell!"

"Life in the way of God following Jesus is;
"I will be with you always", "I am the way, the truth, the life",
"Follow Me", said Jesus. As I have found in my life,
Jesus is enough; all sufficient, unchanging!"

"This book is about life, real people following Jesus in today's world.

This is real adventure as one moment you laugh, the next
you weep, the next life's difficulties seem impossible,
then all works out in glory."

"These are two people you will grow to feel close to.
The end, the book is not the end-
They still go on with their Lord today."

"Be blessed! Read it! Give it to someone else."

-Arthur Blessitt

Acknowledgements

THANK YOU FAMILY AND friends. Mothers and Fathers, sisters and brothers, we are so grateful for each one of you in our lives.

You loved us as we grew, stuck by us when times were rough, and believed in us when we didn't believe in ourselves. There are so many good people who patiently prayed and loved us no matter where we were in life and still do. Thank you!

Our dearest friend Trish, we thank you for investing so much of yourself into our lives. Our whole family reflects the beauty of knowing you.

Mamma Jackie, we love you! Memories of you handing our sons a special cupcake, or roast, when we were destitute, are etched forever on and in our hearts.

Bob and Judy, Chon, and Mary, you helped us to believe this true story needed to be shared and we are grateful.

Our life has been filled with touches from so many people who chose to be Gods hands extended to us, it would take a whole new book to tell every deed and name every name. Know that your heavenly Father has a book of life of all the great deeds done for eternal purposes, and we know He who catches every tear, has recorded your kindness to us.

You all know who you are, and we are eternally grateful. God Bless you.

Dennis Lane at 5 years old

Chapter 1

In the Beginning

THE LOVE, THE PEACE, and the joy that floods my spirit and soul have not always been there. Born fifth of seven children to Jack and Maurine Nickell, I could never have imagined the road ahead.

When I was 5 years old Mama herded all 7 of us kids onto a dusty old greyhound bus that belched its fumes all the way from Seattle, Washington to Fresno, California. Dad had gone ahead of us and found a job at Sears.

When we arrived in Fresno, Sandy, a lady I barely remember took in our whole family of nine until the day we moved to the projects. Now that I have three sons, I know how special Sandy was.

The start of grammar school was uneventful. I did not consider our family poor, but I do remember having refried oatmeal for more than one meal. In school and out I loved to run which was helped by my closest brother Pat's love of chasing me. The fact that I called him names until he was provoked may have had something to do with it.

We lived two miles from the closest community swimming pool. On those blistery-hot summer days we would run and jump from grass patch to grass patch over burning asphalt to keep from burning our feet to get there. We would collect empty coke bottles to sell in order to pay our way in.

One of the family's favorite outings was when all nine of us would pile into Dad's black and gold Nash Rambler station wagon and head to the airport. The ride was filled with anticipation, each of us trying to spot the first plane to come into view.

The whine and vibrations of the engines as those big birds took off and landed right over our heads was truly thrilling.

On our excursions in the car, Mama had a unique way of keeping control of seven children even though she was in the front seat. Her method was a much-feared "fly-swatter" which would deliver a sting that would quiet any kid. It kept her from constantly screaming at us too. Dad, on the other hand...in frustration, was liable to throw his sandwich or anything else he could get his hands on, out the window.

Dad worked real hard six days a week in sales and rarely got time off. When he did, he managed to take me fishing. I believe those were the closest times my father and I ever had.

When I was in third grade, dad brought home the news that we would be moving. Although mom and dad had to be happy, we were sorry to leave many friends behind. Soon, however we had enough friends to play street football at the new home.

Behind our house in Tarpy Village was a big vacant lot. It was dirt, with plenty of weeds and potholes. The lot was a perfect baseball field, which we dubbed "Nickell Stadium." A small plywood scoreboard nailed to a fence, in full view of passers-by, proudly proclaimed the name.

Mama meanwhile worked full-time at Woolworth's trying to help support a large family. Although a necessity, it left plenty of free time for me to get into everything and anything I could.

Christmas 1955

Chapter 2

The Purple Flash

ONE OF MY NEW friends was Danny Hughes. I met Danny while going steady with his little sister Elaine. Danny was a year older than me. He had a get-a-way in the family garage, which had been partially converted to a room. One day I heard my name being called. "Dennis, come over here."

"No!" said Elaine, "He just wants you to try those awful cigarettes."

If I'd only listened! What seemed like a boyhood prank led to 24 years of being hooked. Not only that, but the beginning of a friendship which would end up in some dangerous places. One boring afternoon Danny and I decided that we needed a raft of some sort to ride down the canal behind his house. Danny's dad helped us tar some big dresser drawers so they would not leak. With the raft, plenty of cigarettes and some "Playboys," dug up from somewhere, we had our answer as to how to spend the rest of the day.

With the aid of my brother Pat, stealing candy and cartons of cigarettes became a favorite pastime of mine. The game was to see who could get the most at one time. One day Pat and I were at our favorite store when the owner caught Pat with a carton of cigarettes. Thank God, I hadn't shoved any candy bars down my pants yet! Mumbling something about "See Ya at home," I split. We thought the police had been called, but mercifully the store's owner just called Mom and left the punishment to the folks. When

I got home that night all Mom said was, "Hit the bedroom." Boy, were Pat and I scared!

When Dad got home we heard him bellow: "Pat, come here!" I thought for sure I was in for it, but was tremendously relieved when all I got was a lecture. After the big talk, Pat and I left the local grocery stores alone.

"The Purple Flash" was the name of Danny's '49 Studebaker. It was the weapon used to terrorize the Clovis Police Department.

"Go, Danny go!" I shouted excitedly, as we raced down the canal banks throwing dust in the faces of patrol cars. High bumps caused the back seat, where I was hiding, to fly up and slam me on the floorboard. It would have hurt had I not been laughing so hard. The favorite get-away was to race up a street, slide around a corner and ditch into any open garage. Our hearts pounding in our chests, we would jump out, slam down the garage door and walk to the nearest pool hall to shoot pool. It amazed us that we never got caught by any homeowners or police. Even more amazing was the way Danny's dad kept him in old clunkers while he was in seventh grade.

After a long hot summer, Junior High School reared its ugly head. At the time, I had pictured it much worse than it really was. My fears were a combination of the fact that I was slight in frame (Okay...downright little) and I was terrified of being rejected by the crowd. Prepared for the worst, I began this new experience with attire that would please any girl of those days. My Levi's were so tight I was glad I had a skinny comb. The T-shirt I wore was decorated by a pack of "ciggies" neatly rolled up in one sleeve. To top it off, my hair sported the biggest pompadour you ever saw, complete with handfuls of pomade smeared through it.

Thinking back it seems almost funny to think that my new favorite pastime was fighting. It hardly makes sense to spend two hours fixing your hair, if you're only going to get messed up going to and from school.

Yep, fighting was it for me; my ticket to success, and Wayne, a new guy I met at school, became my best friend because Danny didn't share my love of violence.

I soon discovered dances were held every Wednesday night at Einstein Park and this turned out to be an opportune time to mingle with the wrong crowd. What started out as one-to-one challenges, ended up gangs from different junior high schools, who would come equipped with every weapon from baseball bats to chains. Now, I know what was going on, but at the time it seemed like anywhere or anytime violence was happening, I was in the middle of it. Usually, I was the first one in.

"Hey, Dennis! Meet me over at Cedar Lanes," Wayne would say. Cedar Lanes was a bowling alley, which was the local hangout for Hells Angels. The attraction for the bikers was the pool tables there. Being young, we were intrigued by these tough-looking guys with their chopped bikes. Wayne and I started hanging out around them and soon they took a liking to us. I remember there was a jukebox in there, one of the big old-fashioned ones and they would play their favorite songs. I would jump on top of the pool table and dance with one of their "mamas." These big old guys would down their beer and laugh away. They liked that I was so cocky even though I was so small. Grasshopper was the Hells Angel that took me under his wing. He was the president of the Fresno Chapter of the Hells Angles, but one day he disappeared—he went to the joint, No one told me what for, and I don't remember ever asking why.

When the Hells Angels weren't in, we would either bowl free or eat free. It was like a Peter Seller's movie. Wayne and I would scope out the booths and see who was eating what. As soon as people left a table, with leftovers to our liking, we would run and duck under it. From there, our hands could sneak up over the table edge, before the waitress could get there, and yank the steak or hamburger down to where we were hiding. Not exactly suave, but it did serve the purpose when we didn't have money for food.

Although I had many girlfriends in grammar school, junior high brought a girlfriend that truly won my heart. Robin was blonde, blue-eyed, and looked every bit like a Barbie doll to me. I gallantly fought another boy named Steve for fair Robin's hand and won. As the huge crowd that had congregated watched, she took my hand and we headed towards her home. "Wait up," said Steve who had lost the fight. "What do you want?" I answered. "Can't I just walk with you and Robin one last time? Please?"

Being the nice guy at heart, I said, "Okay, but only if you walk behind us." I felt bad, as he cried the whole way.

Little Anthony singing "Tears On My Pillow" was the backdrop for Friday night skating. Wonderland was the name of the rink and after skating until 10:00, the real fun, and the sock-hop began. Rows of Beatle boots, penny loafers and big-heeled shoes lined the walls. On more than one occasion when you asked a friend to watch your shoes, he'd get star struck, go dancing, and when you got back-your shoes were gone!

I had naturally jet-black hair and wanted half of it to come out blonde. I went over to Danny's house and had his sister peroxide half of my hair. I'll show them, I thought. But, as Elaine rinsed out my hair I knew something was wrong. With a wet towel around my shoulders, I looked in the mirror. To my horror, one-half of my dripping hair was a vibrant tangerine orange. It was the brightest, ugliest thing I had ever seen. This was in the 60's. At school the very next day, my mechanical drawing teacher, who I really respected, walked up and said, "Nickell, that's the most asinine thing I have ever seen!" That day when I got home, out came the razor and off came all the hair, that made the biggest, finest pompadour at school. Now, bald-headed, I wore a beanie to school.

One weekend the whole crew, including the "fly-swatter," went for a ride. Forty-five miles later we drove into the small town of Visalia. Passing by Redwood High School, we older kids joked that there was no way we'd be caught dead going to a school like that. Past the school and on down the quaint little main street sat Sears. You guessed it! Dad got a job at the Visalia Sears and our world was turned upside down. A new town meant new friends, a new school and even more, having to build a whole new reputation.

Right away my brother Pat was singled out at school for the way he walked. His walk looked cocky; and since Pat didn't think so, more than one argument was had over the subject. With that walk, our reputation was on the line. Being the new kids from out of town didn't help much either. Right by the school was a hamburger joint called Gig's. Red and white striped, it looked more like an ice cream parlor. Pat and I went there for lunch one day and a kid named Raymond offered Pat a coke. Since Raymond was such a big kid, we figured why not? Well, he had the coke ready and it wasn't until Pat took a mouthful that he discovered the guy had peed in the cup. To make matters worse, a crowd had knowingly watched, then had a good laugh at Pat's expense.

The next day while walking past the Safeway, which was close to the school, Pat spotted good old Raymond! He calmly walked up to the parking lot and said, "Man, why did you pee in my coke?" Ray just laughed and Pat proceeded to deliver a good punch. Ten stitches in the mouth is what it took to repair it and this time, no one standing around was laughing. "Anyone else want some action?" I yelled. No one stepped out, but this was by no means the end of our troubles.

Known for its race riots, Redwood had plenty of violence between the Chicanos and the Whites. To follow suit, I found the weirdest, craziest guys I could hang out with. The challenging spot was a long cement wall with about 100 Chicanos that squatted while balancing on their ankles. The bravest honkies would walk closer and closer till a Chicano was finally bumped, or his shoes were accidentally stepped on, the fight would then be on. Girls shrieking, people running, canes flying through the air, you name it. Finally, due to the fact that weapons were getting nastier and nastier, plain-clothes policemen were brought in to bust those with dangerous weapons.

One time, Kenny Ray was minding his own business in crafts class, when a group of Chicanos sauntered in with baseball bats and chains. Crack! A bat came down on Kenny's head, leaving a huge knot, and the craft teacher jumped on the attacker's back, trying to tackle him. Instead, he ended up being piggybacked all over the room. This led to a counter- attack. Two hundred-or-so White's met at Foster's Freeze and cruised en-masse from there to the Oval. Armed with eggs, coke bottles, clubs and yes, guns, we were ready for action and all hell broke loose. From what I recall, two people were shot, and it would be useless to record all of the wounds suffered that night. A 1957 gunmetal gray Chevy was what I was riding in to lead the group, with the driver Danny. After the fighting, we talked to one of our guys who had been shot, and we swore to get the sucker. We never could, but the cops did.

Chapter 3

School Days

A DEEP MAROON 1964 CHEVY Impala S.S. was one of the rides I was seen around town in. My interests had expanded from violence and girls, to a love of low- riders. My friend Butch had a really cool older sister named Carol. She had some money, but no knowledge of cars so Butch and I picked out that Chevy Impala for her. She made us a deal that we could not refuse. "Butchie, if you and Dennis will keep this car waxed up and in shape, I'll let you use it when I'm not."

"Great!" was our reply. Carol had a steady who kept her busy every weekend, and we knew the car was ours for the weekend.

Around this time I picked up a dark black '56 Chevy. Before I bought it, it had been used for racing at Raisin City. With a 350 engine and three speeds on the floor, it was something else. With access to plenty of wheels now, I started spending my weekends up in Fresno, my old stomping grounds. There I met Vickie, who was the most beautiful girl I had ever seen. She could easily have been mistaken for a model, and she was also very sweet.

When I was dating Vickie, I was practicing yet another trade. I guess you could say that I had developed an interest in the automobile industry. Ronnie, a friend of mine from junior high, carried a chain, which held about every kind of car key imaginable on it. "What kind of car would you like to go cruising in tonight?" he would ask. My favorites were GTOs and Corvettes. This is not one of the things I got caught for, but I did get caught for others. I had been in and out of juvenile hall about five times already, so Dad was leery about any friends I would bring around. He really sensed something about Ronnie. One day while Ronnie was visiting, he called the police and had them run a check on him. Boy, was I surprised when they arrested him right there in our living room. He had felony warrants on him for stealing cars. At the time, I felt so betrayed by Dad, not to mention how Ronnie must have felt. Come to think of it, he pretty well verbalized how he felt on the way out the door.

The latter years of high school were pretty well spent ditching. Mr. Scott, the dean of boys, once told me that I had the all-time school record for truancy. My sister Penny (yes, mama actually name one daughter Penny Nickell) would write excuses. She wrote so many for me, that one day when I had a real note from mama the school sent me home and wouldn't accept it, because they thought it was forged.

One day I cussed out the art teacher and he was so furious, he literally ran all the way to the office to get the dean. Mr. Scott came to find me. With disgust, he looked at me and said "Nickell, why don't you go home and don't come back until you're ready."

"You gonna call my parents?" I asked.

"I won't even call your parents. Just do me a favor-go home and give me some peace."

So I did, for three weeks, but returned only to keep ditching. I hated school.

Dennis in 9th grade.

Chapter 4

Destinations?

MY SENIOR YEAR ONLY brought more pain. Butch and I were asleep in a little room built in the garage. Suddenly, my mother, who was almost crying, awakened us.

"I've taken your Dad to the hospital." I could tell that she was trying to fight back tears to be strong for me. "He seems to have had a heart attack. They told me there was nothing I could do, so go on home. If they have any news, they'll call."

At 17, I just laid there for a minute not realizing the seriousness of a heart attack. Dad had never had any heart trouble. Overweight, Dad enjoyed his beer and cigarettes, yet I had no idea that could bring on a heart attack. What I did sense was that Mom was trying to be very strong, and managed to hide the pure terror that she must have felt.

Butch and I sat up and comforted Mom, and at 6:00 a.m. the phone rang. A nurse from the hospital told mama to get down there fast. We grabbed my younger brother Billy and he, Mom and I raced down there. I was terrified, running red lights, while Mama screamed frantically at traffic.

When we got there, I must have sensed something, because I told Mom and Bill to go in, while I parked the car. Waiting a few minutes in the car, I got out and headed for the door. Halfway across the parking lot I was met by Mom who gave me the paralyzing news.

DAD WAS DEAD! He was GONE! I've never, before or since then, felt such pain. There are no words to express it.

Violence turned out to be my release for the pain. Running across the street from the hospital, I ran to a tree and just kept punching and punching it as hard as I could. Mom, always thinking about us kids, ran over and grabbed me to make me stop. Still trying to fight the tears, she said we would have to be strong for the rest of the kids. Jack, Sherry, Cathy and Pat were all either married or moved out, but little Penny and my baby brother Bill were still at home. Stunned, I can't remember the ride home, but the next few days were the worst in my life.

Memories of shining Dad's shoes as an anniversary present just the week before came to mind. It was the nicest thing I had done for him in a long time. We all went down to the funeral parlor at different times, and I must admit Dad looked peaceful. To me the whole thing was like a dream. I'm sure I was in some kind of shock as was the rest of my family. The funeral was a final crushing blow to my heart, leaving scars to this day.

I graduated, if you could call it that, in 1968. I didn't give two hoots about the ceremony and three weeks before the big day, I went to see Mr. Scott. "Do I have enough credits to graduate?" I asked.

"Just enough," said Mr. Scott.

"Well, why not let me have my certificate now?" I asked.

"All right. Good luck in life." He said almost relieved to get rid of me.

I finished school three weeks early. I have the sneaking suspicion that Mr. Scott celebrated that night. Oh, he liked me enough, he just didn't agree with the way I did things…or perhaps didn't do things.

After working at the local car wash with Butch part of the summer, we decided to join the Army. A friend of mine had been killed in Vietnam and I was going to make somebody pay. The two-year buddy program was what the recruiter signed us up for. Talk about Naive! The possibility that we actually had a chance of being in a war never entered our brains.

The easiest part of joining the Army was the paperwork. Getting there was another story. The night before I was to report, I was arrested and thrown in jail for public intoxication and disturbing the peace. The next morning my mother, as only mothers can, marched into the Sheriff's Office and demanded my release. "You let Dennis Nickell out of this jail!"

"What was that, lady?" the receptionist said in disbelief.

"You heard me," Mama stated. "My son enlisted and is now the property of the United States Army and you have to let him out."

After phoning the Fresno recruiting office they verified that what my mom said was true. I was released. Freed. I was told later that the Army had said let him out now or we'll come and get him. Poor Mom, she thought I looked so bad she asked me if the cops had worked me over.

"Oh, son, did they hurt you?"

Laughing, I replied "No, Mom. Let's go."

One thing about Mama, even though her kids were far from perfect, she had a killer instinct when it came to protecting one of her brood.

Boot camp was at Fort Ord, California. The system was pretty easy for Butch and me to figure out. DI's or drill sergeants meant business. All you had to do was follow directions. For such a little word, "**ALL**" carries a very big meaning. I was terrible at following directions and never did what anyone told me. God must have known and hand picked Butch to help me. I decided to do whatever Butch did and follow any directions he gave me. It was much nicer learning from Butch; and everything worked out fine.

Two months later we headed for Fort Sill, Oklahoma. A traveler would have thought how "adventuresome." In truth, it turned out to be the coldest place I'd ever been. The thermometer read around twenty degrees below zero at times; and if you were familiar with Army training exercises, you would know it was not fun. One night I was supposed to be standing guard duty. It was so cold I crawled in to the rim of a five-ton truck and fell asleep. The officer of the day drove up and caught me sleeping, which was really a Godsend, as I would have frozen to death. After a minor slap on the wrist, I was informed that had I been in Vietnam at the time, more than likely my throat would have been cut.

By the middle of February my advanced infantry training, as it was called, was over. To tell the truth, I had about enough of playing "Army." Butch got his orders and luckily they said Korea. I thought for sure that I would follow him. Well, my orders were delayed; and I'll never forget saying goodbye to my best buddy. Watching the taxi drive off until it was out of sight, I felt painfully alone. Butch was always there when I needed him. Everything inside of me yelled "Go AWOL!" Some-how I managed to hang in there a couple more weeks.

Then with trembling hands, I opened my letter, with those all-important orders inside. Destination- **Vietnam**! Now I definitely knew I was through playing "Army." At 18 years young my sites were laid on the next good party, not a war. Off I went totally ignoring all my responsibilities and headed for home.

While I was at Fort Sill, Oklahoma, I received a letter from my mom saying she had remarried. The lucky fellow was Dad's best friend, Gene Brown. He and his wife Betty had been pals with Mom and Dad for years. Shortly after Dad died, Betty was struck with leukemia and within two days was dead. Out of their horrible loss, Mom and Gene comforted one another, and out of that led a relationship that led to marriage. Knowing that Mom must be tired of the loneliness, I more than heartily approved.

I continued down my reckless path, but soon ran out of time and money. One Sunday afternoon at a family get together my step dad Gene called me aside. Gene was a veteran of WWII and though not in love with war, was concerned that I should want to defend my country. By now we were officially at war with Vietnam. Respecting Gene, who had always been like an uncle to me, I did some thinking. Deep down I knew I must go. Soon after that I said my good-byes.

Several family members and I took the drive up to Oakland. Joking and laughing the whole way, I fought back a rising uneasiness. When we got there I unloaded my duffel bag and waving, watched everyone drive off. All of a sudden, a crippling fear grabbed hold of me. I didn't know one single person there. Butch was long gone to

Korea and friends and relatives were safely headed home. For the first time in my life I was totally alone, not only alone but headed for war.

Lying around Oakland for a week gave me plenty of free time to consider going AWOL again. Things got a little better after I met a few guys. Then my name was called. As the plane lifted off, my thoughts returned to the days when I watched the big DC10's take off as a child. This time it was far from thrilling and had I known what lay ahead I don't know if I would have gone. The plane ride was thirteen hours long with stops in Hawaii and Guam.

What a difference your destination makes! Eyeing the clear blue water around Hawaii, I didn't feel much like the travel brochures always said you would

Chapter 5

Vietnam

I ARRIVED IN BEN HOA on the 27th of March 1970. Stepping off the plane, the heat was so intense I could hardly draw in a breath. The next of my senses to be attacked was my sense of smell. Only someone who has been there can truly appreciate it. The Vietnamese burned all their garbage, including human waste. I thought I would vomit from the stench. With the smell of burnt sewage burning my nose and heat I could barely move in, I hardly believed what my eyes were seeing. The "grunts", as they were called, looked like absolute maniacs. The name applied to infantry and others who had been in the bush. Stunned, my ears picked up chants from the Vets who were headed home.

"Hey, Cherry Boys," they yelled, picking us out by our brand new fatigues. "You left your mama at home! You better say awake over here or you won't see your mama ever again."

Still wishing I were in a dream, I continued to scan the grunts around me. These guys had machine gun rounds draped around their necks as if they were necklaces and jungle hats of all different shapes and sizes, with hand grenades clipped to the front of their shirts. To top if off, some had adopted live jungle monkeys that leered from their shoulders and others had opted to drape themselves with giant pythons, real 15 foot long **PYTHONS**! Waiting for my orders from this holding place, stories of the GIs who hadn't made it rang in my ears.

My third day in-country, a brand-new GI was pulling guard duty. He was smoking a cigarette when a sniper, who had focused on the glow, shot him. At the time I smoked, but for the rest of my active duty, I never openly smoked after dark. I now knew this place was for real and played for keeps. I served with artillery units and airmobile units for the Ninth and Twenty-fifth Infantry, First Cav and the First of the 82nd infantry.

Sometimes, we would convoy into the jungles and at other times we were dropped in by helicopter. I spent all but my last 40 days in the bush. I still believe that those who did more than sit in a base camp are usually the last to share war stories.

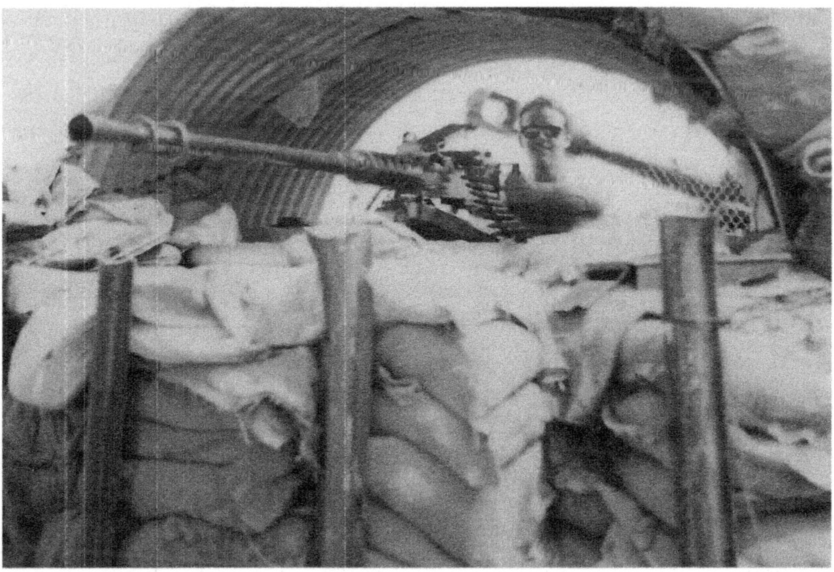

Dennis in Vietnam

During this time, I became really close to several "soul brothers" who were of the Black Panther persuasion. When I first met them, I wondered why I had gotten the meanest tattoo I could find, put on my arm, for the whole world to see while in high school. It is a huge Black Panther's head, with a dagger stuck in it with blood dripping down its face! Wonderful! Strangely, no one ever commented on it.

Yes, I had close calls, including two that I know God spared my life. Every day being blanketed with fear, we all looked for ways to escape. For many, drugs were the way. Scag (Liquid Heroin), Liquid Speed, Opium Joints, and Cambodian Red, to name a few, were readily available. Equipped with my own pipe and a candy dish full of weed I stayed loaded most of the time. Even a full bird Colonial smoked dope with us and everyone tried to cope with being in hell any way they could find.

One of the most talked about subjects among the men were the two planes. Every day both of these big birds would slowly fly over. One was the “FREEDOM-BIRD!” headed for home with GIs aboard. They all fervently prayed to make it past the border without getting shot down. The other was the big “BLACK-DEATH” plane, a sober reminder that there were no guarantees of tomorrow. No matter what we were doing, we always seemed to notice when one or the other flew over. Finally, I ended up going home, leaving from Cam Rhan Bay. Remembering my first day there, I walked over to a new recruit, but instead of calling him names I said to him, “Good-luck and stay alert. This place is for real. If you pay attention and stay awake at night you’ll make it.” I wonder sometimes if that young man was as fortunate as me.

As we were landing in Fort Lewis, Washington I cannot remember being more excited. It was the moment that I had dreamt about for fourteen long months. I’d really made it through alive! Little did I know the price to be paid for going to Vietnam was far from over.

Oh, God! I don’t think I’ve ever smelled such fresh, clean, beautiful air, before or since. Yes-you’d better believe it-we kissed that American soil before we walked on it.

An immediate briefing was held on our arrival explaining the discharge procedures. Some GIs still had active duty left but since I had chosen to do extra time in Vietnam, I was getting out for good! The first thing I did was call Mom.

“Oh, Dennis! Where are you?” she cried into the receiver.

“I made it! I made it!” I’ll need to be picked up at the airport in two days.”

On the plane ride to Fresno a lot went through my mind; and I remember being very nervous. Worrying about the way I looked, I thought back to high school when I had a flawless complexion. Now, my face was solid acne! There was a time in Cambodia when we had gone without showers or even water to wash up with for over three months. The combination of red clay, mosquito repellent and sweat from the climate had ground into my pores and left its mark. The other main change in my appearance was skinniness, due to all the drugs and bad diet. As my pride was suffering, I wasted no time in getting bombed on the plane.

As the plane taxied slowly up the airstrip, I saw 15 to 20 of my friends and my family anxiously waiting. Peering through the window I decided to play a little trick on them. Waiting while all the other passengers got off, I continued to peek at my family. Pretty soon they all looked panic-stricken. With the stage set, I made my grand entrance popping out the door. My oldest brother, Jack, spotted me and let out a whoop! Yelling, we ran to each other and loving relatives mobbed me. It was great seeing everybody. Downing a handful of whites, the post war celebration began.

Debbie, a girl I had dated from high school, was the one I had been writing to from Vietnam. She'd gotten pregnant by someone else while I was away; but convinced me that he was long gone. I was so hurt, but figured she was entitled to one mistake; so, I called her and met her at a party. The party went on for several days, but when the excitement wore off, things were just not the same.

Chapter 6

Hopeless to Helpless

WITH SOME MONEY IN hand, which I had saved from Vietnam, my efforts were concentrated on finding a car and a place to live. Visiting Danny one day (remember Danny?) I saw this beautiful low-rider Lincoln Continental. It was solid white, had spoke wheels and the interior was powder-puff blue. Paying Danny only $700 for it, I thought I had the ultimate low-rider. The only drawback was the low 12 miles to the gallon it got. Well, that took care of my car situation; now I just needed a place to live.

One day my brother-in-law, Johnny, mentioned his two other brothers had an apartment together. Their names were Rick and Garland; and hitting it off, I soon moved in. After a while, Garland needed a little more space so he moved out. I quickly learned that Rick was into drugs just as much as me. In no time at all we were both strung out on uppers.

At the time, I figured we were both saving money on the grocery bill. Neither of us had a job so we started selling drugs to support our habits.

In 1971 there were a lot of suicides connected to LSD, so the next adventure in drugs was to try that. In Vietnam I had become addicted to weed, heroin, uppers and downers. After coming home nothing seemed to help the fear I carried. Trying these new drugs, from Mescaline to paper acid, to peyote buttons to purple microdot, I thought I had found some relief. My brother, Jack, was studying about drugs at Fresno State and came by several times to warn us about the dangers.

Rick and I laughed and invited him to take some. We wanted him to know it really felt like heaven not hell. We even rounded up coke bottles to buy the stuff.

One night, I blew it bad! Really bad! Rick and I took a lot of whites and decided to drop some acid too. One minute we were walking down Blackstone Street tripping out on the lights, skipping along like you do when you are on an acid trip. Coming to our street, we took off running as fast as we could. When we came to a stop, I got a rush that I thought would blow my head clear off the top of my shoulders. It was like when you get really startled, and then magnify that feeling of fear about a million times.

"What's wrong?" Rick asked. I screamed something about losing my head and freaking out. This magnified fear stayed with me not only the next day, but for years to come. Every day it got worse instead of better.

Now I understand why people would jump out of windows on acid. All the talk about drug-related suicides kept running through my head. A couple of days later, I decided to go to the Veterans Hospital for help. When I got there, I received a barrage of questions, which reeked of a third degree. There seemed to be little concern or help.

Pumping me full of Thorazine, I was admitted to the psychiatric floor. This was the 7th floor, referred to as the "Nut Ward" by staff and patients alike. The therapy they started me on consisted of a steady diet of 75mg of Librium a day. Physically, I was prodded from stem to stern and even electric shock was considered. After a one-week observation period, a panel of approximately 15 psychiatrists and psychologists reviewed my case. They decided I was dangerous and crazy and prepared to ship me off to a mental institution for the criminally insane.

They pegged my problems on Vietnam. Let me tell you, I was really freaked out. I now had a clinical diagnosis of paranoid schizophrenia and a destination of some booby hatch in Palo Alto.

When I realized what was happening, I planned and carried out "The Great Escape!" At the time it wasn't funny, but now I have to laugh as I recall that time. Dressed in my little, green hospital pajamas with little matching green slippers; I made a mad dash to the elevator. The long 7-floor descent remained uneventful. With all the composure I could muster, I strode past the opening elevator doors as if I was a doctor or something. Marching past the admissions desk and out into the bright sunlight, my eyes darted back and forth to make sure I wasn't being followed. My heart racing, I walked 5 miles across town, to my friend Jake's house, yep, 5 miles across town in my pajamas.

Rick was at Jake's and was concerned about where I was going to go. As the hospital hadn't helped, I started in drinking. The conversation turned to whose fault the whole thing was; and I started blaming Rick. Angrily, I started throwing anything I could at Rick. A glass that I had just broken made good ammo for Jake's wall.

Next, I tried to punch Rick, but he knew I was drunk, and didn't want anything to do with it. Running outside, I found a defenseless bush and beat it with my fists, while I cried my head off in shear frustration at the fear that would not leave me.

The hospital's treatment of Librium and Valium replaced street drugs, but since I left I needed a pain reliever of some kind. It didn't take me long to find out that booze was the answer (I thought). Man, the alcohol just made me more wild and violent than ever before. I was a walking time bomb.

One time, a guy kicked a friend's car. I carried a 45 under my seat, and my friend had a rifle. We drove to this guy's house. Lights were on inside the house and we just started shooting up this guy's car. We didn't stop there though; and we blew the heck out of his house, never thinking about what we were actually doing.

Bar fights continued for over ten years. Barbiturates (reds), along with the booze, helped to fight my fear. But it was never gone. I made some return visits to the Veterans Hospital through the years, but never could find help.

One time I had a broken hand with shattered knuckles. I told the doctor I had hit a wall, he looked me right in the eye and said,

" Someone's jaw, you mean." Another time I went in with a big human bite on my chest. I told the Doc that a dog had bit me and he said, "Nice try, but that's a human bite, and it's worse than a dog's bite. You might have died if you hadn't come in."

One bar fight stands out in particular. It was when I challenged some huge maniac, while I was on Reds. "Shoot me!" I shouted in his face. So he whipped out his gun and started firing. To this day, the wall behind where I crawled has 5 or 6 bullet holes; and I couldn't understand how he had missed.

By now I was a jobless drug and alcohol addict, full of violence and not very welcome at most my relative's homes for more than a quick meal. Living in my car, I was such a wreck. I had absolutely no interest in anything---not even girls or parties. I was possessed with fighting the fear that gripped me. Since booze was my answer, it became the most important thing in my life!

Chapter 7

Obsessed, Then Possessed

GETTING MONEY TO BUY booze was my motivation for starting college with VA funds. I stayed with Mom and Gene in Merced for about a year while going to school. Thank God for their help and understanding. They lived only a half a mile from the closest bar, which was attached to a bowling ally. One night I was down there drinking and closed it down. On my way home I ended upside down in an empty canal two miles in the opposite direction from Moms'. I was really lucky to find my way home the next day, as I was out in the middle of the country.

My Mom and my step-dad, "Pop", moved up near Redding, California because he had been transferred. They moved to a mobile home park right on the Sacramento River, in a small town called Anderson. Since they had a big beautiful mobile home, they invited me along. They could see that I was totally irresponsible and they wanted so very badly to help.

Work was not easy to find. I applied at every business, answered every newspaper ad, and when I finally got a shot at a cook's job, they told me I was over-qualified. Discouraged, I helped myself to Mom's Librium that she kept on hand since my father's death. Little did she know that a couple of days before, I had literally held a 22 pistol to my forehead. Right as I was ready to pull the trigger, I was interrupted by Mom and Genes' early return from fishing.

Mom was very concerned about me as she suspected that I was downright suicidal. An appointment was made with a shrink, and as usual I was very nervous.

"Is there some reason that you haven't taken off those black sunglasses?" He asked as I walked in.

"I never take my glasses off, unless I'm sleeping," I told him.

I sat down and spilled my guts about the acid trip, the years of violence, etc. He assured me that the acid had left my body within two days after I took it. He told me that the fear attacks and constant paranoia was all in my head! No kidding! That didn't help a whole lot, as I already knew that. He ended up prescribing a generic equivalent to Valium and sent me on my way.

Depression grew heavier and heavier, so I decided to move back to Fresno to good old Danny's house. By now, this being years later, Danny had become an alcoholic, like me. At 17, Danny had lost his brand-new wife in a car crash. Headed for Bass Lake, they had a head-on collision and his wife was thrown from the car. She died in Danny's arms, leaving him with a 6-month-old daughter. Later, Danny turned his daughter over to his in-laws to raise.

Danny learned the plastering trade from his father. Whenever Dan needed help, his father was always there. Danny was living with him when I hit town and his dad invited me to stay with them. I hoped that I could go to work with them when they needed an extra hand.

Ironically, Dan's Dad was very active working with Alcoholics Anonymous in Fresno. Often he would let men who were trying to "dry out" stay with him until they got themselves together.

At one point in time, work came to a total halt. We ran an ad in the paper and for three weeks, no one called. From the time we woke up in the morning to the time we went to sleep, we drank straight Vodka. We would lie in the back yard drunk, and get up only to stumble to the store to buy some more. After three solid weeks of that I not only had alcohol poisoning, but we ran out of booze and money. Danny and I soon got on each other's nerves.

Doug, another childhood friend, dropped by Dan's and wanted me to go to Bass Lake with him. Doug had the money for booze, so off I went. We hitchhiked up there; and at the local store, right down from the Pines Bar; we bought ourselves a gallon of wine.

It was the 4th of July weekend and the bar right next to where we were sitting was full of Hells Angels. Doug and I finished our gallon of wine and headed to the bar for more. We walked right in and sat down in the middle of all those bikers and started ordering straight shots of Tequila. I minded my own business, but they threw Doug out on his ear. Doug went to jail after being chased by the Sheriff and some how I made it down the mountain alive. Once again, I headed for the town of Visalia and ended up at my sister Penny's house. Little Sis was in the middle of a painful separation, so I thought she didn't really mind me staying there.

Chapter 8

New Beginnings

I LANDED A JOB AT the Chinowith House, but my problem with the fear was still there. I remember I used to go to work drunk. My daily routine was to wake up, take some Valium or Librium, down two quarts of beer and then I was ready to deal with work. When I got to work at mid-day, I would hide a bottle of Vodka by a certain tree. As the night wore on and the pressures of work got to me, I would slip outside for a nip.

My brother, Pat, was a bartender at the Depot and I would often go down there by myself and drink as long as he would keep pouring. One fateful night I sat drinking alone at the darkened end of the bar. I remember this very bubbly, kind of loud, little cocktail waitress that kept catching my attention. She was a cute, sexy little thing, with hardly anything on, because of the outfits they were supposed to wear.

Yes, she caught my attention, but I hated women because they had really burned me.

She came bouncing my way and said, "Hi there!" I just stared straight ahead and ignored her.

"Your loss!" she said and bounced off.

My brother said, "What do you think of that little chick?"

Playing the role, I said, "Oh, she's all right. A little dingy though.

Later that same night I was headed for Tulare, a little town 8 miles away.

" Pat, call that little chick over here."

He did. Pat introduced us and after talking a few minutes I asked her for a ride to Tulare.

She shocked me by saying, "Sure, but we'll have to stop by my Mother's first so I can change."

When we got to her Mother's, the first thing she did to win my heart, or should I say craving, was to pour me a glass of wine. Then, on a beautiful stereo, she blasted my favorite group, "The Temptations!" Her parents were out of town so we stayed there that night. We saw each other everyday after that, usually down at the Depot. Her name was Diana, and she made a valiant effort to keep up with my drinking.

One night against my brother Pats' wishes, I started drinking Tequila, which usually made me crazy. "Fine!" said Diana and at that, downed straight shots of Tequila with beer backs, one for one with me.

Diana held her own until she stepped out the back door. I mean, the cold air hit her and she did the classic fall, straight back into the flowerbed. I picked her up and headed for her Mother's house, where I had been allowed to stay on the couch downstairs the night before. She sobered up enough on the way home to invite me up to her room

I said, "Are you crazy lady?"

"Oh, no," she assured me. "My mother sleeps across the hall and it's perfectly all right."

Well, with the life I had led before, I had met some pretty weird moms, so what the heck? Drunk from Tequila, we got undressed and passed out. The next thing I remember was staring into the face of a flashlight and a man's voice ordering me to get up and get dressed. Yelling at Diana to cover up I said, "What do you guys want?"

The two huge policemen standing over the bed politely said, "This young lady's Mother has called us and you have to leave immediately." To say that I was embarrassed would be an understatement, but my shyness was overshadowed by my anger. I was furious. The next day, when Diana called good old Kenny Ray answered the phone.

KR was a high school buddy of mine, whom I started hanging around with. He had literally fried himself on an acid trip, but was the nicest guy you'd ever want to meet. He came over to Penny's every day and we would listen to oldies but goodies and drink anything we could get our hands on. I asked Kenny who it was.

"It's Diana."

"Tell that broad to go jump in a lake," I said.

"I can't Dennis; she's crying man. I mean she's beggin." After Kenny kept bugging me, I went to the phone. I was determined to never see her again, but when I heard her crying, my heart softened.

"Come on over," I offered, as she told me that she had been kicked out and had told her Mom off. By that night she ran into an old friend named Uncle Al, who offered to let her stay at his house. Without missing a day, we continued dating and spent every spare minute with each other.

After about three weeks I decided to call things off. Walking out the back door of the restaurant I said, "There's something I've got to tell you."

"What?" she said smiling back at me.

"I can't see you any more."

"What?" she screeched. "Why not?"

"It's not going to work because I'm really... really starting to like you and if I get burned by one more girl, I'm liable to kill somebody."

Not even batting an eye, she replied, "Is that all?" Are you nuts? You don't have to worry about me leaving you. You probably couldn't get rid of me."

"I'm dead serious," I shouted.

"SO AM I!" she said right back in my face.

No one had ever got in my face before. *She's just as crazy as I am*, I remember thinking. So issue settled, we continued to spend every moment together that we could.

Chapter 9

In Jesus Name

DIANA'S PARENTS HAD LEFT for a week to Hawaii and by now she was on speaking terms with them. I believe now that her mom calling the cops was well within reason and that after reconciling, her mother even joked about it. "What a funny story to tell the grandkids someday, if you end up together."

Totally against house rules, Diana invited me to stay there for a week this time. From the day we met I cannot remember spending one day or night apart; and we desperately clung to each other. My wife shares the following part of my story, to you; and after reading it you'll know why.

Dennis was still drinking beer pretty early in the day as a rule to calm his nerves; but I had talked him out of needing Librium on a daily basis. One sunny August morning I had no idea what was about to occur. The birds were singing a little tune out the dining room window and it promised to be another hot summer day. Looking out over the pool in the back yard the wonderful aroma of freshly cooking bacon seemed to promise a great day.

Returning to the stove to finish making breakfast, I and was totally shocked when Dennis said, "Go get me a bottle of Vodka." He laughed like it was no big thing and laughing back; I said "No way! You don't need that this early in the morning."

Dennis laughed again and said, "Oh, come on. I won't drink it till tonight."

"Good," I replied. "I'll get you some tonight then!"

This was totally blowing my mind, because he had appeared to be doing much better. Dennis was stone sober. He hadn't had Librium for around a week and nothing to drink since dinner the night before.

"No, Dennis" I kept saying.

I was honestly getting worried. I loved this guy and I started realizing he really had a problem. As I refused to go buy Vodka, even though he kept laughing, I sensed he was getting madder and madder. Suddenly, the next thing I knew, Dennis was threatening to kill me, but this was more than that. Even though I had just spent 3 years boozing, drugging and living a non-stop party I remembered I had been taught the name of Jesus was above every name. I didn't consciously think this; it literally burst out of my mouth at the needed moment.

"JESUS!" I screamed out.

I was not touching Dennis and I'll never forget. It seemed like something out of the "Exorcist" when his body was thrown back against the couch at the sound of that name. He was three feet from the couch and was thrown back on his rear. His eyes rolled and looked glazed and the next words he said were,

"What's going on?" Then his eyes got intense with hatred and from his mouth I heard a voice that was not his say,

"I hate you and I'm going to kill you."

If you have ever looked into the eyes of a murdering demon, you will never forget it.

" JESUS!" I screamed each time he tried to get from the couch to come near me. It was as if someone repeatedly came between us; and to this day I'm convinced that angels were watching over me. I remembered the name of a friend that knew about the spirit realm, but I hadn't spoken to her for almost three years. Running to the phone, I dialed the phone number that sprang up in my mind. Just as I got through and said

"Lori—help!" Dennis would slam down the receiver. Through the repeated calls, Lori got across the words,

"Bring him over here."

Every time Dennis ended up back on the couch with me screaming "Jesus," his eyes continued rolling and first the demon spirit would say that it hated me and then Dennis would be weeping and asking, "What just happened?" Every time this spirit would manifest, Dennis would blank. Telling Dennis that I was going to take him for some help, we headed towards the back door.

Walking past the open dishwasher, I had my back to Dennis. DANGER I heard a small inner voice say and as I whirled around I saw, poised in the air, a butcher knife that had just reached the top of its assent. "Jesus" I shouted; and Dennis' wrist literally went limp and calmly, he turned and laid the knife on the drain board. Making it out the door, down the steps, and into the car, I was amazed at the peace I felt. I honestly don't remember any fear through the whole ordeal.

In the car, headed for the Travel Lodge Motel where Lori worked, that still small voice urgently let me know that Dennis was going to try to grab the steering wheel, so commanding his arm to be still in that name, I watched as his hand went back to his lap. The rest of the one-mile ride was uneventful.

As we arrived at the motel I said, "Come on in, just for a minute."

"I'll wait in the car," Dennis offered.

"No," I said, "You really must meet this lady".

Walking into the manager's apartment, Dennis' eyes darted around the room. Dennis later told me he couldn't believe his good fortune. A man named Reed, who was an old drinking buddy of his, sat on the couch grinning away at him. Good old Reed will have some booze, and he'll offer me a drink, Dennis thought.

"Reed, what's up?" Dennis asked.

"Hey, Dennis," Reed replied. Dennis didn't know that Reed was now a believer in Jesus Christ. Reed had literally been the town drunk. Owning the Travelodge he would go bar to bar buying everyone drinks. After his own encounter with the Lord, Reed no longer drank and spent his sharing what God had done for him.

"Sit down and visit awhile," Reed invited. Dennis was no sooner on the couch than Lori smiled and said, "Do I hear you've been having a little trouble honey?"

All of a sudden this spirit rose up in Dennis and glared at Lori.

" I'm going to kill everyone in the room." This gross demonic voice growled.

Lori recognized an old foe and laying her hands on Dennis stomach and forehead declared, "Oh no your not!

"You come out of him you murdering demon and I mean NOW! In Jesus' Name, you've got to go!"

From deep within, this thing started to scream. Later Dennis told me he totally remembered this part of that morning. He'll share from here.

It didn't give a lot of screams, just one long, long scream that built and built in volume; and leaving my body, you could hear it go out of the door of the apartment. Sitting completely limp in an air-conditioned apartment, I noticed that my clothes were so wet that you could have wrung them out. Physically, I was so weak that I couldn't even stand up.

Lori said "Honey, what you need is Jesus" She said He was the only person on this earth who could help me. Well, I'll tell you, I had hit the bottom of bottoms. I truly needed a helping hand from somebody and I didn't care who it was. If He can really help me, then, "Yes!" I wanted Him to come into my heart and to my life.

I didn't pretend to understand it with my mind, but that didn't matter. I came just like a child and said,

"I believe you died for me and are the Son of God. Come into my heart."

Lori, Reed and Diana were weeping and hugging me, which I thought was very strange. But for the first time, I felt such a relief.

It had been years and years since I had felt any kind of relief. After Diana recommitted her life to Jesus, Lori continued to stress that we needed some follow-up. "Study His Word", she said. "You need to know Jesus personally, He's not a religion. Jesus is real and it takes time to get to know Him."

To be honest with you, by now, I was ready to get out of there. "Captain" (Reed) and Lori felt we would be fine, so walking us to the door, they said goodbye.

Have you ever heard of the doubting Thomas? Well that was me. But the Lord sent me out the door with absolute proof that I had not only been saved, but that the whole experience was real. You cannot spend 27 years cussing and have it instantly disappear. Every other word had been four letters for as long as I can remember.

A few minutes after leaving the motel I realized that not one cuss word had come out of my mouth. "Diana, I'm not cussing!"

"I know", she said with the biggest grin. I knew that God had cleaned my foul mouth up, as a direct sign to me. How special that made me feel. I may not have understood why or how, but I knew this Jesus had done more in a couple of minutes than anyone else had my whole life.

Diana and I headed back to her parents house. Walking in the front door, I mentioned that I had to use the bathroom. Diana yelled,

"The wooden coasters just flew across the room!"

"What? Now you are getting carried away", I replied.

As I turned from the hallway to go downstairs, I did notice some beverage coasters lying in the middle of the floor. The house we were in was split-level, and Diana was in the foyer. She could not have even reached the coasters to move them, but I shrugged that off. Jumping down the steps, we got downstairs and headed into the bedroom, where we had spent the night before.

"Oh", Diana gasped. "Look!" There on the waterbed mattress were prints of pigs' feet, in some kind of oily substance.

"Oh No!" she gasped again. Following her gaze, I saw that a black and white silhouette picture of her little sister, Pauline, was hanging almost completely upside down. Walking slowly out of the room and into the downstairs living room, I saw even more pictures that were cockeyed. We headed for the back door, ran down the steps and away from what we were seeing.

Let's go back to Lori's", Diana said. Having nowhere else to go, we did. Reed listened to what we had found and offered to let us stay at the motel for as long as we needed. That night I told Diana to come with me to the Depot. She must have wondered why.

Walking into the bar, I realized I hadn't had my sunglasses on since the deliverance and that was a shock, even to my brother, Pat.

"Hey Pat!" I said. "I've been saved!" Going into great detail about all that had happened, it didn't occur to me how strange it must have sounded.

"That's great", Pat replied. "I'm for anything that will help you."

I found myself bubbling inside; and to Pat's complete disbelief, I ordered two cokes.

"Man, you have flipped." he commented.

Next, I went to the bathroom, which turned out to be funny. Instead of staring at people as if ready to belt them, for the first time I got this urge to visit. Yep, this is the same guy who would go all night on a date without saying more than two words and I want to get talkative with strangers in the bathroom. So I did.

"Hi there", I said to the other guy in the bathroom. "How Ya doing tonight?"

He looked at me like, "you weirdo."

Then a man who had a few too many bumped into me as I was walking out of the restroom.

"Oh, excuse me," I heard myself saying. This really is weird, I thought, but kind of fun.

Chapter 10

Going to the Chapel

SEVERAL MORNINGS LATER AT the motel, I was lying on the bed. "Hey, Diana" I yelled in to where she was showering. "They're not going to let us stay here forever. We need to find some place to live." Answering from the bathroom, Diana replied, "Well, I don't believe in living together. If I love you enough to share the same house and bed, I love you enough to marry you."

Thinking, I paused for a minute.

"Well, let's get married!" I yelled back.

Coming out of the bathroom, Diana said, "Now, don't tease me about a thing like that. I really love you."

Try to remember that this is the same woman that had almost been murdered by me less than three days before.

"Who's teasing?" I asked. "Where do you go for something like that?"

Charging into the room Diana leapt on top of the bed while yelling whoopee and choking me with hugs.

"We could go to Reno. Today!" she said without hesitation

That's what I like about my wife. She never lets a golden opportunity pass! About five weeks was all that we had known each other, but deep inside we really believed we couldn't do without one another.

After packing our things in the motel room we thanked Reed and Lori, informed them of our plans, and headed for Diana's

Mother's house to tell her. Not owning a car, a decent pair of pants, shoes, or a shirt, I had a few minor details to take care of.

First, I borrowed a pair of black Angel Flight pants and matching shoes from my brother, Pat; and then arriving at Diana's house we told her Mom. Ivan, Diana's father was down in Los Angeles, so we asked Dorothy if we could borrow the car. I'm sure she wondered what planet we flew in from, asking her for my future father-in-laws car and a shirt. So many people wait to get married until they have the perfect set-up, and here we were with nothing but ourselves and $60... going to elope. Terribly romantic if you think about it.

I had never had the pleasure of meeting Ivan yet; and he just happened to call before we took off.

"Hello, Ivan? Nice to meet you. May I borrow your car and have your daughter?"

Ivan stayed perfectly calm and replied, "What can I say? Just love her and take good care of her!"

As we got in the car, Diana's mom looked at her and said, "Honey, are you sure?"

"Yes, Mom."

Driving away, I couldn't help but notice that Dorothy looked very concerned. I wondered what she would have thought had she known about the events of the last three days.

Boy, was I nervous, and the more I thought about it, the shakier I got. About one hour out of Reno, we both were so tired, neither of us could drive, so we stopped for the night. The sun rose early and so did I. Fear was really attacking my mind. Sensing it, Diana said,

"Don't do anything you are not sure of."

"Hey, I can get out of it as easy as I got in" I laughed

At a gas station outside of Reno, Diana picked up a brochure advertising the "Starlight Wedding Chapel". The pamphlet was hysterical as it offered five dollars off the ceremony, free parking, dressing rooms, five dollars worth of gambling tokens, complementary champagne and a gift. If that didn't grab you, it was directly across the street from where we had to get our license.

Later, Diana told me she got the pamphlet out of a holder that was sitting on the back of the toilet. What Class!

Applying for the license went smoothly, except for the fact that I had left my identification in the car. The lady filling out the legal papers said, "Oh, no problem. You don't need any." Right!

Walking into the actual Wedding Chapel felt like a tour of Universal Studios. It had all the appeal of a fake television set. No one was at the desk and we didn't know whether to pick up the phone sitting there or what. A few minutes later this lady appeared out of nowhere. Nicely, she took all the information and asked us if we wanted wedding rings. "Definitely", Diana answered. The lady continued to fill out our paperwork and then ushered us into a couple of dressing rooms. Excitedly, Diana and I talked and joked back and forth while we changed. I stepped out of the dressing room and spotted the man who was to marry us. Pouring over a copy of the National Enquirer, he had all of the makings of a wax dummy. I mean this guy was looloo city. He didn't bother to look up, so I headed up front where Diana was waiting.

Being positioned at the entrance of the chapel, the secretary bellowed to the nameless man in the back room, "Ready?" As the 'Preacher' stood at the alter, she galloped through the front office, around back past the dressing rooms, behind the chapel, and plopped onto a piano bench where she banged out the wedding march. Diana and I were halfway down the aisle by the time she started playing.

"Do you have the rings?" The preacher asked discretely.

"Oh, no!" I figured they would take care of that.

"Stop!" yelled the preacher back at his helper.

Cloppity, clop, clop, we heard her gallop back up front. Escorting us out of the chapel, we followed her to a display case, picked out the rings, and paid for them; nothing like a business transaction to break the mood. Then we followed her back to the chapel for a second time.

Making a repeat performance, she dashed madly back across the office, around the back past the dressing rooms, behind the chapel and simultaneously we heard the plop of her butt hitting the piano bench as her fingers started playing the wedding march.

Again, we were nearly all the way to the altar before she began to play.

As the preacher spoke to us, I looked at Diana and noticed she was on the verge of a laughing fit, right then and there. This man's voice never changed in volume, tone, or inflection during the whole ceremony, and sounded suspiciously like a recording. All that was left to do was to concentrate on the words and the fact that I knew these vows were between Diana, God, and me. How the preacher sounded didn't matter.

Well, we had done it! I had made a huge step and it didn't even hurt. We both still drank at the time, so after gambling our nickels, we headed out of town to pick up our champagne and free gift. With 8 ounces of champagne and a plastic pair of salt and peppershakers that said, "South Lake Tahoe," we headed out... destination, Anderson, California to tell my Mother.

Mom had no idea that I even had a girlfriend; and seeing us drive up she probably thought, Oh, Dennis brought home another girl.

"Hi, Mom! Meet your new daughter in-law."

Mom laughed and said, "Oh, sure! That'll be the day."

Diana said seriously, "Mom, look at my ring!"

Mother replied, "Oh, that ring could have come from Woolworth's for all I know."

Mother finally picked up that it was real and realized that Diana was her new daughter in-law. "Oh, you guys, you crazy kids!" Hugging us, she gave us hearty congratulations. Since it was around four in the afternoon, "Pop" was due home soon.

After dinner, Diana and I played poker with Mom and Gene and literally won our gas money home. Diana headed to bed. Both of us drinking, Gene proceeded to tell me that everything I had experienced wasn't real. This being his belief, not backed with any scripture, he hadn't convinced me. Satan's first tactic is to convince you that he doesn't exist.

I guess we really got carried away with the booze and I had forgotten that I had just gotten married. I tried to make up for it when I got to bed. Diana was quite upset and to this day she teases me about it.

Chapter 11

Under the Tree

AS WE DROVE INTO town the next morning, we drove straight to Penny's to tell her. We were so excited to get back home, plus we both had to work the very next day. We had tricked my sister Penny before we left and asked her for $60 to go gambling with. She jumped for joy as she thought I would never settle down, and I was glad to see her happiness, as later she admitted she thought Diana was just another barfly.

Penny lived in a little two-bedroom house on the north side with her children. "Not much room, but you're welcome to it," she offered.

It was summertime; August 22nd was the big day, so Diana and I stayed out under a big tree in Penny's front yard. We didn't mind the lawn; we were in love! I've always enjoyed telling people that we started out underneath a tree.

A couple of weeks later, we located a tiny little apartment. I mean tiny. There was just enough room in the one small bedroom to fit a double bed, which you had to sit on to use the closet. The kitchen was very handy, as you could reach the fridge, sink, stove, and table without moving one step. We used cardboard boxes set upside down for end tables and with one sofa, chair, and a TV, that was home sweet home.

For transportation, we had bought Penny's old, white Ford Falcon. After Pat and I switched the gearshift to the floor, it had only two gears. Running around town with second and third only, you had to be very careful which way you parked, as it had no reverse. I was now landscaping instead of cooking.

Beginning our new life, we pretty well stagnated spiritually. Now, I refer to that as "Band-Aid Christianity." Call God for a Band-Aid when you are hurting. We continued to drink and get involved in pornographic magazines in our marriage. We argued a lot the first year, although regardless of the issue, the root was in the alcohol.

Diana, not out of absolute necessity but rather out of boredom, wanted to go to work. Landing a job as assistant manager of a ladies apparel shop seemed to meet the need. With extra money coming in, we searched for a new place to live, as we had been invited to leave the apartment. Coincidentally, we discovered the two-bedroom house across the street from Penny's was up for rent.

We rented that house for $350 a month--$200 cheaper than the going rate. What a blessing.

Chapter 12

God Will Provide

NOW MY OLDER BROTHER, Jack, was looking for some kind of business to get into, so I suggested landscaping. I had not received a raise in months and when I asked for one my boss just laughed. Laughing back, I spit on his shoe and walked off the job. Jack thought landscaping sounded good, and I reassured him that I could teach him what I had learned in the time I had been landscaping. Well, Jack moved to Visalia and together we formed a landscaping company. We had a good time at first, but then problems. I was still not seeking the Lord and was drinking heavily.

While I was still landscaping with Jack, Diana started work as an aide at a school called Riverbend. This school catered to the special needs of the developmentally disabled. I have a nephew named David with Downs Syndrome, whom I had always been crazy about, so I had a special appreciation for her work.

Things became really tough with the landscaping. I hurt my knee; and after a cold, hard winter, we found ourselves applying for food stamps the day after Christmas. A sack of almost empty flour was literally what was in the refrigerator when we decided we needed help. Sitting down, we realized that Diana's income alone was not enough and my knee was having a heck of a time healing. With no insurance or unemployment benefits, something had to change.

Diana believed God was knocking on our door; and she was beginning to listen. I have got to tell you it must have been hell on her to motivate me. Between my stubbornness and drinking, I was a bear when not working.

Getting a local newspaper, we started skimming the help wanted ads. Diana had mentioned seeing an ad three weeks before about someone needing live-in house-parents.

At the time, I said, "You've got to be kidding." Now, this same ad was back in the paper.

"What would you think about working with handicapped children?" Diana asked. The ad says, "House-parents needed to live in and care for six children. Some yard-work is also included." The timing of this new ad was incredible.

After the first time Diana saw the ad, I had gotten a job at what was known as Sin City, some sleazy apartments. Along with the job came an apartment.

This was going to help meet the bills, so we had already given Bernice, our current landlady, notice. We did not have any money for rent and only had ten days until we had to be out of our house. Two days of working for those apartments was enough. It was a crooked operation and after talking it over, Diana urged me to quit.

"God will provide!" Easy for her to say I thought. Here it was eight days until we had to be moved, with no job, no place to live, and no money. Diana was really shocked to see this same ad come back into the paper. I didn't know anything about taking care of kids, but the yard work looked up my alley, so I told Diana to call the number.

A lady named Mary Jo answered the phone and after hearing of Diana's experience at the school for handicapped, said to come on out for an interview.

Pulling up in front of a ranch-style, country home we almost gasped. The house was out in the country with a beautiful mobile home next door.

During the interview, we discovered the ad had been in three weeks before, but she had found someone. That person was to start days before and just didn't show. So the ad came back in the paper the day I quit "Sin City." Another strange thing was that no one else had called but us, and after offering us the job; Mary had four or five calls that afternoon. Mary Jo told us to go out back by the pool to discuss it.

I asked Diana what she thought. "I don't know, this one's your decision," she replied. The offer was $600 a month, plus room and board. The mobile home was like a mansion after where we were living.

"You pray and ask God, He will tell you," said Diana.

"Who needs to pray, I know the answer. You're telling me someone is offering me money, food, and a place to live....just to love these little kids? Feed them, dress them, and bath them...all the things they cannot do themselves? No, I don't need to pray about that. If I could, I would do it for free." So, by faith we took the job.

We headed home and instead of a garage sale; Diana told me she felt we were to give all our belongings to a local charity that helped the poor. The new mobile was furnished down to dishes, and we felt so blessed; it didn't seem like anything else could be right.

Being very excited, I'll always remember the day we moved in. Our clothes, some plants, and a few personal belonging were all we had kept. Everything fit in the back of the old, primered Chevy truck we were now driving. We wanted to get familiar with our newly adopted family, three girls and three boys, Michael, Richard, James, and Griselda, Laura, and Kami.

Oh, did we do some growing up in those years. We absolutely fell in love with those kids and God knows we loved them just like our own. No one will ever know the precious memories they have given us. Sadly though, I found myself drinking more than ever. It was fairly easy to get away with it, as we had a job that was at home. You had to be aware of licensing, but remember by now I had been drinking for many years and I felt I was a professional. I had always had Diana there. She never drank while working, so I felt some security. This was definitely a high-pressure job, and instead of joining in with my drinking, she drew closer to God. She really turned away from my lifestyle and became hungry to learn what the Word had to say about Jesus.

Chapter 13

Rise and Be Healed

I REMEMBER JIMMY SWAGGART, AMONG other preachers, were on every Sunday morning. The radio always seemed to have on Greg Laurie, Raul Reese, or Bob Grenier, who were teachers of the Bible, who had a way of talking to you, not at you. By now I was back to drinking Vodka, not the proverbial one beer; and was headed for trouble. I was really worried. I knew I was jeopardizing our job and I really loved the folks.

One day Diana said, "Hey, Johnny and Sherri, your sister, invited us to go see Jimmy Swaggart in Fresno.

Would you like to go?"

I heard something come out of my mouth like, "I guess so. Call them and tell them we'll go."

Diana was thrilled and believed God was going to move in a miraculous way. Thousands of people filled Selland Arena; and we found a spot right smack dab in the middle, down on the main floor. In the service, long before the altar call, a man named John Starnes sang a song called, "**RISE AND BE HEALED**." I have always been painfully shy, but found myself pulled to my feet with my arms lifted to God while tears streamed down my face. I felt like someone had thrown me filthy dirty into a crystal clear river and I came up out of that river cleansed head to toe. I didn't know what had happened, and I didn't understand it with my mind.

After the service ended, we said our good-byes to John & Sherri and headed home.

A mile down the road from the convention, I said to Diana, "That place shook me up! I need a drink."

She didn't say a word. She told me later that she started praying. I bought a six-pack of Coors at a little store and it being a hot, summer day, I could hardly wait to get it open. "Yuck!" It tasted absolutely terrible. I spit it out and threw the bottle out the window. Diana started laughing. What happened in that convention was a literal miracle. At this time, I had been drinking almost everyday for over 15 years, not to mention the years of using painkillers off and on.

Another interesting fact was that during our first two years of marriage, Diana had not used any contraceptives and she never got pregnant. For the last six months, due to stress and my drinking, we only ran into each other one time.

Diana had prayed that we wouldn't have a baby until I quit drinking. Yep, you got it; we were to find out later that she had gotten pregnant in that one rendezvous, two weeks before I got set free from alcohol.

Well, I didn't have a drop to drink for months. The Lord had instantly set me free. The rest of the six-pack stayed in the back of the fridge for months. Our joy was cut short when after months of not one thought about alcohol; I indulged in a glass of wine to celebrate our third anniversary. That started my living in hell all over again. If a glass of wine was OK, a beer was OK. If a beer was OK and I could handle that, a quart of beer was OK. If I kept it to a quart a day I figured there was no problem. I wonder how many reading this have experienced the same syndrome. Soon, I was back to drinking Vodka and the drinking led to more trials.

One night, I had been in Visalia at the bar where my brother Pat worked. On the way home, once again, my life was almost taken. I was driving our light blue Volkswagen when another car being driven by a member of the "Mongols" (biker gang) ran into me. All I remember was spinning around. When the car stopped, I got out and saw everything from the car door back totaled.

Diana told me later that she had been watching television when an urgent voice said **PRAY**! She went down on her knees and prayed until the urgency lifted. We knew the timing of that prayer had to be intercession. Both the biker and I were drunk and words flew about whose fault it was. At any rate, this biker went to a phone and called a group of his friends. Up they all roared and they had on their colors, acting like bikers do. I tried to win their respect right away, as I was greatly outnumbered. I jumped in one guy's face and demanded a cigarette. Somehow, rather than getting the you-know- what- beat out of me, I had wrangled a ride home. Jumping in the back of one guy's pickup, I rode home. As I got there, I was furious about the whole incident and by now even drunker.

Once in the house I grabbed an old 22 pistol of my Dad's and raced out the back door.

"What are you doing with that gun? What happened?" Diana frantically asked.

I ignored her and started to aim at the pickup, but I had changed. In spite of being drunk, I aimed at the ground and shot one round into the dirt, then went back inside. The next day I received a call from the guy threatening to blow me, and the mobile home away. The next night it was foggy. Sitting in our living room, Diana and I heard the roar of God knows how many bikers. Even though they had been there the night before, somehow they couldn't seem to find the place. I never heard from the guy again. Our insurance company heard all the details and paid him.

Chapter 14

The Birth of Laughter

NOT LONG AFTER THAT incident, Mary Jo was getting ready to replace us with her husband, so our social worker suggested we open our own home. He was very impressed with the progress our folks had made, and for the record, had even written a letter recommending us to the head of the Regional Center, who placed and monitored the clients.

This was a great idea as Diana was pregnant with our first child. Remember how I related to you how a panel of psychologists and psychiatrists had diagnosed me as a paranoid schizophrenic? Well, this time I had to go in front of a group of professionals that not only included them, but also doctors, nurses, social workers, program directors, etc. This group not only found us to be totally suited for the job, but also within three months of opening our home had placed three clients with us.

Now living in the quaint little town of Porterville, CA, Diana and I had received two of the girls from Mary Jo's; so it was like old home week. Casey was the name of a beautiful collie that perfectly fit the little doghouse and fenced back yard of our new home. Our love nest was pale yellow with white trim. Two big bedrooms, a nursery, a living room with a brick fireplace and a gorgeous kitchen overlooking the dining room, completed the house.

With Diana due, we were excited about the new baby, and I was mainly drinking beer, trying to control my dependency on alcohol.

"Let's go watch Randy (our nephew) play basketball." I said one weekend.

"Sure! And since it's just 40 miles to Visalia, I think I'll take my suitcase just in case" Diana said.

She looked at the main event more like going to spend the night at a girlfriend's house. Since she was three weeks from the due date, I thought she was crazy. Racing all over Visalia, looking for the right location of Randy's game, Diana and I kidded about the amount of railroad tracks we had crossed. Finally, walking into the local YMCA, we spotted Randy dribbling the ball down the court.

"I think I'm losing water," Diana whispered, "Let's go to my mothers."

"Go to your mothers?!!! Call a doctor!" I said.

"That's what I mean, I'll call him from my Mothers' " replied Diana.

Diana and I had been so busy that we hadn't attended any childbirth classes. Her doctor assured her that all the nurses were well equipped for last minute coaching. At Dorothy and Ivan's', we got the word to go on in to the hospital. Arriving around three, I excitedly checked Diana in, to her singing, "Let's get physical." Oh, how little did she know what was coming. Being Saturday, we got whatever doctor was on call.

After waiting and waiting, I said, "Where is this guy?" Meantime, a nurse on duty rudely greeted us, and for the next seven hours complained constantly about missing a break and not getting a chance to stuff her face. Never having given birth herself, her maternal instincts equaled that of a tarantula's.

Sitting on the bed, I said, "Oh, no! Look Diana! If that man coming this way is the doctor, we're outta here!"

This guy looked like some kind of nutty professor. An old faded T-shirt hung on him, his hair looked like it had never been combed and to top off the spectacle, he was in his stocking feet. This man walked, to my horror, directly into our room and without introducing himself said, "We're going to induce labor! It looks bad! We really could have trouble ahead. If the baby isn't here by midnight, we'll have to take the baby by C-section." The way he stated this, it sounded more like an offense to the body, not a helpful medical technique. Turning and walking out the door, he left.

After 14 hours of terrifying, hard, hard, labor, I felt like I had birthed the baby myself. But, oh, what a baby! Being three weeks premature, he weighed only six pounds seven ounces. Diana and I had picked out the name Isaac, which means laughter, and little Isaac had every reason to laugh. He was born circumcised. "A rare medical condition," the doctor explained. "A miracle from God!" Diana retorted.

Bringing brand new baby Isaac home on her birthday, Diana felt like he was the perfect present.

Dennis and baby Isaac

Chapter 15

God Can Do Anything

WITH TWO FOSTER CHILDREN and one baby, our lives definitely picked up. Soon a third girl was placed with us, followed by yet another call from our social worker. "Would you accept placement of Richard to your home?" Oh, Diana and I jumped for joy. He was a little boy we had in our home at Mary Jo's. When we first met, he was 43 lbs. 55 inches tall and ready to die. Diana called him her "baby bird," and she and the Lord nursed him back to health. With a special diet, but mainly love, within two months he weighed 75 lbs. Richard had also learned the words baby and mama.

The only way to accept Richard was to have a bigger facility, and to pass all the licensing and fire clearance requirements. In one week, we had located and made arrangements to buy a fellow care provider's home. The day we were to sign the paper work, a licensing official put a halt to our plans. Another facility was on the same street and we were told two on the same street were not allowed. We were disappointed, although we had not been crazy about the location of the house. It overlooked a drive-in that played mainly grade xxx sex films, and worse, cheap horror films. Looking in the paper the next morning, we decided to drive out and look at a house that was listed.

"How much is it?" I asked Diana.

"Only $90,000" she replied

I about fainted! We were barely making it; and we didn't have an extra dime. The only way we were going to get the first house was for the owner to carry the paperwork.

"Come on," Diana said, "God can do anything."

Sure, I thought. Sure. My wife is the most optimistic woman in the world, and at that time I was the worst pessimist. Driving six miles to a little town called "Terra Bella", we drove to the address and couldn't believe what we saw. The structure of the old country home looked okay. But what a mess! The front porch door was wedged open with all kinds of junk, including an old washer. Weeds stood high at various places on the acre. The house was a faded olive green, there was an ugly redwood stained fence running down both sides of a pool, and the fence wasn't connected at either end.

"I wouldn't give these people $80 for this place," I told Diana.

"There must be a reason they're asking so much. Let's look inside." Diana said. She's blind I thought but I knew what she was thinking. We had always fixed up any rental we had been in, where they needed it. Once on the porch, I saw a different story. A massive door with beveled glass led the way into an open living room with a cathedral ceiling overlooked by a loft. To my left was the largest fireplace I had ever seen. It spanned the main wall through the whole house and was made of massive mountain rocks. The fireplace mantel was literally a full slice out of a whole tree.

The home was 2000 square feet with four big bedrooms, all-leading off from the main living room. Besides two extra large bathrooms, there was a kitchen complete with pantry. The eye-catcher was a big chandelier with a matching mini chandelier at the other end of the living room. As we passed a window box off the kitchen and headed out the back door a twenty by forty-foot swimming pool greeted us.

Diana's first words were, "This is it! This is the place God has chosen for us!"

Now I knew she was nuts. I believed God might get a little involved with you, but we didn't have a quarter. As we were leaving, the realtor showed up. Her name was Alice. She was a real cutie and reminded us of Lois Lane from the "Superman comic books". Alice was headed out of town so she asked if we could come to her office later? Well, my wife, little Miss Optimist blurted out, "Sure. What time?" before I had a chance to protest. Later that day we went to Alice's office. The first thing Alice said was, "Kid's, how much have you got?"

We said, "Money?"

She said "Yeah. You gotta have money to buy a house."

"God will take care of the money, let's just take care of the paperwork." Diana blurted out. She had greater faith than I did.

Alice to my surprise said, "Okay. Let's see what we can do. Are you a veteran?"

"Yes. I am." I mumbled

"Have you ever used your Cal-Vet loan?" Alice asked hopefully

"No." I said.

"Good, the guy that owns this house is a Veteran, and he is trying to switch his loan to another house, but has to have someone else take over this house, who is a Veteran."

"Alright," we said. Miracle number one!

"Do you have any assets to borrow on?" Alice inquired

"What's an asset?" we joked. We had only been married three and a half years since starting out underneath Penny's tree.

"Do you have any relatives that could loan you some money?" Alice retorted

"Maybe a little. How much do we need down?" Diana asked

"Oh, if we offer $84,000, about $8500, just 10% down" Alice said as a matter of fact.

"Great." Diana said.

"Oh God! Great, you say?" I silently thought.

Suddenly Reed came to mind, the man that had been at my deliverance. Just what every smart businessman would want to do. Loan money to a man you'd cast a murdering demon out of that was still drinking. If nothing else, Reed could give us some good business advice. So mentioning this to the realtor I decided to head over to Tortilla Flats, the restaurant Reed and Lori were running.

Before we left, Alice said, "Hey, by the way, I need some money."

"How much?" Diana asked.

"Just $500. So no one can buy the house out from under you. You know. To put it into escrow" Alice said.

"No problem," said Diana. To my shock, she whipped out our checkbook and wrote a hot check for $500. Sure, I liked the house, but I didn't know if this was faith or lunacy! Getting outside she said, "Didn't you hear her? This check won't be cashed until we have a deal, but I'll see if Mom and Dad can lend us this for a week until our paycheck comes in, if that will make you feel better."

Arriving at the Flats, Reed not only gave us legal advice, but now we were much wealthier on paper. Our next move was to be approved by Cal-Vet. We were turned down, flat. No explanation. So we pursued Cal-Vet. After many conversations and getting more paperwork, Cal-Vet gave the go ahead. Finally, there was the problem of $2,000; and so we wouldn't lose Richard, we had to get into the house right away.

My brother lent us $2,000; and the owner of the house said, "Sure, I'll rent to you until Cal-Vet closes escrow." Here within a month of the initial call from our worker, God had provided us with a mansion when we didn't have a dime. Now there was only one small detail----$6,000 for the rest of the down when Cal-Vet was ready to close. Diana had no doubt it would work out and I was beginning to think it was a possibility.

Everything was ready for the big move, except manpower. Packing, Diana took care to pack everything like a professional. To add to the chaos we had received yet another female client on a temporary basis, just in time for the move.

Renting the U-Haul, I drove back to Conley St, wondering where time had gone. Arriving home, Diana and I packed the whole truck our selves, except for the heaviest things. Moving morning, my brother, Pat, showed up and was able to donate a few hours, but had a time limit as he had to work that day. Isaac was three months old by now; and with four of our special kids, we had our hands full.

The first trip wasn't too eventful, other than the new little girl who tried to kick the windows out of the moving van the whole time. The social worker had warned us she had behavioral problems. Diana had the baby and the other three girls in the Volkswagen with her as we went back and forth on the six-mile trip between the two houses.

After Pat left, Diana and I headed back to the house. It wasn't the 110-degree weather or having the windshield of the truck I was driving constantly kicked that bothered me, but moving the final piece of furniture, our king-size waterbed almost did us in. Time was running out and so was our energy. Between changing pampers on the adult kids (they were not toilet trained), Diana would breast feed the baby and try to help me. The last little bit of water wouldn't drain from the bed, so we physically drug it through the house onto the front lawn where it finished draining. Now all that was left was the frame of the waterbed, and we only had the rental truck for another 45 minutes. I was sick when I discovered the screws wouldn't come out by hand as they had used an electric drill to put them in.

I had forgotten that Diana didn't have the strength of a man. As we wrestled the giant frame out of the bedroom and down the hallway, we had to stop at least ten times.

Diana was finally in tears and yelled, "Can't you find someone to help?"

I pointed out that we didn't have one neighbor on the block less than 75 years old. As Diana sat on the front porch crying, I gave her some of her own medicine. "You just pray to God for the strength, cause you're the one He picked to help me move."

Diana cried harder as she knew I was right. Standing up, she let out a karate yell and lifted that thing a final time and got it onto the truck lift. Now laughing, we gazed at the five kids hanging out the U-Haul and the Volkswagen. They were all screaming their heads off. Hungry and thirsty, it felt more like 150 degrees than 110.

Ready to go now, I gave the command, "Follow me, Diana!" Off we went to our new home in Terra Bella. By the time we unloaded the final things, the living room was full of our belongings. Nothing was put away. After returning the U-Haul, I bought Chinese food, and back home in our new house we literally sat in the middle of furniture, boxes, mattresses, you name it, and ate our food.

We were so tired we fell asleep that night, right in the middle of the whole mess. The next morning we both just sat and stared. What a long way we were from under that tree on Divisadero Street.

Chapter 16

God is My Helper

I WAS GETTING MORE INTERESTED in the Lord, and although I was still drinking, He certainly was getting my attention. By now, Diana was on fire spiritually, and when Lori offered to come hold Bible studies, I could hardly say no. Lori taught us so much of the Word and it was truly exciting. She sounded a bit radical with statements like, "We are the church, not a symbolic bunch of bricks on the corner." We believed this as we had seen so many dead, lifeless, loveless groups meeting in buildings.

I remember asking her how I was supposed to remember all this stuff.

She said, "Don't worry, Honey, the Holy Spirit will bring it back to your remembrance."

Diana and I had gotten involved with another care provider who had a son we invited to the Bible studies. Walter was the young man's name, and he brought his girlfriend Leah with him to our home.

Walter had quite a gambling problem, along with a large appetite for drinking. Lori, after sharing for a few minutes, started teaching on the power of the Holy Spirit. Interrupting, Walter excitedly said, "I have powers like that. I predicted the eruption of Mt. St. Helens. Another time I made a lawn mower start without touching it."

"I believe you, Honey, but that power is from another source." Lori said with concern

We all turned our attention to Walter as his voice was getting louder and very challenging. We sensed a violence that was ready to surface.

"See those lights over there," he said, indicating a chandelier. "I can make those lights turn off and on."

Suddenly, we were getting a light show as not only the chandelier, but three other lights twinkled on and off. Some brighter, some quicker, you name it.

Lori, without blinking, firmly replied, "Jesus Christ is the head of this house and He is more powerful than where that power is coming from." Instantly the light show stopped. Enough said!

I remember one Tuesday; I had been cleaning up the property around our home, when I stepped on a 16-penny nail. It was sticking straight up through a two by four; and that sucker penetrated straight into my foot. It took all my strength, using both hands to pull that board and nail out of my foot. My foot was throbbing so badly that night I could hardly pay attention to the Bible study.

As everyone said their good-byes and headed out the door, Lori said, "Honey, would you like me to pray for your foot?"

I looked at her kind of funny and said, "I guess so."

She said, "Well, do you believe Jesus can heal your foot?"

"Well, yeah, I believe He could!" I slowly said

"Well, then, He will." She said with a gentle smile

Lori said a quiet prayer as she laid her hand on my foot, and I told her that her hand was burning my foot.

"I know, Honey," she said, "That's a healing anointing that you're feeling."

I didn't understand so I just said, "Whatever."

When Lori was through praying, she told me to stand up and walk on it. "Honey, you're healed."

I did what she asked and I couldn't believe it. There was no pain! I had stepped on nails as a kid, and I knew the next day was always when it hurt really badly. The next morning my foot looked swollen; and I thought, "See, there!"

Telling Diana to look at the swelling, she suggested, "Get up and walk on it." Even though the swelling was there, I couldn't believe it. There was not one bit of pain or poisoning.

Oh, my. What an anointed lady, Lori is. What wonderful knowledge she taught us out of the Bible about the Lord. When a Bible study is really led by the Holy Spirit, He stirs up, blesses it, and yet, He knows when it's time to grow in different areas. So, the studies ended for a season.

I hired a man to plow my acre; and I carefully planted the whole thing with a hybrid grass. By hand I had weeded and smoothed, rolled in the seed and sprinkled the new seed with water so carefully. No grass had sprung up in three weeks. Jack, my brother who was still in landscaping said, "There is no way Number 1 Kentucky Bluegrass will grow in this land, and if it isn't up yet, you can forget it."

That's all the challenge Diana needed. "Lord," she said, "You promised to bless the works of our hands. Dennis worked his butt off on this lawn, it's not like he just threw seeds down anywhere. Now, You know we can't afford any more seed and I believe You will take care of this." While she was praying, she was carrying a bottle of anointing oil, sprinkling, or should I say pouring it on the soil. One week later, there was grass everywhere. It was so beautiful! Personally, I thought she was carrying this a little bit too far, but I couldn't argue with the results.

Diana had been very active during her second pregnancy, but now the time had come to birth the baby, I thought. I say that because we had two weeks of false labor.

The day of the main event we drove 40 miles to Visalia and stayed late in the afternoon. Labor stopped so we went back home to Terra Bella. I was so tired I crawled into bed at 6pm in the evening.

Two hours later at 8pm Diana said, "Get up, this is it."

"No more false alarms," I mumbled.

"Dennis, this is it," Diana snapped

"Oh, gosh, hurry, HURRY!" I said.

At 2 o'clock in the morning another beautiful baby boy was born; and we named him Isaiah, which means, **God is my helper**.

Isaac and baby brother Isaiah

Chapter 17

Unconditional Love

FIVE FOSTER CHILDREN AND two sons of our own, we now had our work cut out for us. Receiving a higher income, I decided to have my life's dream, so motorcycle shopping I went. After getting an advanced case of "Harleyitis!" I came home and announced that God had told me I could have a Harley. Taking Diana with me, I purchased a brand new 1984 low-rider. To complete the purchase were saddlebags, a 36" sissy bar and two matching helmets. The color was deep purple, with gunmetal gray accents. Boy, I tell you the devil jumped right into my back pocket. At first I played innocent, but then I started living my fantasy that nearly took my life.

Within three weeks I quit wearing a helmet and soon purchased black knuckle motorcycle gloves. The dark sunglasses were back on for the first time in years. I started riding alone a lot. I went camping and fishing with my bottle; and once again in life, I tried to pretend I'd found heaven. As the summer headed to a close, I was drinking heavier and heavier. The conviction of what I was doing drove me crazy because I was trying to hide the drinking from my wife.

On our fifth wedding anniversary, I was five hours late to meet her at the Holiday Inn. After stopping at the bar downstairs, I headed for the room where she was waiting, to set her straight.

"I'm tired of trying to hide my drinking and smoking from you all the time," I said with drink in hand. Plopping down at the table I lit a cigarette, blew smoke right in her face and said, "If you don't want me to drink or smoke in the house, I'll find somewhere else to do it." I couldn't believe how even-tempered she reacted.

"I know you've been trying to hide all these things, but don't do it for my sake. I never asked you to hide anything. I love you. You're having some battles and I'm here to help." Diana gently said .You know it's extremely hard to fight unconditional love.

A few days later I was driving my Harley from a bar in Visalia toward home. I remember just flat burying the needle in the speedometer. I must have exceeded 100 mph easily. When I got home all the lights were out and I slumped down on the fireplace hearth. I remember saying, "What are you doing to yourself?"

A picture of my two precious boys passed before my eyes and that still voice inside said, "You are going to die on that bike if you continue the way you are going!" I told Diana the next day what had happened. "I'm going to sell it," I announced. I told her my boys were more important to me than any motorcycle. I loved my family so much and felt great about my decision. Diana was so happy with the choice I had made and with no influence from her. Once I decided this, like most spoiled husbands, I told Diana, "Since I'm selling my bike, I'll trade it in on a new pickup." By now Diana wouldn't have minded if I had said an airplane.

The pickup I chose was a cream colored 1984 Chevy Stepside pickup, the truck I'd wanted my whole life. Yet even all these new things could not get rid of the fear that still lingered after all these years. One night I came home so drunk I can't remember how much I had drank.

Tired of living with the bondage of fear and alcohol, I fell to my knees and wept. I remember many different feelings and emotions flooded through me. I was crying out to God Almighty Himself. I yelled, "Lord, I've tried all this religious garbage," I began to break everything in sight, including the glass shades covering the bulbs of the chandeliers.

Screaming at God, I grabbed a picture of Jesus that hung over our fireplace and beat it up. "If You're real, why haven't you taken this alcohol and fear from me?" I challenged. In between bellowing questions, my fists would smash against the thick wrought iron gates to the fireplace. Blood was spattered everywhere and once again I was screaming out for help the only way I knew how, with violence.

Diana stayed calm through the whole ordeal. Quickly leading the boys out of the room, she explained that Daddy was having a talk with God and that it was OK. Later she told me at the very beginning God distinctly told her, "Do not fear, as you are going to see the repentance of your husband. I'm allowing you to see this because of all the times you said, God, I can't believe Dennis is turning his back on you." God told her that I was never getting away with anything, and He wanted her to see my heart.

My knuckles shattered, blood and glass everywhere, the spirit of God spoke to me. "Go out to the tree where you've hidden your Vodka, and pour it on the ground."

When I did, all of a sudden I was stone sober. The Lord said, "You are free now. Go and never drink again." Returning to the house, I slumped, exhausted, on the couch, and after Diana dressed my hands and cleaned the blood up; she brought out my two sons to me. Drained, I cuddled them both and fell asleep. To this day, I have faced life's challenges without drugs and alcohol. Praise the Lord!

Terra Bella fireplace and Isaac

Chapter 18

Time To Pray

RETURNING HOME FROM SEVEN days at a James Robinson Conference, at John Wimbers church in Anaheim, Diana told me about miraculous things she had witnessed. Two mighty beams of light had led the car she was riding in home through the fog. A girl that had gone to the conference was instantly healed of a visible skin disease. Seeing the Shekinah Glory as it poured from Heaven over one of the singers was impossible to describe. There was no doubt if Diana hadn't been totally sold out to seeking spiritual growth; she was on fire now.

By now so many mighty things were happening in my personal life that I, too, wanted to know everything about the power that had set me free. One night I was watching TBN, a 24-hour Christian broadcasting station. A man named Shambach was preaching on the baptism of the Holy Ghost. I had heard a lot about it; and although I didn't understand it, I knew I had better get everything God wanted me to have. If I was going to serve God, I was going to serve Him as well as I had served Satan. Since that had been 100%, I figured that was the least I could do for God. After a simple prayer asking the Holy Spirit to baptize me, I went off to bed uneventfully.

About 11 o'clock the next morning, I was in the bathroom; and I was not brushing my teeth, if you get my drift. Suddenly, a language I had never heard before came flowing out of my mouth.

Excited, but still doubtful, I asked Diana if this is what they called "tongues."

Laughing she said, "Honey, that's it."

"Oh, this is stupid," I said.

But an unspeakable joy, full of glory, was flowing out. For three hours I spoke in different languages repeatedly walking from one end of the house to the other as I was bursting with energy. My son, Isaac, laughed and giggled, as he had never seen his Daddy laugh so much. Besides lifting me up that initial time, I've since discovered the tremendous value of praying as the apostle Paul did, with my spirit, as well as my understanding.

With a full facility of six clients and two children of our own, we needed help. Rosa was the name of the young lady the employment agency suggested. Because of the prior experience working with disabled, she worked out super. Usually, when I was working around the house, I would play teaching tapes, and between those and some Amy Grant music, Rosa knew we believed Jesus was the answer to any problems.

One day Rosa began to open up and share some things about herself, and was curious if her problems could be helped. Diana led her to the Lord, and the transformation that took place was so great it would fill a book by itself. Rosa invited a friend over, after asking Diana if she would share some things she had learned from studying the Bible. Mary Lou was the name of the precious young lady that came, and she was extremely surprised by the topic of study. Evidently, it was actually the area she was curious about; and she, too, made a commitment to follow Jesus.

Some day if the Lord wills, I must write a book concerning the many beautiful events that took place over the next ten months. I can honestly say that I never had to invite one person to our Bible studies. Within four months, as many as 30 to 40 people would show up. I've always believed since then, if God is trying to use you in some way, you do not have to work it up, or make it happen.

The Bible says what He has for you will overtake you. That's really what happened here. So many special events stand out. Healings, deliverances, inner healings. In particular, deaf ears were opened, female problems healed, painful warts disappeared, and a severe skin rash cleared up.

In the middle of praying for a young man, he said, "I don't think God can truly forgive me for everything I've done."

I assured him, "Oh, yes He can. What's the problem?"

"I murdered someone," he said.

"On accident?" I said, hopefully.

"No, on purpose," he replied.

"I'll bet you were stoned or drunk right?" I commented, making a last ditch effort.

"No, I looked him right in the eyes while I was sober, and shot him in the face."

"TIME TO PRAY," I suggested. Since then, that young man has been set free from guilt, and is happily married. God can do anything!

From young people that had been eating out of garbage cans, to heroine addicts, to homosexuals no longer thrilled with their lifestyle, all found total freedom in Christ. I think it was the most wonderful time Diana and I had ever spent in our lives. God sent them; and we just let His love pour through us.

Chapter 19

Jesus Our Healer

One morning the Lord instructed me to drive forty miles to Visalia. "Diana, I feel like the Lord wants me to go to Visalia today."

Smiling she replied, "If it's Him doing the sending, don't question it, get going."

"I think He wants me to take Penny some flowers!" I shared. I'd never bought anyone other than my wife flowers for years.

"Well, God will instruct you on exactly what to do. Don't worry. Now, go!" Diana agreed.

Feeling very strange, I headed out the door. On the way, I felt a tremendous presence of power and authority in my car, and I knew it wasn't my own. As I got closer to Visalia, a powerful inner voice spoke to me and said, "Now, I want you to go to the Christian book store!" The only time I'd ever been in a Christian bookstore was with Diana.

"Well, this is really strange" I thought. I didn't even know what my reason for going in was.

Once inside the store, I said "Now what?"

The voice said, "Walk over to that rack." So I did.

My eyes met a wooden plaque that had a little red heart on it that had been broken. I picked it up and read the writing inscribed on it. The voice said, "Buy it." So I did, and had it wrapped. Then once outside, I got in my car and started driving down the road.

"If this is You Lord, what's going on?" I questioned.

The voice spoke very clearly to me and said, "Today I'm going to heal your little sister's broken heart." It all made sense now. Tears streaming down my cheeks, I couldn't believe what I was being used to be a part of.

He now instructed me to stop at a certain grocery store; and I thought, "Why here?" I walked into Albertson's and headed for the cards where I searched and found a beautiful one; and I picked up a little bundle of flowers to complete my purchase. I now headed out to the Holiday Inn, where my sister Penny worked.

The Lord instructed me to pull into a park right across the street from there. I began to talk to the Lord the only way I knew how, from my heart.

I said, "Lord, how can I be a part of You healing my little sister's broken heart?"

He told me He was going to give me some words, which I was to write. Then I was to seal the envelope and leave the card and gifts in her car and go.

I became very unsure and frightened. I said, "Lord, I don't even know how to write. Okay Father, I'll make You a deal. I'm going to pray in tongues and when I finish praying, I'm going to write down whatever You speak to me. If I hesitate or have to stop and think of what to say, that's it. I'll head home.

Praying for what seemed a long time, I finally stopped and these are the words that flowed onto the paper:

" BEHOLD, THESE WORDS OF PROMISE AND COMMAND! TODAY I SET YOU FREE FROM ALL PAIN AND BONDAGE OF A BROKEN HEART! RECEIVE THESE WORDS OF TRUTH AND YOU WILL SURELY KNOW THAT I AM LORD!"

On the way to where her car was parked, I was very excited, as I knew this was the Lord. I'll just stop and call Diana to read this to her, I reasoned.

"No!" the Lord sternly told me. "I'm sending you with this message, not Diana. Just obey Me."

"Whoops," I said. "Okay Lord, I hear Ya." So I dropped the things off and headed home.

Driving home, thoughts attacked my mind. What if this wasn't God? You could ruin your sister forever, telling her something like that. If you are wrong, you know you'll start drinking again and think this faith stuff is a lie. To say the least, by the time I got home I was shook. It was Bible study night, so we got right into teaching and that helped some.

Suddenly the phone rang, and shaking, I picked up the receiver. It was Penny. Crying her eyes out she said, "Dennis, you won't believe this; the Lord sent you today. It really was God who sent you!" "Tell me, Penny," I said. She explained that she had been up crying her eyes out all night. Praying specifically to God over and over that He would heal her broken heart!

Penney healed of her broken heart

What a joy to know I had heard from the Creator of the universe. I guess God was really showing me that it is possible to have a personal relationship with Him. When the Bible states God made Adam for fellowship, it's true. He longs to fellowship with you, too.

One day several friends from the Bible study group were over swimming. One adult was on the deck facing the pool and two were in the water. Playing with my son, Isaiah, I heard a wail from a child that had fallen. Leaping to his aid, I left Isaiah seated on a step with an adult one-foot away. The baby that had fallen on the wooden deck was crying really hard, so I walked him for nearly five minutes around the edges of the property.

Coming back, I spotted Isaiah, face down and motionless in the middle of the pool. Screaming, I dropped the child I had been holding, and raced to the pool. Diving in I grabbed Isaiah and drug him to the edge of the pool. Diana was at the store; and there I was staring at my son, who was completely out of it. I raced around our acre praying. Barely breathing out came the words, "Father, in JESUS NAME, heal my baby! Heal my baby!"

Satan came immediately taunting saying, "Your baby is going to be brain damaged just like the handicapped children you take care of." Immediately I rebuked him. With still no response, I pleaded with God. "You said in Your Word that You would protect my children if I was serving you with my whole heart. Please God, heal him." I was scared to death.

About that time Diana drove up, and screaming at the top of my lungs, I said, "Diana, PRAY! Isaiah was in the pool!" Running to me, Diana jerked that baby from my arms and prayed, also. Instantly, Isaiah's eyes opened and he said, "Hi, Mom." He had been healed instantly, from not only the effects of the water in his body, but also what appeared to be brain damage, if not death. We always credited guardian angels with saving Isaiah's life, but later discovered differently.

Chapter 20

Trust Me

ONE DAY, AFTER MUCH praying, Diana said, "I believe God is shifting us out of the business." A conflict had arisen as more and more people needed ministering to; and we still had our duties to our special children. All of the kids had made monumental progress. One client had been set free from epilepsy. Other clients had excelled in many areas, but for the last two years they had reached a plateau.

There was a conflict of the type of people that we were ministering to, as we had to comply with licensing standards. The Licensing agency would not have appreciated the type of company we were having over. Even though people left changed for life, it was a delicate situation.

Diana was now pregnant with our third baby. We discovered this at the Kenneth Copeland Convention in Anaheim. This baby was very special too, as Diana was taking birth control products when she became pregnant. Giving up our business, by faith, we went to Anaheim seeking the Lord. We sought the Lord day and night, seeking His specific guidance. While there, He gave me the first vision I'd ever had. I saw an enormous hand the length of our 20 by 40-foot pool in Terra Bella. The water in the vision was illuminated in much the same way pools look at night with the lights on. Lying in the middle of the hand was my son Isaiah.

God then spoke to me and said, "Son, that was my hand that held your baby up in the pool that day. I was there all the time. I heard your prayer." Turning to Diana who was in the middle of praising God, I quietly told her the vision I had just had, and instantly the Spirit made witness as she burst into tears and thanked God for yet one more special touch from Him.

Returning from the convention, we felt the Lord was asking us to follow Him much the same way I had followed Him the day I was sent to my sister Penny. A call from a ministry in Oklahoma confirmed what we believed. We had preached the truth, had seen many set free; and as they grew, we taught them to desire a holy, uncompromised walk. To let the person, of Jesus Christ, be formed in them and through them, to help others.

Now the Lord was calling us to a new level of trust in Him. Our house was offered to a church that wanted to have a home for ministry purposes. We offered it freely, all the equity, if they would take over what was owed. They decided not to, so we left it in the hands of a realtor, knowing that if it didn't sell, we would lose it. Walking away from all things, we returned anything we were indebted for, even sending the new car and truck back. We really believed God was calling us on everything we had ever taught, saying, "**Will you walk what you've talked about to so many**?"

Diana and I continued in prayer, and were convinced that our destination would be Oklahoma. After giving away most everything we owned to our Bible study kids, we stuffed the rest into a twelve-foot U-haul. A trailer hitch on the back towed our 1978 Audi that we had purchased for $800 cash; and what a spectacle it was!

"Diana, grab the boys and let's not forget Goliath, our little Cockapoo. Time to roll out!"

Here, I must share with you yet one more miracle that helped to convince us that God would answer prayers. Two years ago we bought Goliath from a local pet store. Born December 24th, weighing one pound, he was the cutest little thing you ever did see. Two weeks after buying him from the pet store, with no warning, Goliath became fatally ill. A veterinarian confirmed the worst. He was blind and had severe coccidia (A dog disease), his distended bloated stomach was ready to pop; and he could not walk. "Take him back to where you got him and maybe they'll give you a refund," was the hope that was offered.

Doing just that, Diana and I dropped him off, trying to figure out what to say to our oldest son, Isaac. Heading home, Diana, with tears streaming down her face, asked God to heal our little puppy; and Isaac offered a hearty AMEN!

Twenty-four hours later a surprised pet storeowner was on the phone. "I don't understand it," he said, "But your dog appears fine. Come pick him up." Glory! We did; and after a thorough inspection by the Vet, Goliath was pronounced totally well, sight restored. It was comical how the Vet seemed almost offended by the turn of events, as he could not explain it.

Isaac and Goliath

So our little dog, Goliath, was always special to us. Hopping into the front of the U-Haul we shut the door and waved goodbye to our special home. We were on our way with $2,300 in our pocket. God said He would meet our needs, so we stood on that promise.

We were so excited and for the first time in years, we felt like a real family.

I'll never forget how beautiful the ride was. I remember one stop in particular that we made at a Holiday Inn. On day two of our journey we were in the middle of the Colorado Mountains. Walking from the motel, we came across a little baseball field.

The grass was a deep, rich green and looked like velvet. Taking a deep breath, Diana and I just laid on the grass, while the boys ran to their hearts content up and down the field. What a beautiful country we live in. As we drove through Kansas with it's never-ending wheat fields, we couldn't wait to see our spiritual mother, Lori.

Yep, the same Lady used by God at my initial deliverance was manager of a restaurant called, "The Branch". It was connected with a beautiful motel called the Salina Inn in the town of Salina, Kansas. Lori graciously offered to have us as her guests for a few days of R & R before we continued to Oklahoma. Lori was very busy at the restaurant; and we tried to share all the wonderful things God had been doing in our Bible studies in a few short visits at the restaurant.

Anxious to see what the future held for us, we said our good-byes and once again headed down the road. We had called Paul and Maxine, the founders of the ministry we were headed for and they were excitedly expecting us, too. Rolling through Tecumseh, we followed directions to find the spot called Harjo. Driving through gorgeous woods with leaves just turning color, autumn warmly greeted us.

Spotting the dirt road that had been described to us over the phone, we turned left. Running up the road to greet us was this young woman, who turned out to be the most sincere human being I think I've ever met. Shirley was her name; and I mean to tell you there was no doubt she loved the Lord.

"You're here! You're here!" she shouted. "Praise God, Thank you Jesus. Oh, Lord, I'm so thankful you're here.

By the way, any of you all an evangelist?" I just love to tell people about Jesus! Oh, Praise God, Praise Gold!"

Subtlety was not Shirley's way, but I'll tell you, she wasn't just running at the mouth either. She meant every "Praise God," and you knew it.

Leading us up the hill to where the old school was, Shirley shared why she was extra bubbly that day. She and her husband had been without transportation, and had no money to fix their broken car. At midnight, the night before, someone unknown had driven up the lane and in the dark, had left a car.

When Billy, Shirley's husband, checked the car out he discovered an envelope with their names on it. Inside was the title to the car showing Billy and Shirley as owners and a car lot receipt marked paid in full. Billy went so far as to go to the car lot to see if a well-meaning friend had done it, but never found out who had given it. Needless to say, they were very happy.

Arriving on the school property, we headed for a small, white house on one corner of the property. Inside, I was introduced to an elderly man, who carried the name of Paul. Greeting us with hugs, it was only moments until his wife, Maxine, arrived on the scene and welcomed us with Oklahoma fervor.

Chapter 21

Trials and Tribulations

THE MOBILE HOME WE were to live in had not arrived yet, so our belongings were loaded into the gym, up the hill. Paul and Maxine insisted that we take their house and they retired to a little trailer parked up a ways on the property. It was a wonderful place to study the Word; and Diana and I were still reveling in our newfound freedom.

We both showered our boys with attention, and thanked God for such a wonderful opportunity to enjoy our family. The mobile home arrived, and so did the rains and cold weather. Here I got my first experience at playing plumber. The mobile home that had arrived had virtually every pipe leaking from some point or other.

Not being familiar with galvanized plumbing, I had my work cut out for me. To this day my wife teases me about the red stains I got on all my clothes from that red Oklahoma clay. For two full weeks I fought plumbing, and now I think I could probably tackle plumbing a whole house by myself. During this time Diana had lots of opportunity to sing and preach which she thoroughly enjoyed.

Maxine felt the Lord would keep us based in Oklahoma about a year, yet there was turmoil in my spirit. After roofing parts of the gym, I continued to pray and shared with Diana that something was about to happen. "I don't believe God has sent me to remodel buildings."

Diana replied, "Well, if the Lord wants us in Texas sooner, He is able to make the way, so don't worry."

Driving down the road after getting some things in town the next day, I was stunned to hear God say, "You'll be leaving here soon. Very soon."

Getting home I told Diana, who an hour later received a call from Maxine. "Honey, the couple in Texas has had personal problems and I'm afraid we'll need you to go down there soon. How Soon? In about three days." Once again I had heard directly from the Spirit of God, whom I was learning to appreciate.

Two days away was Isaiah's second birthday, and also, what turned out to be a home going for our precious little Grandma Frank. When I first met Diana, we traveled to where Ivan's mother Sarah lived, and visited for a few days.

Grandma wouldn't go anywhere and had not been well. Her body had recovered, but she just had lost her sparkle. I asked her a few questions, which led to hours of looking at pictures when she was a young girl. Transformed with memories, Sarah giggled and told wonderful stories. Wouldn't you know that the next day she agreed to go to a museum out of town, that had a plaque dedicated to Diana's' Grandfather.

Sarah ended up having the time of her life. From that time on she decided she still wanted more in life. I remember Diana telling me that Sarah had asked her "Is he the one?" Diana quickly replied, "Yes, Grandma."

Hearing the news that Sarah had died, Diana had a beautiful experience. Fall was changing the leaves into brilliant colors so taking a walk outside Diana found tears starting to trickle down her cheeks. She told me later that just as grief tried to take a hold of her heart God gave her a vision. She saw Sarah full of joy, laughing and running across a field of flowers, Grandma appeared to be about thirty again; and as Diana saw this, the Holy Spirit said, "Are you really going to grieve?" "I guess the only reason to grieve would be for myself," Diana thought. That seemed hard to do knowing we will see Sarah in Heaven again and the parting is temporary. Seeing Grandma so full of joy and life while remembering how happy God must be to have her back home, it hardly seemed right to mourn. In just a few seconds God had shown Diana the reality of how different He can make any situation when you let Him.

Grandma Sarah, with Isaiah, and Isaac"

Gathered in the dining hall where we had attended Bible studies and fellowshipped with some very sweet people, I ate some birthday cake and reflected on more blessings that had occurred in our six weeks in Oklahoma. Leaving many things at base camp there, we headed for Odessa, Texas the next morning.

Trailing Paul's long yellow Cadillac was a six foot brown trailer, holding just bare necessities. Following in our Audi, the 14-hour drive seemed longer, due to our car being packed to the hilt. I remember Isaiah perched on top of a microwave, and Isaac, surrounded by pictures, plates, and stuffed animals.

"Bare necessities," my wife had said.

Pulling in at midnight, Diana and I were thrilled. The neighborhood and apartments weren't as bad as we had expected. It was a bad part of town but we had envisioned hookers on our doorstep, with derelicts hanging out of every tree, not so. Walking into our sleeping place for the night, a reality of the needs sharply loomed in our faces. A gutted apartment with a filthy couch covered with cigarette burns greeted us, complete with a rolled up joint left by a transient. Too tired to care, I saw a mattress on the floor in one room, and to heat us that night was a gas stove a room away. Broken windows and a urine stained toilet glared at us from a corner. A single light bulb hanging from the ceiling on a cord finished the view. Mission begun, I thought to myself.

Unpacking a few blankets, Diana attempted to find a clean spot for the boys. Goliath happily snuggled in, thrilled to be along for the ride.

The next morning the wildest thing happened, that to this day I don't fully understand. God literally told me I couldn't stay. The catalyst and events that led to this were not important. What was important is that I had to make a decision between a compromised walk, or to trust whole-heartedly in Him. I chose the latter. We informed Paul and Maxine that even though we disagreed on some things we dearly loved them, but had to do what was right between the Lord and us. So here we sat in the tip of Texas, penniless with not an idea in our heads about what was next.

The Lord, in His infinite wisdom, tried and tested us. Patiently He waited for me to learn current lessons, and then would move me on to another refining. A door opened for us to head back to Kansas, so packing for a third time we waited the seven days until we could go back to Oklahoma. Meanwhile in the very midst of the biggest battle, the greatest Glory of God took place. A man named Ken was at the door. He had been the previous manager and was obviously bound by alcohol.

"Come on in," I offered and, to my surprise, he did. Maxine shared a few words and then turning to me said, "You know, Dennis was an alcoholic. Perhaps he could share what helped him."

As the Holy Spirit poured, I had real compassion for Ken. He was a typical big old Texan that stood 6'3" with a twang you couldn't forget. What a teddy bear he was, though. I told him what a difference Jesus had made in my life and that if he wanted to give the Lord an opportunity; Jesus would help him, too. A voice had told Ken the night before that he was going to die if he didn't repent and give up alcohol and give his life to the Lord.

It was absolutely glorious leading that big old Texan to Jesus Christ. Ken was instantly delivered and set totally free from that awful bondage. Diana and I often talked about Ken, saying if the main purpose for our going all that way was for one soul to find abundant life, it was worth every test and trial. Last time we saw Ken he was waving away with a big ole glass of orange juice in his hand. Straight juice that is!

All packed, our hearts lightened with that salvation, we drove back the 14 hours to Oklahoma.

Isaiah and Isaac in the packed Audi

Although arrangements had been made for Lori's son, Greg, to pick us up, bad weather made it impossible. During those next two weeks, I fellowshipped a lot with Billy and Shirley, and their three adorable kids. Talk about some good times. I really wish that we had shared more time with them. Our little families had a blessed Thanksgiving. Diana offered a ham that Paul and Maxine had bought us, and Billy provided deer meat, fresh beets and macaroni and cheese. The weather finally lifted, and giving even more possessions away, we were escorted out of Oklahoma with one small trailer filled with all of our belongings.

Arriving in Salina, the snow was so beautiful; it looked surreal. Greg, and Patty his wife, had offered to let us live with them and welcomed us into their home as if we were blood relatives. Since Patty had three wonderful sons, our boys were thrilled. A few days later Lori called and asked if I would wash dishes. She needed the help and knew we needed some money. After having had two successful businesses, not to mention 5 years of cooking experience, I did not joyfully anticipate washing dishes. In other words, my pride (which I thought I didn't have) and I met. Lori had also worked it out that Diana could do some hostessing. Biting my lip, I mumbled, "Sure, thank you."

Within two weeks after arriving we were not only gainfully employed, but had been introduced to a man named Ken, who was a Realtor. Offering us a chance to rent-to-own, he even offered us free rent for the first month, if I could do some minor work for him. The little house was tiny but cute. I could hardly believe that within two weeks, I was going to be in my own home, after leaving Texas without a penny. God did many great things during our eleven weeks in Kansas.

Because Greg and Patty did not have a phone, no one knew the day we were moving into our new little house. The morning Diana and I left Greg's house, the snow was falling at a good pace. Arriving at our new home, we moved our belongings in and realized we had two sons who had a habit of liking to eat, but we had no food and not one-dime.

"God will provide," Diana said. Barely getting theses words out, she turned and cried for joy. Up the walk came Lori and a cook who worked for her named Kenny. Their arms were full of grocery bags. There must have been twenty bags of food and household products. What a mighty God we serve. Many other blessings occurred, including several strangers walking up to me, handing me money saying the Lord had told them to. This always happened when it was most needed.

The restaurant I worked in was one of the prettiest I'd ever seen. The decor had been brought in from Mexico and second hand shops. Bright, big, paper flowers from Mexico decorated the walls. Spray painted branches, with colorful macaws were mounted around the room. Only five weeks after I arrived in Kansas, I had worked up to night manager and was overseeing the cooking. Nursing my wounded pride from washing dishes, I had learned a lot about myself.

Being with Lori was wonderful; and Diana and I were really content in our new home. Working away, once again came the order to move. I came home from work and told Diana more shifting was going on. Little did I know that just that day, Dorothy, Diana's Mom had called. "Diana, if you guys ever decide to come home, we'll help you in any way we can." she said, "We sure do miss those grandsons."

As Diana was recounting the conversation to me, to my amazement, the owner of our house came by and said, "Would you be horribly disappointed if I had sold the house? We wouldn't leave you in the cold. There's a mobile home I think you could move to." Even I can take a hint. Call your mom back I told Diana. Briiiiiiing! As the phone rang, we could hardly wait for her Mother to answer. Memories of loved ones and precious times flooded my mind.

"Hello? Yes, Diana, I was serious!" said Dorothy.

"Has someone been praying?" Diana asked

"Well, come to think of it, Dennis' Mother said she had been specifically praying for you to come home." Dorothy replied

"Well, Mom," Diana shouted from the background, "Tell Maurine her prayers have been answered."

"Great, I'll tell your Dad." Dorothy commented and with that Diana's Mom hung up the phone.

Counting the stay at Greg's, this was our sixth move in four months. Thank God Diana was having a healthy pregnancy. I was amazed at the way she could hustle a tray filled with several dinner plates, up and down stairs to the banquet rooms. After all the moves, packing was not a big chore, and as always, the hardest part was saying goodbye.

Chapter 22

Homeward Bound

WE STARTED OUT ON our long trip back, but this time we had a moving company haul our few belongings. It was so nice just to pack clothes and jump in the car and go. We had grown to love Kansas, but the thought of being close to loved ones was really exciting. It had been a very busy four months, but oh, what an education we'd gotten!

When we left Kansas we knew our windshield wipers didn't work, and we were trying to outrun a storm. We would have had them fixed, but we had already sunk a bundle into getting the lights fixed, and didn't have the extra money. After driving all day, we pulled into Dalhart, Texas in the middle of a snowstorm.

At the motel I discovered the radiator was cracked at the top, around the cap. The car was really over heated, and I felt fortunate to have made it to town. Catching the news, I was not thrilled to learn, we were in the middle of severe weather with more snow on the way. The following day was spent in our motel room, as there was no way we were going anywhere.

That night, Diana and I both awoke at 2 a.m. "Do you think we ought to head out before the storm gets worse?" Diana asked. "I don't know, but we could give it a try." I agreed.

To this day I really believe God used little Goliath to save our lives. With the car packed and engine running, Diana called Goliath. He was nowhere to be found. We even drove up and down a two-mile stretch calling, "Here boy, Goliath, come on." But Goliath was not to be found. Since he had always come whenever we called, we were really surprised.

Finally, I said, "Let's go back to the room. We can't leave him here." I also saw that in about 10-degree weather the car had heated up too fast. Unloading the boys and carrying them to the room, Diana and I were joined by Goliath! Later when we found out the true condition of the car and how bad road conditions were ahead, we knew Goliath had saved our hides.

Rising the next morning, Diana said, "What are we going to do?"

"I can't do anything," I said angrily.

"Well, we could be getting the car fixed while we're snowed in, then it would be ready by the time the storm lifts." Diana retorted.

Wonderful! Just wonderful! It must have been 9 degrees outside as I headed out looking for a radiator shop. I was sliding down the street looking for a gas station or somewhere to ask directions. I couldn't see anything because of not having any windshield wipers. My left arm hung out the side door; and I attempted to wipe off the windshield over and over. Frozen, and blinded by the snow I had to pull over.

Sliding into a parking lot, I found myself at a donut shop. The man was in the process of closing the shop due to the storm. I felt like I was in the "Twilight Zone".

"Hey buddy," I yelled. "Do you know where there's a radiator shop?"

"You're in luck," he replied. "The only one who works on radiators is right across the street. It's a gas station, but they do that kind of work to."

Hoping the car would start, I turned the key, thanked God as it did, and drove across the street, where the car died. A huge cowboy sat in his chair.

"Can I help y'all?" he drawled.

"Yes. It's my radiator." I said with frustration

"Well, Tex should be in soon," and with that this good ole boy struck up a conversation about storms in the year 1902 or something. My mind was obviously on a stranded family. Four hours later, after Tex arrived, the man offered me a ride back to my motel. He said Tex would call me as soon as he finished, maybe 3:00 or 4:00 o'clock that afternoon.

When I got back, Diana was frantic. Day two of constant commotion with two small boys, the storm, and the discovery that there were no taxis, no cars for rent, and no way to get food was driving her nuts. At six, I gave up hope that I'd hear from the gas station guys that day. Meanwhile Diana had discovered a market in the yellow pages that would deliver.

The night passed with no word from these guys, so by 9:00 am the following morning, I called the police. It was the only way I could get a ride back to the gas station. Tex had fixed the radiator, but to let the sealant dry they had to leave it out overnight. So now, here I was again, waiting for Tex to show, to install the radiator. I wasn't allowed to install it because of insurance reasons. The snow was lifting a little and all I could think about was getting out of this town.

Crossing the street to the Laundromat, I loudly offered money to anyone who would give me a ride to my motel. It's incredible how a room full of people can suddenly go deaf. Declaring it a shame how a man could fight a war for his country, but couldn't get a ride 5 miles down the street I attempted to shame someone into offering assistance. As I raised my voice with each new comment, finally, the owner of the Laundromat offered some assistance. Diana said he was probably afraid I was about to come unglued, if I wasn't already. Asking the man who gave me the ride to the hotel to hold on, I bundled my wife, kids, suitcases, and the dog into his car and requested that he now take us back to the gas station.

I figured if I parked the whole family there at the station, Tex might get off his duff and do something. It worked. Hurrah! "I guess Tex isn't coming in today," the other tall Texan offered 'so maybe I better do it so you folks can get goin." Getting the radiator back in place the good ole boy threw me the keys and pointed to the car. I jumped behind the wheel and turned the key.

Nothing! Dead! Dead as a doornail! NO LIFE! Are you getting my drift?

Numb, I said, "Come on Mom, grab the kids. We're going to this little cafe next door, feed the kids, and discuss this situation." Diana was totally silent.

A young man visiting his wife, who managed the cafe, overheard our conversation and said, "Hey, I'm a mechanic here in town. I've got a shop to work on it, and can get it towed over there, no problem." Coincidence? I doubt it. He fixed the car in under two hours and only charged me $25.00. That included the tow. The car was fixed by 11:00 a.m. Since we were going to gain an hour of time heading to New Mexico, we decided to leave right away. God bless that little couple. Heading out, we just knew our troubles were over.

Within 10 miles we ran into traffic and the worst road conditions that I'd ever driven in, my entire life. Diana was now over 6 months pregnant and how she endured all those bumps only God knows. The road was so narrow that two rigs could hardly have passed going opposite directions.

A snowplow had only managed to chop up all the snow, which had then frozen. Our Audis frame was in constant contact with the ridges left by the snowplow. If you've ever gotten a flat tire you might get an idea of the conditions. To add to the overall view, we had no chains and still no wipers. The snow had stopped falling but the rigs going by marred the visibility, as they threw shovelfulls of dirty slush on the windshield. My little Audi had a sunroof, so with no other choice, Diana hung out the top, and standing on the seat wiped her arms back and forth like wipers.

There was no way to turn around, and as we passed more than one car that had slid off the road, we knew to be careful. The temperature was around 14 degrees; and I know Diana got slush directly in the face several times when she didn't duck back inside the car fast enough. At the time this experience was very serious and we prayed more than once that our car would not stall. We averaged 10 miles per hour as it took us 8 hours to travel 80 miles. Seeing that the Tucumcari motels were sold out of, we made the decision to go as far as Santa Rosa.

We were now on the bigger highway. Before we left Tucumcari, we found that the frame was solid ice, and there were icicles above the tires. After about 30 minutes we knew there was only about an hour of daylight left. As we saw a sign indicating a gas station, over 5 miles away, Diana and I heard a clunk. It sounded like the whole transmission was gone. Somehow, the car was still running, but oh, it was hurting. It sounded so bad I thought the engine would blow at any minute.

That was the longest 5 miles I've ever driven. Pulling onto the off ramp, we saw one, dinky, run down station with probably several hundred cars and trucks. Most of them were waiting out the storm, or so they thought. It was getting colder and colder. We had a flat tire and discovered that our tire jack was broken. I began frantically asking people to loan me a jack. Finally, a young man from my hometown of Fresno, CA. offered me his. The spare tire in place, we had about 20 miles to go and our lights were not working regularly.

Jumping behind the wheel I turned the key. Repeatedly I tried to get it to turn over and finally, the battery was almost gone. By now I was very quiet and Diana hung her head and wept. Even though she was weeping, she was reminding God of His promises to us.

Isaac said, "Dad, start it the way you did back in Kansas."

"What do you mean, son?" I said

"Back up and do it, Dad!" Isaac said again. Suddenly, I knew what he was trying to tell me. When the battery was low, I would turn the key on, pop the clutch, and off we'd go. Looking at Diana, I said, "It's our last chance." Diana held her breath, Isaac cheered, and even Isaiah joined in as the engine barely started. Out of the mouth of babes!

"Oh,
He brought forth his people with joy,
He brought forth his people with joy,
His chosen with gladness,
He brought forth his people with joy!"

This was our theme song every time we were being tested. We all sang loudly as we beat it down the road for Santa Rosa. It took us an hour to go the last 20 miles. Pulling into the town, we saw literally hundreds and hundreds of trucks everywhere.

A Holiday Inn was the first motel on our left, and I told Diana to run and go get us a room. Within a few minutes, all their rooms were gone and we had gotten one of the last ones. There were people sleeping in the hallways, on the steps, sprawled on couches in the lobby, you name it. The National Guard was called out, and Santa Rosa was declared a national disaster area.

Well, here we were, our fourth night on the road, and we were only as far as New Mexico. Our money had dwindled from $600 to $80; and we were in a motel paying $40 a night.

"Mother, Help!" Diana cried out on the phone. Feeling like college kids calling home, Diana explained the situation.

Dorothy, Diana's mother, was so neat. "I'll send you our credit card numbers and don't you budge until those roads are safe. Don't take my grandsons on those roads until the storm has passed."

Later, Dorothy called and said, "I talked to Ivan and we figured you may need some cash. We'll send some of that Western Union too."

Now that Grandpa and Grandma had given us strict orders, along with financial support, we decided to take a forced vacation. Snow fell for the next two days straight. We could see the highway from our room; and we were told that traffic was backed up in several cities. Schools had been opened up for people who were stranded to sleep at.

The snow that had been so deadly while on the road was breathtaking from the safety of our motel room. We enjoyed the R&R, lots of room service, and visiting others who were stranded. Diana talked with a trucker who had taken the same highway that we had taken out of Dalhart Texas. "I've driven over 40 years and I've never been on a road that bad!" he commented.

By the end of the sixth day after leaving Kansas, we were ready to be on the road again. Clear skies, Wow! Nothing can stop us now! After spending the night in Arizona, we started out at 5 am in the morning for arrival day home. Laughing hysterically, Diana headed out the sunroof as the worst rainstorm to hit California began to poor in on our heads! Wipe, Wipe, Wipe. What a trooper!

Chapter 23

He Will Rule As God

OUR WELCOME HOME WAS wonderful. My in-laws, Ivan and Dorothy, welcomed our family into their home. Diana and I started looking for a way to meet our needs. Since we needed a place to live and a job, it seemed to make sense to apply for management jobs. Still praying that God would shut every door that was not correct; it was incredible, not one reply to our job applications.

Once again we began house hunting. We found the cutest little white house on Myrtle Street, placed exactly halfway between both grandparents. Diana's parents, sticking to their offer, continued to help us with mental and financial support.

Selling the Audi, Ivan offered us his Datsun. Set now with a home, the start of a business (I decided to take an ad out for handyman), once again we were on our way. On May 24th, the arrival of Israel Jonathan Nickell brightened our world. Trusting God with just two of us was one thing, and now, our little Israel brought the family count to five.

Isaac, Israel and Isaiah

Bringing all work to a literal halt for four weeks, Diana and I sought the Lord, yet another time.

We believe that was when we heard God say, "By the word of your testimony, share the wonderful things I have done for you." I always preached that if the Lord required my material wealth, it would not affect my trust or love of the Lord one bit. I really do treasure my spiritual blessings far above any thing the world has to offer! Three healthy, happy boys, a wife that is a joy and loves God with all her heart, and a spirit, soul, and body full of love, peace, and joy that only Christ can give. Yes, I knew I was the richest man on Earth.

Summer was drawing to a close, when one afternoon; I arrived home to find my sister-in-law, Cathy, had stopped by. "Diana, Cathy's ready for a deliverance!" "Oh, Praise God!" Diana blurted out, and tears streamed down her face. If you had watched this beautiful woman turn into a vegetable, you would have wept too.

My mom, who had stopped by with Cathy, offered to take the kids to her house for a while.

Now we had been involved with a few deliverances, but we by no means drum them up to entertain ourselves. So heading off to the den we were prayerful as to what the Spirit of God wished us to do.

You see sometimes, a simple prayer of repentance, on the part of an individual needing help, and they would be set free. At other times we experienced commanding literal demons out, similar to my deliverance. We never anticipated what was to follow. Seating Cathy comfortably in a chair, Diana and I laid hands on Cathy, and instantly, literal demons started manifesting. Several hours later and obviously tired, yet relieved, Cathy smiled and said she thought she'd head on home for the night. I did not get a peace about it, yet being unsure what else to do, we said fine.

Cathy called repeatedly through the night and we knew something wasn't right yet. "Diana, go ahead and take the baby. Visit Cathy and see what's going on."

"Sounds good, " Diana said and headed out the door. Driving towards Hanford, a town 20 miles away, Diana felt an urgency to pray in tongues. Half way there, she found her words switch to English and commanded a spirit of suicide down from its stronghold over Cathy and Sam's house.

When Jesus said, "I've given you the keys to the kingdom. What so ever you bind on earth will be bound in heaven, and what so ever you loose on earth will be loosed in heaven," He was not kidding! The power and authority, which the prayer was being prayed with, was not her own. Diana was overwhelmed with an urgency to get to Cathy. Now for those of you, who don't believe you're in a war, as Jesus said, let me share one more little confirmation of the reality of the enemy. Driving down this two-lane highway, right as all this praying was going on, the Holy Spirit jogged her, and she looked in the rearview mirror to see a huge sliver gray low rider Cadillac bearing down on her at over 100 miles an hour. In front of Diana was a whole line of cars and coming in the opposite lane was a semi.

"BLOOD OF JESUS over me," She cried, and swerved off the road so as not to be rammed. That death machine careened by and within 50 yards had pulled onto a side road and proceeded at about 30 miles an hour. Not a coincidence! Arriving, Cathy answered the door and not only looked like a total zombie, but also immediately said she had just been fighting off thoughts of suicide.

"Cathy, sit down," Diana told her. With the baby hanging over one arm Diana sank onto the couch next to Cathy.

Starting to comfort Cathy, Diana placed her hand on Cathy's shoulder and instantly this demonic voice wailed out,

"Nooooooo!" Hands off! This was not to be dealt with now. As Diana took her hand away, Cathy's face stopped contorting, and Diana mumbled something about rest, and that she was going to call me.

"Honey, I don't understand it, but Cathy needs help. This battle isn't over yet."

"Well, bring her over with you," I said. So after seat belting Cathy in the back seat, baby in front, off she headed for home.

Arriving at naptime for the kids was perfect, so off we headed to our den once more. "Diana, I think you're supposed to pray with Cathy alone." I said.

Kneeling together as I left the room, Diana asked Cathy the simplest question, "Can you say Jesus?" Now, this was a woman who had accepted Christ and had experienced the power of God in her life more than once. Her mouth quivered and her face started shaking. Stuttering, she could not physically say that name.

"Dennis!" Diana yelled. "This one's for you, too!" Coming back in the room, I began a battle that lasted for hours. We had seen people contort before, but this was a first.

Cathy slid off the chair, mouth open, eyes bulging and a gross raspy voice gurgled, "She's mine! You can't have her, I'm going to kill her!" The mighty power of God rose up in me and I stared that lying devil down. "You loose her in the name of Jesus. Cathy belongs to Jesus Christ." Physically sitting on her body so it wouldn't flop all over the room, I continued to command the spirits out!

One by one, the spirits were called out. "Rejection, Rebellion, Suicide, Go! In the name of Jesus!" Afterwards, Cathy was not only Cathy again, but there was joy, smiles, and the name of Jesus being praised from her mouth. Oh, God, You are real!

That night Cathy started the steady process of getting used to herself, physically and spiritually, from a whole new perspective. Physically her body had gone months with only 2 to 4 hours sleep a night; so there was some time involved for her body to get back to normal. Penny gladly came over to help, and that night we visited. Now, Cathy was consuming home made chicken soup by the bowlfuls.

The next day and night were emotionally draining, as Cathy's body wanted to stay on the old schedule, but the chains of bondage were broken.

Constantly Satan attacked her mind with doubt and unbelief, but deep inside she knew a big change had happened. On the third morning you would not have recognized this woman, heading home with unadulterated joy! That night and following, she slept 6, 7, and 8 hours as her body got use to the new schedule.

Cathy later told us that she had watched us go from a $70,000 a year job to nothing, possessions gone, etc., and no matter what state she saw us in we had a peace and a joy that she didn't have. That's why she was drawn to us. After 18 years of sleeping problems, suicide bouts, 26 different anti depressants, Cathy was free!

Later we discovered that Sam had fasted and prayed for three days to break the demonic stronghold. It was just a few weeks prior that he had petitioned God on setting his wife free. Praise God, also, for a husband that is one of the most sincere men I've ever met. Not enough can be said about that kind of love.

Oh, people, the Bible is true. Ephesians 6:12 say, "We wrestle not against flesh and blood, but against principalities, against powers, against the rulers of darkness of this world, against spiritual wickedness in high places."

Jesus said, "For this purpose I've come. To undo the works of the devil." Jesus was the embodiment of all truth. If He referred to the devil, the snake, Lucifer, the fallen one, He knew he was referring to a real fallen being. How people twist and say, "Oh, He meant the devil in us," is unbelievable.

How can intelligent people continue to refuse the truth of who we are in a war with? Yet, Jesus commanded His followers to heal the sick, cast out demon, etc. That is what His kingdom is about! Letting that which is in His believers, flow through to the need. And those who do not accept Jesus Christ truly have not looked at the price that was paid.

A few weeks passed, when I came rushing into the house. "Diana, I'm going to the coast to pray! I believe God just spoke that to me." "Good, go!" Diana replied. Within two days, I had a wonderful experience with God, who instructed me to be diligent about spending time with Him. During the second day of fasting, early in the morning I walked down to the beach. I sat down on a huge rock

As my heart cried out to God, the Glory of God descended and lit up the entire beach. I was the only one on the entire beach and God's presence was so awesome; no words could ever do justice to what I experienced. I need direction, now Lord, I need a job, and I pleaded. As I sat there in awe I heard Him say, "Come with Me!"

He led me up a path towards the street. I thought I was heading back to my hotel room. Instead He said, "Look up on that hill." As I looked, I saw a help wanted sign in the window. The sign advertised for a maid and I thought to myself, the sign says maids - what does that have to do with me?

Strongly, God repeated, "Go up there," So I did. Walking up to the front desk, I inquired if they needed a manager, as I had seen a sign hanging in the window. "No, just a maid," a man said. "Well, my wife and I are looking to manage something." "Get his number," a lady's voice yelled from the back room. Two days later back at home, we got the big call. Hired! Now we looked forward to a new job and a home one block from the ocean, with a view.

Chapter 24

We Wrestle Not Against Flesh And Blood

ONCE AGAIN, HAD ANYONE told us what was ahead, I'm not sure I would have obeyed the Spirit and moved to the coast. Oh, it was beautiful enough. Who wouldn't want to live one block from the beach in your own private house complete with seagulls and all? The owners of the motel we were to run forgot to mention one little thing, it was plagued by it's own personal witch. After five months there, we left not knowing if the owners themselves were practicing witches.

The funny part about this was prior to moving to the coast; I had a very vivid dream where I ended up in a room full of witches. In that dream I wanted to get up and rebuke them in the name of Jesus, but the Holy Spirit wouldn't let me. He said, "Dennis, you are here to learn something."

Now, I know what you're thinking. Diana and I had gone off the edge because of past experiences with deliverances, etc., but that just isn't true. Many times in our lives we have gone months and months without seeing or being involved in any kind of that activity.

Well, anyway let me tell you how this began. Diana was taking walks early in the morning at 4:30 a.m., and was proclaiming Jesus as Lord over the town, the motel, etc.

On one of these occasions she felt led to turn to Morro Bay Rock and command certain spirits down from their strongholds out over the heavens. After speaking in tongues, the spirit identified was witchcraft. Suddenly something connected. Diana could not put into words the force that came through her as she addressed that spirit. It seemed as if Christ Himself was speaking through her; and she knew there had been a tremendous shaking in the spirit realm. The Word says that ALL of hell shakes at the name of JESUS!

The next afternoon Diana was walking on the beach and a poor, pathetic looking woman was walking along the shore. She seemed absolutely driven, and physically was much older than her years. As soon as Diana's eyes rested on her the Holy Spirit revealed the woman was a witch. This woman was over a quarter of a mile away down the beach from Diana. When the Spirit spoke to Diana and identified the woman, it shocked Diana, and she said, "My God, there is a witch!"

This woman was out of earshot, yet she hurled around and started shaking her fists and screaming at Diana. What she was screaming couldn't be made out, but that's ok! This was a first for Diana and all she knew to do was to start pleading the blood of Jesus over herself and over the woman. The spirit of witchcraft challenged Diana for about five minutes during which time Diana just continued to speak the name of Jesus. Defeated, the witch turned around and went off at the same agitated pace. A little shook up but thrilled at God's power, Diana continued in the opposite direction and headed back to the motel. Diana told me what had happened; and I responded with, "Yeah, right."

Well, it didn't take long for me to get the picture when the witch showed up at the edge of the motel property. There was a pay phone there and she would come and stand next to it, not use it, but would scream curses against us as her arms were madly waving in all directions. Usually we ignored her, but sometimes I would get mad and turn, and command those demons in her to go away. When I did she would immediately run to her car and peel out like a bat out of...well, you get the picture.

Now as all this was going on, Diana and I discovered that our idea of manager and the owner's idea of manager were two totally different things. For the first two months Diana and I worked every day, all day, and were on call at night. We did all the work for the motel. Although it was small and had 17 units, that's a lot of beds to change.

Our first week there I had built a fenced play yard for the boys so they would have a safe place to play. Baby Israel was about 6 months when we took this job. We would watch all three sons, rent rooms, do all the bookkeeping, all the maintenance, all maid work, and even wash the laundry for the whole motel, ourselves. Thank God it was the slow season.

On occasion Diana or I would try to get to the beach for walks. While the work was going on, and our personal witch was trying to keep our attention, we tried to keep our eyes on the Lord and what He was doing; and that was plenty. So much was going on, the days flew by. Remember Cathy, my sister? Well right before we moved to the coast we had the privilege of leading her stepson Scotty, and his girlfriend Tracy, to the Lord.

They were so precious. They came over to visit several times. One time Cathy laid hands on Tracy; and Tracy received the baptism of the Holy Spirit. How exciting knowing that only recently Cathy had been unable to meet her own basic needs, let alone help others. The Lord was sending people over to the coast to be ministered to. In God's wisdom, it was always when the motel was slow. Since we had a separate house from the motel we were able to minister without interrupting any guests.

Penny, my little sister, was over one time with her children. They had a nice visit and were preparing to leave. Penny's brand new car wouldn't start, and so walking back into our house I said, "OK, Lord, what's going on?" Her oldest son Brian seemed a little uneasy and my heart started to move with compassion towards him. He had been listening to our stories of all the exciting things God was doing; and as a teenager I'm sure had a million questions. He was old enough to remember his Uncle Dennis drunk all the time, and had seen his life dramatically changed.

That morning the Holy Spirit spoke to Diana and said, "Brian is not absolutely sure of his eternal destination." So asking him, she discovered she had heard the Spirit of God.

"No, Aunt Diana. I'm not sure." Brian responded. Well, Joy unspeakable was ours as Penny and I led Brian to not only recommit his life to Jesus, but also let him know that Jesus would never leave him.

Diana and I continued to encourage people as the Lord led. Finally after two months or so, I took a day off to help my sister Penny. She was in the middle of another trial and the Lord used me again for direction in her life. Driving off, I was hoping it would be calm since Diana would be covering the motel for two days by herself, with all three children.

About five minutes after I drove away the witch was back. Diana later told me the curtains were drawn, but there was about ¼ of an inch crack that she could see the witch through. Diana really started to have compassion for this woman. This woman couldn't have been over 35 but she looked 60.

Diana started weeping and asked God why wouldn't He set this tormented soul free? Then Diana started to get really angry that this woman appeared barely to have any mind left.

Standing back, Diana faced her direction (curtains still closed) and said, "In the name of Jesus, I come against every spirit that is holding that mind captive!!!" The witch took two steps sideways; and all of a sudden, Diana was literally thrown on her behind by a spirit of fear. Gasping, Diana pled the Blood of Jesus and commanded the spirit of fear to leave her house, now! Which it did. Still shaking and on the verge of tears, she called and left a message for me to call immediately. When I returned her call, she told me what had happened.

You just found out a valuable lesson about compassion, I told Diana. You tried to operate in your own power, not God's! And you don't have any! He didn't tell you to do that. Your compassion did. Now get your eyes off that witch and ignore her. You'll be fine. And she was.

October through December, the months flew. At Christmas Dorothy and Ivan came over and brought Isaac and Isaiah two motorized motorcycles! Oh, how the boys loved those. With Christmas Eve approaching Diana and I were surprised to find no business at the motel. So, we prepared for a quiet holiday.

As I went to close the office and lobby Christmas Eve, I sensed something strange. I was bending over to unplug the Christmas lights when my eyes saw a pair of boots; and it startled me, as I had not noticed anyone upon entering the lobby. Sitting in the corner was a person, who I thought was Satan manifesting in person. Scraggly, twisted gray hair that hung down his back gave him the definite look of a drifter that made Charlie Manson look like a wimp. Pointing at the Christmas ornaments he said, "See those worlds? I've been to every one of them. I have been all over California, up and down the coast. I died along highway 101 at least 7 times."

At this, I came to the house and said, "I think Satan is manifesting in our lobby. Come on Diana, let's go over there, you won't believe this." No kidding; this was one character who was totally possessed and we didn't really know why he was at our motel.

Diana and I went over to the lobby and spoke with him a little while longer. Gene was his name; and as he continued to blurt out violent statements we decided to call the police. As I was calling, Diana did the only thing she knew to do. "Gene, do you want to know Jesus???" Diana asked. "I know who He is," he said. "Do you want to know Him personally?" With that Gene counted, "One—two--three" and then took his hand and made as if cutting his throat by pulling his finger across his neck.

"Oh, great!" At that, Diana tried the last ditch effort. "Here Gene, take this sandwich. You need to eat!"

"NO, NO, I don't want that."

I told him since he didn't want Jesus and he didn't want food he might as well go. The police arrived shortly, and even though we pointed out which direction he'd gone, they could find no one. Diana saw Gene the next day in San Luis Obispo, by a traffic light, talking into the air and to anyone who would listen.

In January the city of San Luis Obispo mailed out labor laws for motel owners. The motel owners had received a copy of the labor laws; and knew darn well it was illegal to work us 24 hours a day, for 4 months with no breaks for $600 dollars a month. So they gave us notice that they were broke and wanted to lay us off.

Once again, here we were being tested in our faith. With a 30-day notice we owned nothing and had nowhere to go! For weeks we applied at every motel up and down the coast, we even checked the mountains above Fresno. Nobody had the right set-up for a family of five. Deciding to take only what fit in our car, we had a yard sale, and guess who came? Yep, you got it! The witch. Walking boldly into our fenced yard she acted as if she had never laid eyes on either of us. Picking up a spider off of a plant leaf she looked at me and said, "How pretty!" Then she turned and looked through all the clothes for sale and picked out the dress that Diana had gotten married in. Paying for it, she left. Diana and I immediately prayed for the Blood of Jesus over the dress and that it could not be used for any evil purpose.

On one of our trips looking for a new job we had trouble with our car. It took us eight hours to limp it from the coast to Cathy and Sam's in Hanford. Having to put it into the shop, Cathy's husband Sam, offered to let us use his second car. Now as thankful as we were, we determined that we wouldn't let anything happen to this borrowed car, as car trouble was Sam's worst pet peeve.

Driving back to the motel we discussed how we just had to trust God with our life; and it came to the day we were supposed to leave and we didn't have anywhere to go, so be it.

Pulling up to the motel I parked the car. As we unloaded suitcases Isaac and Isaiah headed for their play yard and we stopped to take a deep breath. "Well, let's unload Israel and get back to work," I said.

With that done, we put the baby in his crib and called the boys in for a nap. We proceeded to head for the office door, turned and looked again past our little house to the beach.

I don't remember the exact conversation but I believe it was concerning God's providing us with transportation through Sam, when all of a sudden; Sam's car took off. It went across a driveway, down a planter, over a curb, and out of sight. The minute it started rolling I ran after it. Shouting to anyone below to watch out, we looked as the car teetered over a curb and on to a street below.

Missing two people and five houses it smashed into an old MG that someone had meant to restore but never did. "WHEW!" Thank God no one was hurt.

As people looked on, I came back up the hill where Diana was and she said, "Call the police, insurance company, and Sam!"

"Oh, no, you can make that call," I told Diana.

When the police arrived, Diana and I went with them to survey the damage.

"Who touched this car?" the policeman wanted to know.

"No-one!" Diana and I told him.

"Well, you tell me how it got here with the emergency brake on????" As Diana and my eyes met we knew it was no accident, but as you probably guessed we were not about to tell him what we really thought.

Waiting for Sam's voice to come on the other end of the line, Diana prayed he would not be too upset. "Sam, you're not going to believe this." After hearing the whole story and that we had insurance, Sam understood.

Now that our car was fixed we used it to get around while Sam's was being worked on. Packing our car with every last belonging, the day had arrived. There we were once again, nowhere to go, no job, willing to work, and anxious to see what God had planned.

Chapter 25

The Birth of a Vision

OH, LORD! SINCE I gave You my life, my path has not been easy. Never dull, never boring, very exciting, full of life, but definitely not easy. Arriving in Visalia, precious Scotty and Tracy (who are now married) invited us to stay with them. I wanted to spend some time fasting and praying, and so with our daily needs met, I headed up to Mt. Shasta.

While I was gone Diana also fasted for three days and asked the Lord to confirm whatever He showed me, to her too. For three days God gave Diana this scripture:

"Pure undefiled religion in the eyes of God our Father is to meet the widows and orphans in their distress, and remain unstained by the world!"

On my arrival back I had several things to share. "Diana, I was in the middle of the mountains and I kept hearing God say widows and orphans. I'm not sure what it all means, but I heard him say over and over during these three days, widows and orphans. I was way back in the forest of Mt. Shasta when all of a sudden the Spirit said,

"GO—NOW!"

"What?" I said.

"GO—NOW! Get in your car and leave!"

Wondering why, I obeyed the voice. As soon as I got in my car and headed down the road towards civilization, guess who manifested in person in their car? The owners of the motel we had been running.

Upon seeing me, they went to make a U-turn. At that I punched the gas and never looked back until I was safe and sound in the motel. Then I tried to call Diana to tell her and couldn't get through. Hearing all this, Scotty and Tracy watched the kids while we went to a nearby orchard to walk, talk, and seek the Lord, yet another time.

Diana said, "I kept getting the scripture about widows and orphans, too." The next word the Lord gave us in that orchard was to get a house. Right, no money to speak of and we were supposed to get a house. For the next couple of weeks we were bounced around and stayed with several people. Finally, depressed and wondering if we weren't completely nuts, Diana and I, our three sons, and our few belongings pulled up to a local park.

Weeping, Diana confessed to me that all she knew was that she still loved God and no matter where He wanted us to go, she would be willing to follow. I agreed.

With a car on empty, $7 to our name, no food, we were prepared to continue in faith. Well, if the Lord asks us to leave town again, the boys should see their Grandma and Grandpa, I said. So, heading over to their house we were prepared to do whatever the Lord asked.

Arriving, Diana's mother invited us to stay and have a BBQ (which seemed like an excellent idea). After that we were invited to stay the night. As we had been in this position before with them, it was extremely hard for me when I believed through no fault of my own we were in this position again. Jesus has a way of stripping men of their false pride—If they will let him.

For two days I basically stayed in a bedroom downstairs, not having a whole lot to say to any one. Diana and I finally talked and decided to obey what the Spirit said about going to find a house. We figured He knew our financial affairs when He said it. "So, let's go looking."

As we drove around one house had caught our eye but it had no sign or anything. It was apparently vacant. Smack in the middle of town, it was a beautiful Spanish style home. It was on the edge of what had been a very elite neighborhood years ago. With a park on one side and a gorgeous brick church across the street, it would be ideal. Let's just call tomorrow since today is Sunday, and see if the county can tell us who owns it. So, the next day, after getting a name and phone number, Diana made the miraculous call

"Hi, my name is Diana Nickell and I noticed your house is vacant. What plans do you have for it?"

After hearing they had just been talking about how it shouldn't be left vacant, Diana explained the facts. "We have no money, no job, and no furniture. But, we are a family of five and we need a home. We will look for work immediately."

At that, the woman on the other end said, "Meet me there at 2:00." Around 1:45, as we were getting ready to go, we'll never forget Diana's precious father who has basically operated in the realm of logic and fact.

"Where are you going, Honey?????" asked Ivan.

"To look for a house Daddy," responded Diana

"With no money Honey?" queried Ivan?

"Dad, God doesn't need money to get a house."

With a concerned look Diana's father muttered something about good luck!

Arriving with our three sons (as spiffied up as I could get them) we were shown an absolutely beautiful home. Hard wood floors, 1930's glass blocks in the kitchen, even down to a special built-in tile fountain in the solarium styled back porch.

A separate Spanish garage was out back, with stairs leading to an Italian style roof where everyone could view the city.

"What do you think?" said the nice lady.

What could we think? I replied, "It's beautiful!"

"When would you like it?"

"Well, I explained to you about our situation," Diana reminded her.

"Oh, don't worry about the rent. When you get a job you can pay me $400 dollars a month. Would you like the keys now????"

"Would we like the keys now?" You bet!

As we continued to visit, Diana shared what her maiden name was and come to find out, she had known Diana's father; and Diana had gone to school with her son.

I can't tell you the expression on my father-in-law's face when we arrived home and Diana tossed the keys on the table.

"What's that?" Ivan asked.

"The keys to our new home Dad, Diana responded.

Want to see it?" she asked?

With Diana's mom laughing and the children dancing, we immediately went back to our new love nest. After a thorough tour, Diana's father headed toward the back of the property. I've always wondered if he asked the Lord about what happened.

Hall street house

I'm not saying it has been easy for either of our families to understand the way in which God has chosen to work with and through Diana and I. We affectionately referred to that home as the Hall street house. Our children were growing and I did odd jobs, handyman, whatever, to get us by. During this time the country was going through a terrible rate of unemployment. One of every three families received some kind of aid. I went through three weeks of training to be a driver for disabled people only to be told that they only wanted me as a standby (they hired all women).

This was a very trying time because even though God had just shown us His love, it was very hard not to be independent. To be in a position where others help you constantly has got to be one of the hardest and humbling trials to go through. If you don't think so just try it some time.

During our first 6 months in our new home we started Isaac in private Christian school by faith, and God always provided. The Lord used many to bless us. Diana's very special Uncle Lonnie and Aunt Loretta brought us groceries more than once.

Though we received help, we were determined not to beg. One morning we were totally out of milk and Diana was in the kitchen reading this scripture over and over to Isaiah, "He who comes to Me will never hunger or thirst." God as my witness, our friend Greg Gibson, drove up at 6:15 a.m. with a couple of gallons of milk. (The couple that had helped us in Kansas was now in California) Another time, both of our families were struggling and Greg laid his hands on our refrigerator and said, "God bless this fridge." Within 24 hours a precious couple we knew brought by more groceries than our cupboards could hold; and we immediately shared them with Greg and Patty and their four children.

That August we felt led to write the chapter about Cathy's deliverance and for four months prayed about what to do with the manuscript "Products of Love". While on Hall Street, Diana and I met and befriended a widow named Judy. Her daughter was going through trials and she needed help watching the grandbaby. Well, after two weeks of watching this little boy I found out the neatest thing.

Years before, while we were still in Terra Bella, Jackie (Lori's sister) called me. "Honey, please pray. There is a young woman on her way to the abortion clinic soon. We need to pray that this precious little baby will not be aborted." After Jackie hung up Diana was overtaken with a spirit of travail. She lay on the ground and moaned and wept, as she seemed to be in intercession for this baby. In Diana's past she was a victim of this same tragedy and many times had asked God to please let her make a difference in some other baby's life since she had discovered how wrong it was.

For about 20 minutes Diana was so consumed with agony on this baby's behalf she was totally unable to do anything but call out to God. The next day Diana received a call saying the young lady had not had the abortion, and all was well. Well, here two years later, guess what? The baby we had been watching was that same child. Oh, don't you know, nothing happens by accident.

No one will ever know the joy we felt finding out who he was. Judy had started dating a man named Bob and soon our home hosted a wedding shower for this precious lady. Bob, the man she married, truly loved the Lord; and God used him on more than one occasion to bless me like a son. One thing led to another and Bob, Judy, Diana, and I were convinced that the Lord wanted our first book, "The Product of Love" in print.

When it was printed, we wanted to sell it to finance a ministry to widows and orphans. It seemed in our lives, even way back to when we worked with the developmentally disabled, we were always involved with these precious people. We met, so many hurting divorcees; children without daddies. We met hurting, hurting people with little or no hope. Diana and I had originally tried to give a copy of our manuscript to Paul Crouch.

We visited TBN and were told by the "guide", that you had to make an appointment months in advance, to see the founder Paul Crouch. I said, "Well, if this is God, we'll see him." Since Diana and I had gone early no one else was at the studios and we were privileged to pray in their original prayer room, which is normally off limits. Again, the Lord broke Diana. As she knelt, God showed her a birdcage; and the Spirit told her, "These are My people, they are bound up like this little bird." Weeping, we became more convinced than ever that people needed to hear that there is abundant life now.

Coming back to the studio that night for the taping, Diana and I took our seats. Before going on the air, Paul walked out, stood in front of me, looked at the crowd and started to visit! Diana was elbowing my ribs to pieces as she put the manuscript in my hands. On the cover we had written, "To the Body of Christ."

Slipping it into Paul's hands we told him it was a love gift to the body. Well, mission accomplished, we thought. We settled down to enjoy the fellowship with our friends in the Lord.

Later, we received the manuscript back, saying that since their call was to Christian TV they could not read all of the manuscripts sent, but please try to send it to a Christian publisher. So Diana and I knew Paul didn't realize it was a personal thank you for all the years that TBN fed us; and we said, "Well, Lord, we tried to give this freely to the body; what should we do?

Thinking then that perhaps God did want us to make money from it to give to widows and orphans, Diana and I approached Bob and Judy about printing it.

We really believe the Lord told them to invest their time and money; and during our get-togethers the Lord continued to bless us all. I had the opportunity to minister to Bob and Judy one day at their house and God set Bob free from some idols.

Being slain in the Spirit, as I laid hands on them I was excited to know God was working in all of our lives.

One day in Fresno, where we were checking into mail order marketing, Bob spoke sharply to the owner of the company. This sweet lady had been worried about her children and was speaking all negative things on them and about them. Bob, out of nowhere, said, "STOP THAT! That's bad confession!"

Diana and I were shocked by his boldness and had to trust God that our brother was in the Spirit.

With a shocked look this lady said, "What???"

Bob asked her how could she ever let God do a work on her children if she continued to speak nothing but problems, and negatively about them?

Basically he taught her she was cursing them with her mouth, instead of blessing. Moving right along then, Bob led her in the Baptism of the Holy Spirit. Oh, good! Our brother was hearing the Spirit. As he explained to her the power that was available to all believers, he laid hands on her head and as Judy and he prayed, she started praising God in another language. Pat was her name; and it was a good thing she owned the company because she carried on for quite a while under the anointing of the Holy Spirit. All of us left knowing God was definitely working in all of our lives.

Diana was convinced that marketing the book through the National Enquirer would not only get the book to the people it was meant for, but would guarantee a hefty return. "20 million people read the Enquirer," said the marketing people. A 1% return would be over 200,000 copies. At $5 a piece, that should help quite a few people.

Diana and I were convinced that God would financially bless Bob and Judy back. Only a handful of letters were sent in off the ad. Statistically what happened was impossible. Only a handful of responses tricked in to the special PO Box we had rented to handle the volume of mail.

Believing God had more in store, Bob and Judy were extremely gracious, giving us 1,000 copies. Diana and I gave everyone of them out freely as the Lord led. From salvations, to emotional healings, and changed lives, God confirmed this was a very special book.

Chapter 26

Around the Mountain

At Christmas time a young woman my age came to our home. Penny was there and told me to give her a book. The next morning at 7 a.m. we received a call from that young, weeping lady who in the middle of reading our testimony gave her life to Jesus, and had been greatly changed. I was thrilled and further led her into total deliverance over the phone! Well, as the book did not snowball as we had expected, Diana and I sought the Lord, yet another time.

The school year was coming to a close, and Lori, back in Kansas, had called and offered me work. So, at the first of May once again our little family headed for Salina, Kansas. I was willing to do anything to feed my family; and here was an opportunity. Unemployment was hitting 19% in our town, so our choices seemed few.

"Well, kids? How about going to Kansas again?" I asked. Excited for a change, all the family agreed this was what we should do. Making arrangements to take a train back, we thought it would be the thrill of a lifetime for our boys. My goodness, how could anyone be ever so wrong? Sorry, Amtrak, but this was our experience.

One day before we were supposed to leave for LA to catch the train, our transportation arrangements had to be changed. So Ivan, (Diana's father) agreed to see our little family safely to the train station. The ride to Los Angeles flew and there was an air of anticipation all around. Entering the big train terminal we checked in our suitcases, (once again, everything we owned with us) and made sure our tickets were ready. Ivan and Dorothy had agreed to send

Goliath (our puppy) out via the airlines, as animals were not allowed on trains. Time marched on and before we knew it, we found ourselves boarding a 26-hour train to Wichita, Kansas. Bumping into everyone, trying to keep a hold of the stroller, two kids and a baby, and four pillows, we were off. Finding our seats, we settled in. We had requested "No smoking" so they put us in the last " non-smoking" row. The row behind us started smoking. Yechhh!

Then we discovered because they hadn't charged us for the baby, he didn't have a seat. All the while we remembered we hadn't bought sleeper berths, so we would be sleeping in our seats. Oh, well, make the best of it, right? Wrong!! Our car was the party car. 90% of the people were either drunk or quickly getting there. Smoke was so thick you thought it was a winter fog. As the day wore on, the booze flowed on, the stories got louder and raunchier. To make this a special test, our son Israel just had to be teething. Finally, midnight came and the drunks were passing out.

Hooray! Sleep came. Then, in the middle of the night, transpires a scenario that only someone like Steve Martin could re-enact.

"Ahhh!" A lady screams

"What are you doing?" Someone else yelled,

"★!#★#!" The first lady screamed louder, "GET THAT %#★#! BACK IN YOUR PANTS!!! OH, MY GOD! He's peeing all over me!"

"Ahhh...He got me too.

Someone get the conductor." Another person hollered.

Passengers were hysterical and conductors raced in.

"Here's a towel." Someone said as they offered it to the woman who was still crying.

"What did I do??" said the drunk as he was dragged out.

"You used the woman sitting next to you as a urinal," the conductor explained as they disappeared down the steps and out of sight.

Oh, my! Right, "See America" – Well, we did and that will do it for now thank you!

Someone very wise once told me, if you don't get it right the first time, God will many times give you the opportunity to go back and try the same thing over.

Arriving in Wichita, we were greeted by Kenny. He was working at the motel as a cook the last time we were there and now was the full time maintenance man. Since we had arrived around 11:00 at night and still had an hour's drive to Salina, we went straight to our motel room upon arrival.

Waking up to a beautiful spring day in Kansas, it felt great to be alive. Visiting Lori over coffee, the events of our train ride were told amidst laughter and giggles.

Well, here's the plan Kids, said Lori.

"Dennis, you're gonna paint this motel for me. On days that Ken has off I may use you to do maintenance."

"Sounds great," Dennis replied.

"Diana, I have an opening on Sundays at the front desk. Would you like to work it?" Lori asked.

"Yes absolutely." Diana replied.

We knew that Lori would keep our hours different so one of us would always be available to be with our sons. Remembering the huge swing set and the big lawn the motel had, the older boys were out the door in a minute headed to play.

Memories quickly returned of how kickback and nice people in the Midwest can be. Diana and I were truly prepared to stay and live there as long as the Lord led. We weren't too thrilled with the California pace. Even though all people are different, there really is a different pace in the Midwest that is perfect for family life.

We wanted to find a house; so Diana applied for a waitress job at the 24-hour truck stop across the street from the motel. Hired within two days, Diana explained she could only work after 4:00 in the afternoon, and not on Sundays. No problem they said.

I was in heaven. Unlike the first time in Kansas, I not only was not at a fast paced job, I basically was in solitude. Everyday I would get up and see what room Lori needed painted, and she would tell me over a cup of coffee, a few hugs, and a "Have a nice day, Honey!" After that, I would paint the day away listening to teaching tapes. Oh, what a wonderful feeding time for my spirit. I've heard it said most of us have fat bodies and skinny spirits. Well, my spirit must have gotten obese that summer. We would give copies of our book out, as we felt led.

While I was in heaven, Diana was now running herself around the tables from 6p.m.to 2 a.m. in the morning, 5 days a week. You talk about a mission field: Sweet people, hurting people, and crazy people. You ever want to see a soap opera, just get around a bunch of waitresses. One girl was an anorexic. She was 5'8" and about 90 lbs, and ready to drop. Another one was real nice but an alcoholic. Three were divorcees. I think the owners' son was the only stable person there. When we got an opportunity, we shared Jesus by actions more than words.

The boys were having the time of their lives. Since Diana worked until 2:00 in the morning, she'd get home and crawl in bed by three. That was always after a shower because it seemed everyone in Kansas smoked. She would come home just stinking. After a quick shower she'd fall into bed with me. At 6:00 a.m., I would leave to work. It was nice living right there on the motel premises, and while Lori graciously gave us free rent, we tried to save for a house. My sons would pop up at about 7:00 a.m. Hopping on Diana and dragging her out of bed, she walked down to the motel coffee shop. There, Diana would purchase fresh home made cinnamon rolls, go back to our motel room, crawl into bed and sleep till about 10:00 a.m.

The kids watched TV while she slept. Then around 10:00 they would all head outside to swing, take walks, visit me for a few minutes, or go to town to shop. Around 4:00 in the afternoon, Diana would start dinner. We'd all have a family dinner, and then off to work she would go. Lori gave Diana her car to use so she wouldn't have to walk home when her shift ended in the middle of the night. Days flew by and there were many wonderful moments of fellowship with Lori.

Many exciting things happened at the restaurant where Diana worked, but none as dramatic as this. There was a cook by the name of Tracy. He had been divorced, had a daughter, lived at home, and seemed pretty sweet. Late one night around two, he started having symptoms of a stroke or heart attack. After he literally lost his sight everyone was in a panic. Diana offered to drive him to the hospital.

As they got in the car, Tracy started asking her all about Jesus. Suddenly he started screaming and convulsing as if dying. Diana led him to the Lord, and as he finally started crying out the name of Jesus, he slumped over as if dead. Laying her hands on his chest Diana called out to God to let Tracy live. As she raced to the hospital, she rebuked a spirit of death, and told him, you can't die. Rushing into the emergency room Diana called for help. Two orderlies came out and took him away in a wheel chair. She headed for a phone to call me. Once again here she was in a great situation. "Yes, dear, that's right. It's after 2:00a.m. And I'm at the hospital with a guy who tried to die in Lori's car… Yes, Dear, I told him he couldn't do that." She knew she would have a rough time explaining a body in a car that wasn't hers. Seriously though, it was scary.

We prayed and then Diana told me she'd be home soon. Well, about 15 minutes later, Diana got the report. Tracy tested fine and was released. He didn't show any signs of anything unusual. Needless to say that was a changed young man after that night.

After about six weeks Diana and I rented the cutest house. It was on a little cobble-stoned street where the trees actually met and made a canopy over the middle of the street. Getting our furnishings from an auction, we were ready to stay nestled in Kansas. The only problem now was we needed a car since we no longer were living at the motel.

On our first day in our new home, while I was at work, Diana looked for a car. She counted all the money we had and it was $500. Looking in the paper, Diana read, "Plymouth Scamp-maroon, rough but runs great. Cost? Five hundred dollars." Whoopee!!!!

Within two hours we owned our own car. And it did run great. But, oh, was it ugly.

I think I'll always remember it as another pride tester. After Diana bought it she drove up and showed me. Three of the fenders had holes where the snow had eaten through or something. And it was an old faded maroon.

"What is that?" I asked.

"Our new car!" she said.

"You're joking!" I hopefully replied.

"I'm serious," she said.

"Does it run?" I questioned.

"I drove it here and it's paid in full."

"That's what counts," I said.

With that we decided to call it our California Raisin. Why, you might ask? Because it was wrinkled, purple, and ugly. But it ran great.

After finishing my painting I had started landscaping the Salina Inn, and what a job it was. Lori gave me all kinds of wagon wheels, old farm tools, yokes, and tons of railroad ties. Add to that lots of flowers and the motel looked brand new.

Around this time I was beginning to realize we couldn't play missionary forever. The painting was completed and I felt the Lord was urging me towards a career and stability. Answering an ad in the newspaper I went and took tests to see it I could attend airline school. After several exams I was accepted! The only catch was that the school was in Washington. Oh, my! What we wouldn't do to make sure we were doing all we could do to support our family. I had finished all the painting so giving a two-week notice, we called our relatives and told them we were headed for Washington in August and would stop by on our way through.

All the Grandparents were excited about seeing the grandchildren and responded in favor of our heading back West. Unlike our first time, we left on very good terms with the motel owner, Lori, and with lots of good friends.

The week before we left, another really exciting thing happened. One of Diana's last nights of work at the truck stop, she believed the Lord told her to give a lady who was eating in the restaurant, the book "Product of Love". Diana later told me the urge was so strong; yet, she ignored it until she couldn't stand it anymore. By then, this woman was heading out the door of the restaurant.

"Excuse me," Diana hollered, as she ran after this total stranger and her husband.

"I hope you don't think I'm nuts, but I believe I'm suppose to give you this book about my husband's testimony."

"Well, thank you!" the lady replied, and off she went.

Two days later, as Diana was working the motel desk, the same couple that had been at the restaurant came up to check out.

"Oh, I'm so glad to see you," said this lady. "I sat up all night and read your husband's story from cover to cover. My husband and I have just been traveling for some time seeking God about some things in our life. We told the Lord we weren't going home until He spoke to us. Your testimony blessed us and spoke to our needs; and we're headed home now. You tell you husband thank you so much for this." Praise the Lord!

This time with a car we owned, money in our pockets, and a career ahead, we left Kansas at midnight after Diana worked her final shift at the restaurant. Hugging dear folks, with our sons sound asleep in the car, we were headed for certain success.

We think it can, we think it can, we think it can. After a week stop in California, the Nickell family was headed for beautiful Washington. With dreams of flying all over the world for tax only, we were determined to settle in as soon as possible. The airline school that had accepted me had all my financial grants arranged. They knew we were coming, and with $1000 we knew God would provide a home.

Our little Plymouth had driven uneventfully all the way out from Kansas and was now zooming up the biggest mountains in the US with no problems. Oh, we did see a little water from the radiator on the windshield at the very peaks. We also watched the temperature gage climb to just below boiling and then right when it was needed the road would start descending and the gauge would plummet back to normal! Arriving in Portland Oregon, which was right across the river from Vancouver, we rented a motel. Immediately, we bought newspapers and called rental agencies, etc.

For three days we searched 12 hours a day. The story was always the same. We don't accept dogs (Goliath was still very much part of the family), or the rental agencies would allow two people per bedroom, so we needed to rent at least a three bedroom; and we don't have any available right now.

The same afternoon we arrived in town we called the airline school for suggestions. "Housing is extremely hard to find up here," they said. After all the searching, on the fourth day, we literally checked out the housing projects. We said, "God, if this is another test, we are willing. The projects had a five-year waiting list. No one bothered to tell us about the housing situation

Parking in a parking lot I looked at Isaac. Remembering how God had used our children on more than one occasion to direct us, I asked my son, "What do you think? Mom has called every single ad in the paper, we have contacted every agency, and no door seems open?"

Now remember, this is a family who had seen God provide a home with no money, etc.

Little Isaac said, "Daddy, I want to go home!"

Where's home son?" I wondered

"Home is where Grandma and Grandpa are, my school, and my friends."

Sweet, sweet Isaac, had so willingly gone back to Kansas and all, but in his heart of hearts was ready to settle down in Visalia.

"No," Diana screamed, "I just knew it." Having a royal fit, she told God we would move anywhere except Visalia. She was tired of people judging me, and our life. We truly believed that we had been obeying God; and no one we knew really understood. That left some wounds that were not yet healed. We discovered often the way to your healing is to go down the same path where you got hurt before. That way, as life was lived again, hurts were erased and new good memories made.

After her fit, Diana apologized to the kids and started to get excited about Isaac being able to start back at his favorite school. Isaiah and Israel were ready for anything. I took a deep breath and said, "Ok, Father, Here we go." Back on the freeway we headed home.

Chapter 27

There I Am

RETURNING TO VISALIA BY the fifth day we had less than an enthusiastic response. The general consensus was we were at least a little strange. Of all the people to receive us wouldn't you know it would be my sister Penny? Without hesitation she seemed truly glad to see us and invited us to live with her for a few weeks. We only had about $600 left and knew it wouldn't last long.

Getting up at 6:00 a.m. every morning I would head out the door dressed in my best suit, not returning until late afternoon. After a week of no responses, this was the hardest time of my life not to go back to the crutch of alcohol. But, what a mighty victory and testimony to the power of God! What a God we serve. With a week to go and knowing we did not want to wear out our welcome with Penny, we started to house look, as well as job hunt.

One day we were driving around a cute neighborhood and again spotted an empty house. We called the county assessor and found out it was owned by a church. After calling the church and speaking with them, they agreed to let us rent the cottage until they found a new pastor. It had been empty for some time. The prices was $350 a month (in 1988); and believe me, you couldn't rent a nice three bedroom for $350. The very next morning, Diana, the kids and I were driving down Tulare Avenue when I said, "Let's pull in here."

The place was Good Shepherd, a state licensed facility for developmentally disabled. After I went inside, I came back out and had an absolute smile on my face. For the first time in weeks I actually felt joy. I was on the verge of putting an application in when I started to laugh. I was so happy to see precious people like we had the opportunity to serve before.

"Diana, guess what were are going to do?" I said

"What?" she questioned, ready for anything.

"Remember when the Lord said widows and orphans? That's really who we dealt with back in Terra Bella. Why would I go to work for minimum wage at Good Shepherd when we could have our own care home again?"

Talk about blinders being lifted. Of course, that was the career. That was what we had been willing to give up when the Lord beckoned. No one said He wouldn't return it someday. As I shared my revelation Diana was so happy to see the joy in me as I spoke. Quickly, though, reality set in. More faith time. All we needed was a home big enough for 11 people, a state license and about $6,000 dollars. Piece of cake, right???

Now I don't know why, even though we had seen God intervene in our lives so many times before, each new time that He demands total trust again it seems you've forgotten all that you had learned. Returning to Penny's, Diana and I told her of our new found revelation.

"Great," she said, encouragingly.

Within the week we were moved to Burrel Street. I was working for my brother, Jack, and still applying for other jobs all over town, and Diana was hired as a waitress job at a local restaurant.

The boys, knowing we were committed to stay in Visalia grew more happy and secure. What a wonderful house it was, but Oh, No! Within two weeks we were given the word, time to move.

After months of waiting they had found a new pastor. The little church felt so bad they offered us our money back to help us financially; and Diana and I house hunted with every spare minute. Isaac was in second grade, Isaiah started kindergarten, and Israel was three and running full blast.

Once again Diana's father was involved in our faith walk. Diana said, "Dad, we can't find any where to move!!! We have looked everywhere. There is one place, but they won't give us an answer until the day we are suppose to be out of the Burrell house."

Ivan instructed, "Diana, you'll just have to go somewhere."

"I know Dad, but I believe the one on the line will say yes."

"Well, I'll help any way I can..." Ivan offered

"Oh, good! Daddy? Two things! I need you to drive your car full of stuff, and Daddy? (Now dads who are called daddy by their 33-year-old daughters know to be suspicious) We need you to write the check, we'll give you almost all the money, but Dennis will get the rest from work in a couple of days. OK?"

"Sure honey" Ivan graciously responded

Moving day arrived. Diana had to be at work at 4:00 in the afternoon and at 1 o'clock we were still circling the rental company waiting for an answer. We were out of the place completely and still had nowhere to go. Finally, around 1:30 they said okay and handed across the keys to an adorable condo. It had a back yard for Goliath, and we discovered the previous renters had even left a doghouse. This condo was small, but homey and provided for a very protective nurturing atmosphere. We had been through quite a walk and still had plenty to go.

Living in a home that was intimate was very special. Diana and I shared an open loft that overlooked the fireplace and our three sons shared a huge bedroom downstairs. It was big enough for three twin beds. I had started full time home health care for a little grandpa who needed a home health care worker. For many months the Lord provided through that, and Diana's waitressing. Once again there was some good opportunities to share with people at her job.

During our two months stay at the condominium we found the perfect house for a care home. My brother, Pat, who was now a realtor, gave us a list of about 30 homes, and as we started to leave, shouted out, "Hey, I forgot one. Write this down."

Then he told us about one more house he knew of. Well, after checking about three houses we were sorely disappointed; and Diana said, "Let's just look at this one your brother mentioned."

Driving to the neighborhood we were pleasantly surprised. The house in question was really neat. Peach colored with a white picket fence. It had over 2100 square feet and was on a big corner lot. We could see it was vacant; and there standing in the yard was a woman with her two boys, one, who obviously had Downs Syndrome. Diana and I could not believe our eyes.

Stopping, we got out of the van and greeted the owners. After exchanging pleasantries we walked through the home and found it to be perfect. The bedrooms were 13 by 16, a must for two people to have enough room. The house had three baths and an apartment size addition over the garage. Diana and I would have a bedroom fit for a king.

Asking if they would even consider a lease to buy option, Diana and I were thrilled when they said yes. As we chatted we discovered the woman, Wilma had been a school nurse where my two nephews had gone to high school. She had been avidly sharing Christ with them in deed whenever possible, and after they graduated, in Word also. She had also heard of Diana and I through the one nephew. The fact that they had a child with Downs Syndrome they realized the importance of our desire to open a care home. It was absolutely a miracle.

With the promise to get together soon to discuss details we left knowing we had just been in our future home. Diana's Dad and Mom graciously loaned us $5,000 to have running money and to get into the house. So many miracles took place it's almost hard to re-count them all. Within days of speaking to the owners of the house we had a signed lease agreement in our hands. But as the actual agreement day approached a financial backer didn't feel they could allow us to use the funds.

They had hoped to hear a firm commitment from the agency that places folks in homes like ours, prior to releasing the finances. Heartbroken, we called the owners and told them that even though the funds were in our bank account we were not allowed to touch them yet. So the owners of the house said sorry and put the house back on the market. The for-sale sign went back on the property, and Diana and I drove by again and again.

"God told me that's our house!" Diana told me.

"Yeah. Well if it is for us it will not sell!" I replied.

"I know," Diana said.

Those were some of the hardest months we ever spent. Christmas time was approaching and wondering if we would ever own our own home again and feel stable, Diana collapsed on the floor in tears. No one was home but Diana.

"God! Where are you????" she questioned.

"Open your eyes Diana. And I'll show you where I AM

See the Christmas tree your brother -in-law Jack freely gave you? There I AM; and see the couch you're looking at that Dennis' mother freely gave you? There I AM. See the VCR your parents gave you? There I AM. See the dinette set that your sister-in-law Penny freely gave you? There I AM, and see the very Christmas decorations that Craig (Penny's boyfriend) gave you? There I AM, also. I've been with you all along meeting your needs, watching out for you. How could you ask where I AM?

Engulfed in tears, Diana thanked God for His tenderness and mercy. We are so blind sometimes. Shortly after that, a day or two before Christmas, Diana ran into the owner of the house we thought we had lost while grocery shopping.

"How are things going?" asked the owner.

"Well, we're still interested in your home if it isn't sold!" Diana replied, hopefully.

"Well, we did have a buyer, who even had the money, but we just didn't want to sell it to him. So, why don't you give me a call when you get home?" Wilma invited.

One call later, one call to our backer, and one signed lease later, Diana and I had a move-in date of January 13, 1989. Once again, we were moving, this time hopefully to stay put for a very long time. The big challenge now was supporting the home while we got it licensed. Licensing takes a 90-day process, and then the placement agency will hopefully start showing your home to perspective clients. At $700 a month strokes, we had our work cut out for us. Much of our start up money went to furniture, equipment, and start up costs. Diana ran ads in the paper for me to do one-time cleanups and I also provided home health care for a great little grandpa.

One month towards the end of the 90 days we got the opportunity of a lifetime. We could make $700 in one day moving a lady to the coast. It would save her a ton of money; and somehow we managed not to hear the words that she was moving to an upstairs apartment. So in one day Diana and I filled a medium sized moving van full of tons of stuff. Diana commented she never knew a small condo could hold 14 dressers. We had loaded it, driven 3 hours away, unloaded it and by 9:30 that night, almost crawled into a Chinese restaurant we found open. Slumped into the booth from exhaustion we agreed that it was the best food we'd ever eaten.

We'd made it the 90 days, we were all ready to get our license, and instead we received a letter from licensing asking, "Where are your three months running monies?" Oh, no, just a small matter of $6,000 more dollars needed. In tears, Diana read the letter to me and I said, "Leave me alone!" Walking back towards our garden I wondered how and we were supposed to come up with another $6,000. After a few minutes, the Lord spoke a name to me. Diana called the person whose name I had heard and within one day we had a check for the $6,000 dollars. Finally with everything ready, we were well on our way to being established. Four little seniors, all basically orphaned, a young mother with cerebral palsy, and her baby, who is healthy as can be, was whom the Lord chose to fill our home with.

Chapter 28

Happy Thoughts

EIGHT YEARS HAD PASSED since the Holy Spirit prompted me to write down the word of my testimony. Yet the story was still not finished, as we were finding out.

Something was still missing. Our lives were being poured out to everyone except the One who really counts. Somehow in our busyness we had less and less time for the Word of God, less and less time to hear the Holy Spirit, and somehow we seemed to forget who was responsible for all these blessings. I believe the Word says you have lost your first love.

Changes started and soon Diana and I were losing everything. Two of our clients left, which amounted to one third of our income. For months we struggled and did everything we could think of to keep our sinking ship afloat. At the same time I was having serious chest pains, stress-related symptoms, etc., etc.

During this period Diana had made some serious realizations about our priorities and wanted back the wonderful close relationship we had with the Lord in Terra Bella. Wanting to know that peace in the midst of the storm again, we didn't know how to get there!

One morning I physically could not sit up, and had not eaten in weeks. Not knowing what else to do, we closed our care home. No one but the Father will ever understand our pain and disbelief at all that had happened. We had been totally successful and blessed, giving all we could with our actions, love, finances, and had lost everything again.

We had forgotten the One responsible for the blessings! There is a scripture where God says, "Once you have all my blessings, don't forget and say my hand has done this, or you will lose it all!" (Paraphrase) AND WE DID!!!!

Leasing out our home with a 2-year lease-to-buy option with some folks, we moved in with a friend and prepared to move to Oregon. It's a whole other story, but the people who owed us $10,000 to go on this trip did not follow through. They were very sorry but there was not much we could do.

Everything we owned and still smiling

So here we sat with a family of five with nowhere to go. I was still so very sick with a relapse and was addicted to the stomach pills that enabled me to get a little something on my stomach. No income! Totally stripped (everything we owned fit into our van)! To add insult to injury, our precious Goliath died; and two days later, our other pet, Angel, got hit and also died.

I will never forget when there was nowhere else to turn; we chose to turn to God's Word. Isaac, Isaiah, and Israel, our three troopers, would all get in a circle around their Daddy, who they had never seen so weak, and lay hands on me and pray. Every night Diana would get out the Bible and read verse after verse of God's promises concerning His children. Less than 2 weeks of putting our priorities back in order, I threw away the very pills (by faith) that were allowing me to eat. Several weeks of withdrawals followed; but I stood and had a wonderful victory. Slowly my strength started returning, but I would

still tire easily.

Now, this was probably the first time in years, that we felt that there was no one to rely on, but Jesus. Since I was so weak, Diana was making all the decisions and kept speaking God's Word, in spite of what she saw. There was a new deeper relationship being formed between the Holy Spirit and us.

One morning in the midst of all this Diana was absolutely compelled to start a business. Yes, you heard right, start a business, with no money, no supplies, and no experience in what she was about to do. The Spirit of God spoke clearly, "Diana, get a brief case (empty, except for a pencil and piece of paper), and start calling corporate businesses. Tell them you will make corporate thank-yous for them. They must put 50% down (so you could buy the supplies) and the rest on delivery!!!!!!" I am not exaggerating when I say every single door Diana knocked on loved the idea and bought at least one gift basket.

Huddled together one night watching "Hook", Diana and I concurred we now had the name for our new business, "Happy Thoughts." Since our sons are our treasures and have been the greatest gift in our lives, we decided to use that name to remind us of our treasures, who had helped inspire us when there wasn't much to smile about. Thinking of them always provides a "Happy Thought."

Diana and I were not the only ones going through tests, speaking of our sons. They had been attending a Christian School, but when our finances went so did the private schooling. This was one of the most heart wrenching experiences of our lives. For years we had put every penny in the direction of their education, wanting the very best for them. Now making the best of the situation, we prepared our sons for a new school experience. Gathering in a little circle every morning we would pray over our children and ask the Lord to use them in a very special way. Bring the love of God to those they meet, we would pray.

The first week in the new school our precious Isaac had an experienced Diana refers to as being lambed (as in Jesus, the Lamb). Isaac has always had a very sweet, pure-hearted spirit. Sending him off to school that day we prayed as usual and thanked God for our blessings. After school, to out absolute shock, we discovered our eldest had been publicly humiliated for the whole playground to see and told to keep it to himself. Instead of hiding his feelings or ours we chose to confront the child who had felt this was so funny; and to make a long story short, Isaac was used to break up a ring of boys who had been terrorizing those littler than themselves for over a year. At the end of it all, Isaac was a hero, and some other young men thought twice before physically assaulting their peers. Needless to say this was a hard introduction to public school.

Life went on, and with the boys in school and my strength slowly coming back, a new test for our faith was around the corner. We had 30 days to find a new place to live; and being Thanksgiving, we were just ready to see what would happen business wise that Christmas.

Once again, by faith (we had about $200), we went house looking and found a beautiful little home with a swimming pool and fireplace for $600 a month. The only catch was the landlord wanted first plus an $800 deposit. So just like the good old days we put a deposit down hoping some how we would come up with the rest of the money.

Christmas was busy with little baskets, big baskets; and all the business was coming by word of mouth. At the same time we were continuing to hear from the Holy Spirit about certain areas of our lives that He wanted given to Him. Christmas was approaching, and now less than 3 weeks to save to get into this house, charging Christmas presents seemed the only thing to do. Yet, we knew that getting in debt was not God's best provision.

Sitting in the living room one night, Diana burst into tears and called our three precious sons to our sides. "What should I do? We believe it is wrong to get indebted and yet if I don't charge these bikes there won't be any for Christmas."

"Mom," little Isaac, now 10, said, "That's simple. You can't do it. Don't charge."

"It's ok," Isaiah chimed in, "You have to obey God, Mom." What love! What great kids.

Christmas came and went. As always, due to generous Grandparents, and relatives our boys were far from empty handed. Now the big test was on. Christmas had been good and Happy Thoughts was slowly growing. Yet, we were still $400 short, and the new landlord was adamant, no keys without the full amount. By faith we packed our belongings and prepared for the great moving day, still uncertain how all this was going to work.

The morning we were to move, Diana went outside at 6 a.m. to get the paper, and there on the porch was an envelope with a letter and yes, a check for exactly $400.

"PRAISE GOD, PRAISE GOD! Dennis," Diana shrieked through the house, "Guess what? God did it, He did it!" Much rejoicing was had as even the kids skipped around in circles praising God for His faithfulness. As tired as we were from all the battles, moving day was wonderful. Now instead of 2 bedrooms, we had a whole house again, with a fireplace and a pool, all on a big corner lot. Meanwhile I had gotten a landscaping job that was going to meet our needs. With thoughts of the business growing, we looked great on paper. Still the test to come would reveal even more about ourselves.

Chapter 29

Total Reliance

RAIN, RAIN AND MORE rain. It was a very wet January and instead of the $1,200 a month income I had anticipated, I was fortunate to see anything. Meanwhile when I did work, the crew I was on was doing jobs as quickly as possible. Finally, the weather eased up and several good weeks of work waited ahead. But something was wrong. I was coming home at 3 o'clock in the afternoon and passing out. From time to time the old stress symptoms would return; and we stood our ground and refused that sickness. Finally, we discovered that due to all the rains and many other factors, my body was saying enough.

Just like most men, I was convinced if I could still crawl, I would provide for my family, no matter what. Repeatedly, Diana begged me to quit, stop, and cease! Diana knew that it wasn't God driving me; yet I was terrified that I must do all I could do to support my family. Awaking one morning with shoulders, arms, and wrists totally numb, I even had to admit something wasn't right. The symptoms came after a day of putting almost 5,000 feet of sprinkler

system, in one day. If that wasn't enough I had been digging in mud, due to rain. After about an hour, the symptoms lifted a little and I still reported for work, but thank God, the crew was rained out. So by the next morning my arms were worse and we knew I needed to see a doctor. The prognosis: SURGERY! I had injured my nerves. In less than two weeks I had done the type of damage most people have only after years of overworking a certain spot. With both arms in braces and instructions not to use my hands, Diana couldn't help but ask me if I would trust God now. There was literally nothing I could do, and I finally realized my faith was on the line. What ensued was a yearlong battle with workman's comp. We had an insurance worker that hated men, and people, with no faith, surrounded us.

All the while the Holy Spirit said, "Watch me!" Finally, after surgery, and rehab, and court hearings, two rehab counselors, two attorneys, etc., we emerged from this experience with not only our faith intact, but also some answers to some very real questions. We learned about spiritual warfare anew. We discovered what the blessings of Abraham had to do with us, as believers. We saw God literally remove people who were in the way of His purpose and place people in key positions to help us. I guess you could sum it up by saying, we discovered there is a kingdom that Jesus referred to that is not the same as this worlds. It is more real than what you see because it is eternal.

So with workman's comp finally done, a new Happy Thoughts brochure, paid for by rehab, Diana and I were now serious again about our relationship with the Holy Spirit.

Now, after the boys' second year in public school, our sons were requesting to be home schooled. Oh, they had acclimated well and were quite popular, yet their education was lacking; and we were really starting to pray about what the Lord would have her do. Isaac was heading towards 7th grade and she was increasingly aware of how most of life's lessons that are eternal did not come from a schoolroom that cannot even say the name of JESUS.

Her heart was sincere, and she really wanted to hear from the Lord concerning His desire for our sons. One night she had the most beautiful dream: Jesus was standing behind her shoulder and looking across the room to where our three sons were said,

"**TELL MY CHILDREN**, I'm well pleased!" then speaking to Diana He said, "**TAKE CARE OF YOUR TREASURES**!"

Well, that was all she needed. Decision made, Diana was to have the privilege of teaching my own sons.

There was lots of swimming and barbecues through the spring and summer, lots of growth and many miracles for our business, Happy Thoughts. One day while driving along, the Holy Spirit spoke the name of a business to me.

"Diana, you have to make a basket and go to this business now, today." I was very bold and certain Diana had to do what I was saying; so even though I had no idea what to expect, she followed my instructions. The Result???? A basket account supplied 300 baskets a month. The timing was crucial. The client's words?

"I can't believe your timing! We need your service."

Repeatedly through the growth of Happy Thoughts, the Holy Spirit would create business connections in unorthodox ways. In the middle of these tests and growths the Lord spoke to Diana so clearly, "**When I AM through with you, you will know Me, and that this is Me. You will never take credit for what I've done**."

The Lord revealed that even though we didn't mean to, before in Terra Bella, as we shared all the exciting things happening, people thought we were taking credit for what was happening. They got offended.

It made sense now. We had forgotten the Author of our faith; and we prayed to be back at that wonderful place in Him.

TOTAL RELIANCE! Reliance is an action word. Ask, and keep Asking, Seek, and keep Seeking, Knock, and keep Knocking. **Faith without works is dead!**

Chapter 30

Restoration

TIME WAS DRAWING NEAR to move back home as the people who leased our home decided not to buy it. This was a whole other story of faith and battles and on December the 5th, 1994 our weary wiser family found ourselves circling our wonderful Cambridge house.

Entering the home with the weight of knowing the tenants had left us owing 3 months back rent we had no idea how we were going to pay for it. Within 2 weeks we discovered that because they had trashed the house by pulling out towel bars and making lots of unauthorized changes our insurance was going to pay for all the past debt and repairs! It was absolutely incredible. If they hadn't been malicious the insurance wouldn't have covered the changes but since they had purposely torn some things up we were totally covered!

Our Happy Thoughts gift basket business had now grown from a divine idea in a 5 by 6 foot work area to a successful company with over $50,000 sales in it's 3rd year.

So many things we have been learning about God. One of the most profound is what the true "Gospel" is.

Jesus said that He came to GIVE LIFE and that we should have abundant life. God is Love. He wants you well, blessed, prosperous and yielded. Most importantly He wants you! **All of you**!

You have the opportunity to choose this day whom you will serve. You can choose blessings and not curses. You have been bought with a price and you are no longer your own. Have no idols, no other Gods before Him. You do have free will and it is your choice.

Chapter 31

Growing Up!

WHY? OH, WHY IS it that when you just think you've got things figured out, you find out how much you don't know? Whether 8 or 88 there will always be room for growth and always reminders of why God is God and we are the children!

To pick up where we left off, Happy Thoughts was truly prospering, times were good, and Dennis and I had everything covered once again! Ahhhhhhh!

Arthur Blessitt's words from the foreword rlng out with new meaning:

"The end? The book is not the end!

They still go on with their Lord today."

Other words stood out with new meaning...

"One's walk in life with God is not the absence of struggle."

Is anyone getting the idea yet? Getting that feeling in the pit of your stomach that a new test is about to begin? Well, this is how it happened!

Christmas 1996 was a memory maker with lots of presents and the promise of an even better business year coming up. Dennis and I had figured out that if we could have our biggest account pre-buy for a year we could be debt free, have a great buying trip at the world famous San Francisco Fancy Food Show (with Diana's parents Ivan and Dorothy), and build the business. Packing excitedly for the trip to the Mosconi Center, we imagined how many more corporate accounts we could sell and talked about how fun the trip would be with Ivan and Dorothy.

Stopping in Old Sacramento on the way north, we breathed in the sites of the old paddle wheel steamboats and the old frontier town. Joy comes in the morning and I could hardly wait to confirm our next year's business with our largest account!

Years before, we had stumbled upon a situation where we could produce a $10 Mini basket that was to be given to every new mother that had a baby, and still make $5 per basket. Due to the numbers that were needed we had a really good monthly base to operate from while we marketed other corporate businesses. In December, which was our normal time to approach this account to confirm for the next fiscal year, we shared our concerns that for several months we had become aware that they were not getting the baskets to everyone. Then we actually did a survey and discovered many of the minorities were not getting the baskets.

We knew at the time; and had even talked about it before hand, that if we made "waves" it might cost us dearly. As we checked the yearly birth count with what had been ordered there was a definite problem and breach of agreement. Thinking that the way through this sticky wicket was to be honest, confront, make sure everyone got a basket; we even offered a business deal where everybody saved money by bulk- buying for the whole next year.

Well, guess what folks? Here Dennis and I were standing at the Fancy Food Show calling long distance as the purchasing person had promised an answer by that day.

"Oh, do we want to order? Oh, No! As a matter of fact we don't want your services anymore!" the woman stated abruptly!

To say joy was not my response just might be accurate! Trying to be the hero, I didn't tell Dennis until after we were back in Visalia and I had made an appointment with the purchaser, as we had an agreement through the end of June; and we were going to expect them to finish the year! What ensued were several horrible stress-filled months with the only nice memory of San Francisco being the fellowship with Ivan and Dorothy. They always had loved to travel and were great fun on trips.

As March came around Happy Thoughts had another client who had demanded samples and designing meetings with Diana for two solid months, agreeing to make a major purchase. It was to be for over 500 farmers at around $30 - $60 each for a special appreciation gift. Since two companies were involved in pulling this together we were being run from one town to another; and we never would have imagined what was to come. After months of searching for special farm products, deluxe knifes, cowboy items, on and on, one VP finally set a day for ordering! Dennis and I were so excited. Wow, here was a possible $15 - $30,000 account. Boy, would that help make up for the other company's breach of contract!

I will never forget the feeling as the VP asked if we could supply him with something like 100 $3.49 imprinted lunch sacks.

I remember mumbling something about I'll check into the screen charge and hung up the phone. What was wrong? Our products were tremendous, our service personal and professional; nothing had changed; yet we couldn't sell anything!

A loan! That would fix everything. A loan! June was here and it seemed only a dream that last summer our family had been guests of my parents for a wonderful paid vacation to Hawaii. Dorothy had retired; and after 20 years all the Hershey girls were treated to a week in Hawaii with their families. Now, summer was approaching, and frantically, we scrambled not knowing what else to do.

Dennis started looking for other jobs and I filled out every form I could get my hands on for a second mortgage for the house. Happy Thoughts was drying up, and it was painful.

Relief came as we managed to get a small second on the house and hoped that business would pick up. Dennis and I marketed every other hospital in central California hoping to make up for the account we had lost. **You know, being out of money really is a time that reveals character.**

We went through phases of anger and disbelief, and checked with attorneys about feeling so violated. In the end we truly believed that we were not to sue! Through it all there was some incredible learning about the value of taking one day at a time; but still Dennis and I tried to believe that something good would break soon!

Chapter 32

Heart Attack!
"Oh, My God! Help!"

DENNIS STUMBLED OUT OF the bathroom early one morning bent over in excruciating pain and said, "I think this is hospital stuff. I don't want to scare the boys by calling an ambulance." As I bent over to pray and help him make it downstairs, I heard the words "Dennis will be all right." I was filled with such a peace and told Dennis that God had just told me he was going to be all right! Struggling to walk down our stairs to the car Dennis mumbled "be sure to tell the boys I love them."

Sticking my head in Isaacs' room I said, "PRAY! Your Dad's going to the hospital but he'll be OK!" and with that helped Dennis into the van. Thanking God for what I had heard from that time, it never entered my mind or emotions that Dennis might not make it. I knew what I knew, thanks to the precious covering God was putting around me.

In the emergency room our precious family Doctor started ordering different tests to try to find out if this was indigestion or a heart attack. Dennis was given a huge cocktail of all kinds of upset stomach medicines; and while this was happening I felt like the Holy Spirit instructed me to call just a few prayer partners to pray. Next, I called my mother who showed up while Dennis was still going through the tests. Our family physician turned the info over to a heart specialist who was supposed to then take over Dennis' case. Hearing a decision to hold Dennis for observation was made, Dorothy headed out, after some encouraging words, while Dennis was being admitted to a room!

The next 24 hours I was given specific instructions by the Lord: Contact no-one until there was a good report; have Trish, our very good friend, drop off praise tapes and a recorder; and literally keep the soft praise tapes going all night, changing them every 20 minutes. Dennis pan during this time was excruciating as he was given more and more morphine, to no avail. While fighting the pain and praying, Dennis prayed for a nurse who was in the middle of a divorce. Afterwards, I discovered that the hospital had made several major errors. Tests that were taken to check Dennis's different counts were not returned on time; and then the wrong tests were read. As we were rejoicing that the counts did not indicate a heart attack, in the wee hours of the morning a nurse returned and said, "Whoops! I read the earlier test. You are definitely having an attack, but we have missed the special window of time in which a drug to counter what is happening should have been administered."

The heart Doctor, who came by in the middle of the night, ordered more morphine and didn't know Dennis had even had an attack or was having another and said, "Probably about noon tomorrow if this hasn't lifted we might take a look, by the way how bad is it?" Dennis was so exhausted from overwhelming pain that he just kept saying, "It's really, really bad!" From 7 a.m. the one morning to the next morning he was in non-stop pain.

Early the second morning I walked out of the room just in time to overhear the group of heart doctors saying something to the effect that no one had notified them of the test results and Dennis had literally laid in the hospital through several heart attacks without any intervention other than morphine. As I overheard this I finally vented and told the two Doctors that quite frankly I was aware of all the screw-ups and that I was totally aware of the legal ramifications. I then told them not to worry as I was convinced that God Almighty was sparing his life in spite of the "wonderful care." Finally, for good measure, I informed them that I had called on the Blood of Jesus over the situation, including their hands, and that I wanted them to know that when Dennis went into surgery, that as far as I was concerned, it would literally be the hands of Jesus over theirs.

Do you know those two grown men didn't say one word and said, "All right!" then scheduled Dennis for an immediate angioplasty. By now the family physician, sweet Elizabeth, had shown up only to find out she hadn't been kept updated; and she suggested we pray for Dennis, as he was being wheeled towards surgery. How wonderful to have a caring friend and doctor who knows that there is the supernatural as well as the natural.

Once Dennis was in surgery I made several calls to let his relatives know that he had come into the hospital with some symptoms; and now we were waiting to find out what the problem was, as at this time there still was not a diagnosis of what was wrong.

The Doctors had stated that if the surgery took longer than 1½ hours there was a phone on the wall to use to find out what was going on. Permission had been given to do whatever needed done, as I still had that incredible peace in my heart. I will never forget that while I was waiting several people came to visit and then left. I remember ministering to another woman who was terrified about her husband who was in surgery. **The reality of God's presence in and on a situation makes such a tremendous difference!** The clock kept ticking and about 20 minutes after the time they should have been done, I went to the phone to call the O.R. and ask what was up!

"Well, the good news is Dennis has had the blockage cleared from a main artery and he will be fine."

They never said a word why the delay but something very interesting happened as Dennis was being wheeled to his room from recovery. They had given a short-term memory loss drug to Dennis who was awake and talking.

"I saw heaven! Diana it was soooo green, the most beautiful green you could imagine. I saw Jesus, I was talking with Him and I told Him I couldn't leave my boys yet, as they needed me. When I said that, He disappeared!"

Tears filled my eyes and I wondered what all they had talked about! Whether Dennis was lost on the table I'm sure we will never know in this life; but I was so grateful for his encounter and for the Lord's goodness to allow us to keep him here longer!

The next four days were continued warfare as Dennis was lost in the shuffle and was supposed to be receiving intensive care level of attention. He was put in with less intensive patients. To those readers who are familiar with heart surgeries of any kind, if the doctors go in through the main artery in the leg, there is a 24 hour period where they leave a plastic, hollow, straw-type of shunt in the leg right by a main artery. After heart surgery, the patient, who is no longer on morphine, but still on heavy painkillers, is supposed to have the leg weighted down and or tied so the leg cannot be kicked. If the patient were to kick the leg while high they could bleed to death in about 2 minutes. It amazes me how God protected Dennis by simply asking me to stay in the room with him non-stop. Wouldn't you know that since Dennis had been forgotten for 24 hours, for the higher level of nursing care, no one tied his leg down. About 8 hours after the surgery, as night was falling, I was changing the praise tapes and realized that he was wildly kicking the leg with the plastic straw still in it at a direct right angle. "Stop", I yelled grabbing his leg while ringing for nurses. When help arrived, the nurse on shift couldn't believe that no one had tied his leg down. To this day I cannot tell you how that plastic straw didn't break that artery!

Three days after the surgery, proved to be one of the most awesome days in our lives! Shunt removed; Dennis was looking forward to his first real walk. Oh, how we laughed and talked as he took his first steps holding the little IV holder. Ever so slowly he walked and we both were so grateful for the good reports and the time we were spending together. Finishing several laps around the nurses station Dennis was ready for a good night's rest. What happened next can only be described as an encounter with God. Dennis had been off the morphine since the surgery.

Closing his eyes, I heard him describing what he was seeing in a vision, talking in the first person:

"I see swords, beautiful swords..." what followed was over an hour encounter as Dennis went from an open vision, to the Father speaking through him, as surely as he did through Moses to his people! Some of what was said can be shared and some not.

God said, "Tell my people this:

My people do not trust me!" He shared that the problem in answered prayer is not on His end but ours. He said He was sick of repetitious prayer, He hears every prayer the first time! He also said that if someone considers himself spiritual but does not have PEACE on his feet, "HE IS NOT HEARING ME."

Among other things, we were instructed to never run in our flesh again, as that is what leads to things like heart attacks! Great men of God, who have forgotten that it is "He" in them, need to stop and understand His ways are not our ways! He told Dennis that when He took him before great men; tell them it is not their job.

Dennis and I can say from experience, having God's presence show up, it is truly "awesome."

The rest of our stay in the hospital was busy as we gave out free copies of the book "Product of Love", prayed with nurses, counseled people, and basically did the kingdom of darkness as much damage as we could! This hospital was the same one that had breached the contract with us for the baby baskets; and yet there was some sort of sweet irony about being in the middle of the heart floor, sharing Jesus and loving everyone in site, even after they probably were a contributing cause for the reason Dennis was there!

In the Bible, people were always in trouble for not listening! My earthly father is a schoolteacher who truly fulfills the word "teacher". I bet if you asked him, his greatest pet peeve might be when someone can't learn because they won't listen to instruction. It is true that we have all been given a free will and God has given us a tremendous brain. Like the teachers though, it must be incredibly frustrating to be thrown out of the equation, when those who He created refuse to have a teachable humble spirit...

Little did Dennis and I know we did not possess such a spirit; but because our heavenly Father loves us so much, he was about to do some incredible revealing, using life's ups and downs as our teacher.

Chapter 33

My God, My God, Why have you forsaken me?

WITH FINANCES GONE, A prescription for no new major projects for a very long time, the words rest and recuperation were everyone's suggestion. Great! Wonderful!

After faithfully serving God with all of our heart, soul, and mind, we now were once again going through a wilderness experience equaled to none that we had ever been through. Leaving the hospital Dennis and I had gotten a very strong word from the Lord regarding our immediate actions. I was reminded of a very dear friend, named Lisa, whose husband had gone through a tremendous fire, losing everything. At the time I didn't understand but she used to greet us at the door heading off our well-meant visits like a watchdog. The day before we were to come home I "saw" a picture of this woman and believed I heard the Spirit say, "I want you to guard your husband like a ferocious watchdog. He has been physically attacked and needs left totally alone for a period of time. Well meaning visitors will literally suck the life out of him when he needs to be with Me."

With that, I placed a call to Trish our right hand, and basically said something to the effect to put everyone on alert, no visitors for several weeks. Dropping by meals or helping financially was great but Dennis was under a mandate to separate himself to the Lord.

Arriving home, Trish had cleared out houseguests that had stayed with us for several months. The boys and I literally set Dennis up downstairs in a totally private room. Of course that didn't stop Dennis from getting up his second day home and putting on a suit headed out the door to try to find work. Dennis' brother Pat drove up

"What are you doing?" Pat questioned

"Going to work", was the reply!

It took about 2 hours for Dennis to figure out his body would simply shut down; and he really did need recovery time! The boys said hi quietly once or twice a day; and other than that we kept the house very quiet. Dennis immersed himself in the Word for hours and days and weeks. One precious couple that used to come to our bible studies gave us a financial love gift they certainly couldn't afford, making it so hard to accept. All other doors seemed shut!

Talk about feeling abandoned.

Couldn't people see how badly we were hurting? Didn't they know the bills were piling up, as Happy Thoughts was now totally dead? I was home schooling three sons and nursing Dennis back to health. Looking back now, we believe the Father was staying their hands as we were headed for another year of education in "God's University Street". At the time we tried awfully hard not to be heart broken. Then, right when it seemed all was lost, another tremendous show of Gods love and compassion.

There were just a couple of days left until the home was going to start foreclosure and a friend showed up at the door.

"Hi! Have you been praying? He asked, " I was out in my fields and the Lord said you needed this."

This man handed us a check for not one, not two, but THREE months mortgage payments, over $3,000. Not a loan, A GIFT!

Oh God, why do we doubt! How soon we forget!

Shortly after that, another friend called and said, "Honey, I don't understand this! You know how I feel, about Christians working, and no work- no eat! But I believe the Lord gave me a word for you and Dennis. He is requiring, like Moses at the Red Sea, that you STAND and see the salvation of your God! You cannot defend yourself and you cannot attack the enemy. Just be obedient to what God says daily, and watch to see what He does!"

How special these little touches are when you are feeling so alone!

One morning Dennis said, "Diana, we are supposed to go to a convention in Texas! I don't know how or if my body can even stand the ride but let's pray about it." Talk about faith stretchers! Barely milk in the fridge and an invitation for what would have to be an 8-day trip to Texas. Within a few days, Dennis's Mother handed Dennis a bolo tie that she said had belonged to Dennis' Dad. It had a cowboy hat as the decoration. No one had mentioned anything to her about Texas, and we both thought it interesting. Next, I asked the Lord how we would pay for this. Then some friends stopped by and gave us a gift that they said they were impressed to give! Then another friend gave a gift. So with that part of the question answered, we decided if we had to sleep in our van we would, because if God said, "**Go**" we had better go.

Meanwhile I continued to try to market anybody who might possibly need a gift basket; but it was abundantly clear "Happy Thoughts" was not happening. All this while Dennis was getting rested but was having horrible reactions to some of the medications that the Doctors had prescribed for him. So after visiting "Dr. Lively", yes, that was the new Doctor's real name, Dennis made an agreement with God! "Lord, I will not live the rest of my life sick! If you want to take me home great, but not sick!" So gone were the last of the beta-blockers, while a simple aspirin a day was the new therapy.

The other hug through all of this was that in the hospital God told Dennis that the Devil had tried to kill him and he hadn't succeeded. As a matter of fact, the heart surgeons were amazed that not one bit of Dennis's heart was permanently damaged due to the attacks and usually when there has been a total blockage there is dead tissue and lots of damage. Dennis's stress test showed minimal damage! To God, be All the Glory!

In the natural though, even with all of these reports confirming what Dennis thought God had said, "that he was healed", there was a walking out period for his body to catch up with the glowing reports.

Fighting extreme fatigue, muscle spasms that imitated the feelings of an impending attack, and severe indigestion, Dennis had to continue to walk out his healing.

Now about Texas! Driving away from California for the mid-west we tried to imagine what this could all be about!

"Honey, do you think if "Happy Thoughts" had been going strong and God had a change for our lives we would have listened?" "Probably not!" came the honest response! A real break from all of life's cares for this convention had us so excited, we left California early one morning and arrived in Texas two days before the convention. Since we had supported this ministry through thick and thin and sent many sacrificial love gifts, time and time again, we were very excited to "see" what God was ready for us to learn.

The day we arrived for the convention we were just in time for church. Dressed in jeans and excited to meet some new friends Dennis and I joined the service. The minute I walked inside the doors I felt like someone had placed the softest warmest comforter around my shoulders. It was so real I could barely stand up; and I started trying to tell Dennis what I was experiencing! Next, as people were singing songs of worship, I was reminded that God had supernaturally covered me through this recent attack on Dennis. One moment I was sitting on a pew thinking of God, and the next, I felt like someone had lifted a covering. I was allowed to feel for a few minutes the reality that most people must feel who walk through these kinds of crises. All of a sudden it was very real to me that I could have lost my husband and I was hit with grief, fear, and sorrow- of how close it had been; and what if he had died. Sobbing uncontrollably, I couldn't get the words out to explain what was happening; and all I could do was grab him and hold on as tight as I could. Then I thought I heard the Spirit say, "This is what I covered you from." How can I explain how wonderful the true Comforter is? The name of God's Holy Spirit is "Comforter", and I had experienced it first hand. Dennis and I had also arrived in time for communion, so the morning was wonderful.

After the service was over we checked with an usher to see if we could stay on the ministry grounds even though we were a few days early! He directed us to a "security" building and said to check with them! I was met, by a security guard for the property who said, "Follow me!" Her name was Debbie; and she was joyful and made us feel very welcome. Next, I was introduced to a precious man who had not seen our car, nor had he ever met Dennis or me before in our lives. Debbie had taken me into the main security room with TV cameras and I noticed ours was not in view.

Wayne was the man's name; and after a hearty welcome he got a funny look on his face and proceeded to "read my mail" so to speak. I hadn't seen someone operate in the gift of knowledge like this man in my life! As Jesus told the woman at the well how many husbands she had, this man spoke some incredible things. From the fact that we had come from California to the fact that we would be speaking and ministering on many TV stations some day, world wide; I would have given anything for a tape recorder. He had no way of knowing we had just had a book printed, or the fact that the Lord had spoken over 12 years before that someday we would be ministering on TBN, among other TV stations. Crying my eyes out, the final icing on the cake was when he said, "The devil tried to kill your husband but he didn't succeed!" Blubbering like a child, I listened. "You are being called here for a time of comfort, a season to be covered by a blanket of the Lord!" After what I had just experienced in the service that morning all I could keep thinking was that I wished my husband was here, because he would never believe this and I wanted him to be as blessed as I was getting! So after hugs and permission to go on down and set up at the campsite, I decided to give Wayne a book of our life! When Debbie, the security guard, and I got to the van, I asked Dennis for a book! Next thing I knew he came in with me to give it to Wayne. Well, some prayers are answered quickly; and Wayne no sooner set eyes on Dennis then he shared what God was giving him to speak. Words of confirmation, encouragement and life!

The rest of the eight days were just wonderful, spiritually, while in the flesh, Dennis fought symptoms daily!

Meanwhile we started thinking, “Could it be?” Fort Worth, Texas was booming with commerce, one of the nation’s major growing cities. People moving here by droves! How could “Happy Thoughts” not make it where there were as many corporations as cows?

Had God himself shut the door to California so we would go on another missionary trip?

Would we have listened? Was there more to be learned?

Chapter 34

YeeeeHaw & Texas Bound!

Returning to California, Dennis and I made it home again in just a day and a half! We must have talked for eight days non-stop and then some. With hope, and the feeling that there was transition in the air we got yet one more confirmation!

Isaac came to our room to chat and had the funniest look on his face! "Dad, Mom, I thought the Lord told me something! That we were going to Texas! -Like really going, not just visiting."

"You're right Honey, we just talked; and if God continues to shut every door here and confirm this move, we believe we are supposed to go." Since Isaac our oldest was 15, we were so excited. We knew that being a teenager and leaving friends would be hard. If the kids truly believed God was doing the sending and gave them peace, it would be much easier. Since it was only October we put the house on the market, Dennis continued to look for jobs, and the bills continued to stack up! When we were in Texas we had met a man who had told us if we ever moved to Texas to call and he would be there for us if we needed anything! Since it seemed like everything we were trying wasn't working, and Texas represented a new start, we were so excited to get going! In the process, Trish, our precious friend, had joined our little family helping to pay bills as we discipled and mentored her.

Now, for those of you who say, " Here I am, I want to be like Jesus; I want to learn how to have those wonderful qualities like

patience, long suffering, gentleness, kindness, and so on." Be careful what you pray for. Dennis would never have accepted help from a little widow woman had he not had a heart attack! Trish would have never given up her freedom to live with a family and be mentored 24 hours a day; but to help financially, she would. So Dennis and I accepted the plan knowing Trish was open to one-on-one mentoring; and Trish accepted the plan knowing her giving financially would help us make ends meet while Dennis recuperated.

Ha! Has God had the greatest laugh ever since. We all have learned so much about His nature and about true friendship, and true covenant that literally would have simply been talk and good theology. But I am here to tell you, we lived, and still live, New Testament covenant Christianity with those who God "SENDS".

Now, Trish had heard from God that she too was to go to Texas! Greater love has no man than to lay down his "life" for his brother. So in answer to the call of God, Dennis, Trish, Isaac, Isaiah, Israel and I, chose to put all personal ambitions and dreams on hold, to lay down our lives in service to God and each other, to see where the good Lord was taking us! January 17th the largest Penske moving truck made, followed by our big Van, and Trish's Oldsmobile all pulled away from an empty home. The house never sold, so no nest egg was had to move on!

Oh, Dennis and I had chanted all the right phrases, never broke stride, and just knew we were headed for great success! Of course we were about to learn that **the greatest success is to be in the center of God's will**, no matter where that might be. For Paul, the Apostle, his greatest successes included surviving shipwrecks, standing while watching a viper bury his fangs in his hands, and eventually having his daily needs met by being incarcerated! Oh, lest I forget, remember to count his 39 stripes numerous times and the famous stoning, where he had the honor of being left for dead. Over and over again the Word teaches that God gets the greatest Glory when He sovereignly moves on His children's behalf. God never gets Glory out of fleshly accomplishments, because any flesh can do them! But when there is no answer and you are Moses at the red sea, or staring at a dry rock, (that you'd really rather crawl under than face), then it seems God gets the greatest Glory by supernaturally intervening!

Didn't Paul say, "In our weakness He is made strong?"

To truly appreciate the growth that was about to come, one would either have had to be there, or have had one's own incredible story of betrayal.

We were off to new places with one little black kitty, named "Christmas Kitty". Even though funds were so limited, the doors had slammed so tight in California; anything would have seemed more welcoming! So with all of the past memories of God's supernatural provision we were ready for yet another great "new" faith experience.

Chapter 35

Betrayal

WHAT A PARADE OUR little family must have looked like crossing the highways and byways headed for Texas! The ministry that we were going to fellowship with identified with so much of what we had walked. We just knew we would be welcomed with the same loving arms that we had experienced on our first visit to Texas! It would be heaven on earth no doubt.

Arriving on a Monday with about $600, we were looking forward to seeing God blow the doors open in Texas! Oh, we had all expected to have close to $2,000 at the least, but last minute changes took our finances to less than $1,000. The good news was Trish had an interview for a job at a major hospital and Dennis and I were willing to do any odd jobs as soon as we had a place to call home, while we got "Happy Thoughts" up and running!

"Let's go straight to the ministry office, tell them we are here and that "God" has 'Sent' us!" I said.

Now, with all we had been through, it never occurred to us that we might appear flaky! After all, we had seen the dead raised, we were missionaries, we had supported this ministry and sent "love gifts" when our own family was sacrificing everything! Not only that but my husband who operates in the prophet's calling was absolutely being "sent" to a ministry who constantly spoke that God was going to be sending prophets, apostles, and many, to them! We were a gift to them and they were a gift to us! We were in "Covenant one to another". These were our true "brothers".

Oh my, I could see my Father shaking his head now saying, "Diana, oh, Diana!"

Walking into the main administration building for the "ministry" we were met by a receptionist who ushered us into an office. Quietly waiting, we had such an air of expectancy! The lady who finally appeared seemed less than pleased at our arrival. As we shared our hearts, what we believed we had heard, her face grew more and more concerned. Our timing, in her eyes was not convenient

There was a big Minister's once a year conference, where the elite and important people sought God! Great! Perhaps we could go to it and God's timing was perfect since Dennis is a prophet! "Oh No, partner or not, you didn't receive a 'special invitation'!" As things were going from bad to worse, I looked over and just happened to notice a copy of our newly published book, "Product of Love", in the ministry library. Grabbing it, I waved it in the ladies face and she took it and seemed very unimpressed. It did seem to help a little as she told us to go away until Friday, after "the anointed" had met, but shoved $80 in food coupons in our hands for a local store and dinner for 4 to a local buffet.

Well, shut my mouth! If Dennis' steam wasn't showing, Trish's broken heart was hard to hide. Ah, well, no biggy; no room at the inn has happened to better people than us. Let's go away until Friday and see what God did during the week.

Driving away from our "covenant partners" we decided to go get a motel room and grab a newspaper! The headlines on the morning paper for Fort Worth were some that I'll never forget! Over 300 churches had met to discuss were they their brother's keeper and should the church be responsible for social help programs, for housing the poor and feeding the needy? The newspaper reported after the conference, the response was a resounding "NO". Even though George Bush had managed to get government funds, and laws had been passed federally to no longer discriminate against giving moneys to Christian organizations that wanted to help people, the consensus was "It's not our job."

The week slipped by as we went motel to motel, looking for a place to call home and scouring the newspaper daily. We were on a deadline to unload the moving truck so as not to incur other charges; so, we basically spent almost all of our money waiting for "Friday". The street where we found a motel was named Ephraim, no joke!

Parents don't mind going through hard tests but there's something about seeing your "children" being stripped and disappointed that is horrible. Trish had just come out of a legalistic church background and was so excited to learn about the relationship that was available direct with the Lord, the Father, and His Spirit. Yet she was seeing a whole lot that wasn't adding up! Meanwhile, Dennis and I offered at this one large motel to work in exchange for rooms, and even though we had already paid for the night, the clerk came and wrote down our license plates in front of us like we were going to steal something. Not exactly what we expected.

That night Dennis was up all night and God allowed him to feel totally abandoned and alone. As he cried out and asked, "Why are you allowing me to feel this? Why are You hiding Your face?" The Lord shared His heart for widows and orphans with Dennis! "I never want you forgetting this feeling of abandonment. That's what all these single women who have been left, feel, trying to raise a family single handedly, all alone. It is a terrifying feeling; and when you get a call for help, even if it's three in the morning, I want you never to forget what they are feeling.

As the sun rose, I was still naively looking "forward" to Friday, as this was the day we had been told to return. Now our finances were one $50 check that Isaac had been given from Grandpa and Grandma for his birthday, which was the next day, and a $100 check from Lori's sister, Grandma Jackie, that we hadn't cashed yet! We were almost totally out of gas for 3 vehicles and had nowhere to go. We had combed the papers looking for apartments, rentals, etc. and Trish was supposed to hear the final approval on her job by Monday!

There was another Friday morning in history that was famous for another crucifixion and I must tell you what happened was so far from our thinking!

Arriving at the ministry "Headquarters" we were told to "get real" and how much did we need? Simply enough to get into a little house that would enable us to unload our belongings and get started! Explaining to our "sister in the Lord" that we had been combing the papers there was nothing available in the area. "Well, find a place today, and we will get a check cut. Make sure it's not too expensive, start where you're at." Were these the words of faith I had been taught? The message was go find a dump because God is limited and so are we. What if we can't locate a place in one day, could we unload our stuff into one of your storage places until we find a place (this ministry had hundreds of acres)? "Heck no, and remember we close at 5:00p.m. It's Friday, the weekend's coming!

By the way, here's one in the paper for $400 a month in a town over 30 minutes away, but we are close to being out of gas and we are supposed to be fellowshipping here! Well, check it out and get back to me", the lady matter-of-factly told us.

Since our appointment wasn't until 10:00a.m. Friday we had waited all week to be told go find a place in a few hours. With no other leads, we drove all the way to this town over 30 minutes away and found an absolute dump. Now, if we had been being "sent" there it wouldn't have mattered; but what it would have cost Trish in time and money to drive daily to work, and then add travel time to all the church activities each way, this just wasn't God. Arriving back at the ministry office, where we had left the Penske moving truck parked while we went "house hunting", we ran for the doors as it was approaching 4:30. "Maybe they will let us sleep in one of the buildings tonight," I said hopefully!

This was after all an international ministry, our covenant partners, with unlimited resources on hundreds of acres with many, many buildings!

Being January in Texas, temperatures were dropping; and it was hitting close to 20 degrees. Well, around 4:30 p.m. this woman looked straight into Dennis' eyes and said, "Too bad, you didn't find a house today; we are closing!"

Dennis said, "Are you telling me you are turning our family away into 20 degree weather with no gas and nowhere to go?"

"Yep", was the firm short retort.

Oh, God! Are the prophets always to be rejected and despised?

Here Dennis had gone from selling his life out to Jesus with so many victories, only to be almost killed with a heart attack, and then totally betrayed by our brothers. Dennis' immediate response was "I'm not surprised." Striding away with his family in tow, Isaac had food for thought! "Daddy, if 'so and so' was here he wouldn't have turned us away into the cold!" (Isaac had named the brother we had supported for so many years.)

Isaac and I pulled away in the van followed by Trish, Isaiah, and Christmas Kitty, in the Oldsmobile, followed by Dennis and Israel in the Penske. To say we were all numb would have been an understatement. During the week and up to that day we had been trying to connect with the brother who had told us to call if we needed help; yet for some reason that door was closed, also.

Leaving the property I remember not knowing even which way to head, when a semi coming the other way on a little two lane road decided to pass, and literally ran Isaac and I OFF THE ROAD. Instantly without any thought I gave the driver an extended finger, and couldn't believe it. Isaac, in shock, asked me what on earth I had just done! Trying to make a joke of it all, I explained I didn't mind almost losing his father, or being turned out into 20 degree weather by our "covenant partners", but when the devil tried to kill me and him just then, I had taken it personally!

Heading back into a little town on the outskirts of Fort Worth, I was thinking, "What Now?" And just as that hit my mind I saw a sign that said "Hurting? Need help? Call!" And there was a phone number! "Isaac, write this down, now!" and while Isaac wrote I pulled into the first gas station I found. Grabbing a quarter, I didn't even look back to see if Trish or Dennis had pulled over, I was absolutely driven. The man's voice that answered on the other end of the line was so warm. I explained we had just come from California and things weren't working out quite as planned. BEFORE I COULD EVEN ASK FOR HELP!!!! Precious Danny (the pastor's name) said, "Let me guess. You could use a warm place to sleep, some food, and some gas!) "Oh thank you. Thank you, Thank you," tears poured down my face and hanging up, I ran to the truck to tell Dennis what had happened. By the time I finished talking, Pastor Danny had already arrived. Grabbing Dennis and giving him a hug, this precious pastor, sent straight from God, told him how sorry he was that we had experienced such a rejection from our "partners". Here, a man who we had never met, never sown one seed into his ministry, never had heard of, offered us food, shelter and love, without question -no matter what the cost!

He didn't ask us to fill out a form, explain our theology, or make us promise to come to his church. Like the Good Samaritan story he simply loved us in word and deed.

Hugging Dennis, he told us to "FILL UP" all 3 vehicles and to get the groceries out of the van he had brought to us. Laughing, the boys all transferred about 6 or 7 bags of groceries to our van. It's always the little things that are so special. Seeing the boys break open a bag of chocolate candies that were included, they seemed oblivious to the fiery trial we were in the middle of. Groceries transferred, cars filled with gas, Dennis placed one more call to a man named Rick we had met when we visited Texas in October. Dennis told him that God had provided a place for us to stay for the night. The good news was the friend offered his shed to unload the Penske the next day so we could return it to avoid any additional charges.

"Follow me", said Pastor Danny; and driving to a little Baptist church a few blocks away pointed to a little Sunday school room. It's not much, but it's what we've got! There are some mats you can pile up and we'll bring some pillows and blankets.

"Welcome". It was so cold out and the little room was so warm. The boys were so tired; and it had been a long day.

As all of us surveyed the room, we were delighted to find a little coffeepot we could warm some hot cocoa or tea in; and even though we couldn't find a can opener for the cans, the boys heartily munched down on some peanut butter, jelly, and some crackers. Since it was now getting dark and we were left alone, our crew nestled in for the evening. Opening to the book of James I read to everyone in the room as they laughed and ate!

"Count it **ALL JOY** my brothers when you encounter various trials and tests knowing that the testing of your faith produces endurance (patience). **Make sure to let patience have it's perfect result so that you will be perfect and complete lacking in nothing!"**

Oh man! As I read I was reminded of a prayer I had prayed back in California for my boys! I had been feeling that there had not been any fresh spiritual experiences in their lives for quite a while, and was concerned that they were wonderful and all but kind of living on yesterday's relationship with God. My prayer had been that no matter what it took, please help my sons to each have his very own, very personal relationship with God so that He would be real to them, not because of me and Dennis and our experiences.

Was it possible that all of this fire was actually an answer to prayer? Everyone received as I continued to read the whole letter from the apostle, James; and we all laughed in a manner like I think perhaps the first disciples did, when encountered with the unexpected.

Saturday morning was Isaac's 16th birthday! Oh, how we had wanted to show our love by some material thing to bless him, yet what his heavenly Father was investing in him was far more valuable than any man made gift. Writing a huge thank you note on the board Dennis taped his last $1 bill on the board. Heading out we looked for a place to cash our last check from Jackie, and Isaac's check from Ivan and Dorothy. Isaac was a great sport and said, "I know we're down to these 2 checks and all I really want for my birthday is a paint ball magazine, if it's not too much." Precious moments and costly gifts!

In an Albertson's Store we found a woman who would cash the two checks; and even though we had no idea what was ahead, Dennis and I bought Isaac his own personal lemon-meringue pie and a paint ball magazine. Hand delivering it to the car everyone cracked up as Isaac, as only he could, started in humor singing the most pitiful round of Happy Birthday to me! Everyone howling, we now needed to touch base with our friend, Rick, who had offered the shed for our stuff. We didn't look forward to double-moving, but now with the offer of a church to sleep in, and a place to unload our stuff, things were looking up.

Hallelujah! God uses tests and trials to reveal our hearts to ourselves, to show us once again why we need Him so badly, and why He is so wonderful. Dennis was on the phone to Rick who sounded so heart broken. "I cried all night as I realized my heart, not helping your family." It was like all the words of "covenant", and "brother" had been ringing in Rick's ears and God was saying these words all sound great but what will you do when someone needs help! He couldn't believe that he had not responded in our hour of need and he literally wept all night at God's revealing of his heart! His honesty only endeared him even more to Dennis and I; and Rick said "Please bring your family to our home and we will give you a place to stay while you find a home." A true brother!

Unloading everything from a giant Penske to Rick's' shop we were amazed that it all fit. Returning the truck exactly when it was due, we now started looking for houses, by faith! Trish had the promise of the new job and here she was now walking through a place of trust she had never been before! Being Sunday, the Lord told us to go on back to fellowship with the brothers who had turned us into the cold. To love them, forgive them and not to go away! Talk about being handed a plate full of your worst vegetables-for the vitamins! The Lord said I am sending you for a reason and I have not told you your job is finished yet! Yuck! Ow! Time to grow some more!

Monday through Wednesday Dennis and I left every morning looking for a place to live. From hovels to mansions we asked the Lord to guide us. Rick and his family were precious and we would find a note with $20 for gas to continue looking and Rick's' wife even made a belated birthday cake for Isaac. Two days later was my birthday and I couldn't believe it when I was presented with a beautiful bag filled with new lipsticks, and a candle, and all kinds of goodies!

One more special moment was when on our second day at Rick's, the boys kept asking Dennis and I to bring in the computer from the car where it was still packed. We were trying to be as low key as possible and hadn't let them "set up" anything that might seem intrusive. Getting a little quickening Dennis decided, it would help keep them occupied while we searched for a home! We still had paid for our online service and in our e-mails the boys found a note from the worldwide television network, Trinity Broadcasting Network!

"You have been invited to appear on the program Back on Course, with Gavin & Patty McCloud!" If we hadn't plugged the PC in that day, the server would have dumped the e-mail. TBN had tried to contact our California number to no avail and was looking for us!

Here we were homeless, rejected, hurting, and yet on the other hand in the middle of the greatest times with God imaginable! Picking up the phone I called immediately and said "You bet, is it in Texas?" "No, we'll need you in California." Of course, now that we had just moved to Texas, we were needed in California! Makes perfect sense!

With a tentative date of May for the taping we continued to look frantically for a home. The problem in finding a rental was that very few rentals were available compared to California. It was as cheap to buy a home in Texas, as it was to rent. Finally, spotting one little ad for an 1100 square foot house in a little town half way between Fort Worth and the "ministry" we were sent to, we went to check it out. Calling, I made an appointment, and then made an immediate call to the ministry that had turned us away! Acting like it was the most normal thing in the world I informed the woman who had turned us into the cold that in the week we hadn't seen her we had managed to find a house. It was $750 a month and did they still want to help us get into a house? "Yes" was the reply.

With that in mind, Trish joined us for the walk through. Now she had read all about God's intervention in the book, "Product of

Love", and had experienced some wonderful miracles of her own, but it was so awesome to see what happened next!

The widow woman who owned the house was named Billie! She was pure Texan with an accent and boots to match. We walked through the little 3-bedroom house and figured out that if we gave the

boys the master bedroom, Dennis and I could fit into one, and Trish could fit into the other one! Trish shared about her new job she was starting Monday and when her first paycheck was due. Since it was Friday I shared that a local ministry was willing to pay the first month's rent but that they wouldn't have a check until Monday. God as my witness, this woman handed Trish the keys to the house without so much as an application being filled out, and said something to the effect that she didn't know why she was doing this as she didn't trust anybody, that she had been burned so many times, but that we could move in immediately and pay out the deposit over time!

As Billie drove away, Trish, Dennis and I couldn't stop laughing with joy. Going back to Rick's we informed him we would be moved out by morning and could we start moving now!

"How much money did we need?" he graciously offered

"Nothing" we joyfully shared!

Since we had come from an almost 2,700 square foot home full of furniture, we had a lot to move. Since Rick was a journeyman tile layer, carpet layer, repairman, he had a van, and we had our van, so moving commenced immediately! No paperwork, no money, just keys and a lot of very grateful people! I did call the ministry, shared the good news, and they assured us they would have a check for us Monday morning, first thing!

Saturday morning, as we finished our moving, we discovered that Texas was almost all electric! I had a brand new gas oven and a gas dryer! It seemed like the most normal thing to tell Dennis to park them by the curb; it's Saturday, perhaps we could sell them and get some money we could use to buy food, or even an electric dryer. The house came with an electric stove, so that was covered.

Within just a few minutes of setting the 2 appliances by the curb, WITHOUT A SIGN, this man came whipping up in a car and said, "Hey! I need a gas stove!" Great! I replied. I gave him about a $500 new stove for $250 and asked, "You don't happen to need a gas dryer do you?" "Well, yes, and I just got through going through my electric one! I'll trade straight across!" Now, with a way to do laundry and pay the utility deposits all that was needed was a little food and the deposit for a phone! Rick showed up with a couple of sacks of food with lots of tapioca pudding mixes. To this day, our family jokes about eating tapioca pudding for what seemed like weeks on end.

Monday morning came quickly and what a change had occurred! Dennis and I were treated like royalty! A check for $750 was very lovingly handed across, and then to our amazement we were asked would we mind taking some groceries that someone had donated! About 12 bags full of everything from cornmeal to oil, beans rice, on and on! You don't think this was because I had told them we had been invited to share our "true story" on a program that reached millions?

Before leaving the property you will never guess whom we ran into again! Wayne, the security guard! He closed the door where we were waiting for the check and looked deep into Dennis' eyes!

"Oh, Yes, Oh, Yes, the LORD says you've been through an incredible fire, be not surprised at what has come, but rejoice knowing the standing and the trying of your faith has produced a sweet smell in His nostrils. **You trusted Him! You trusted Him; and He has counted that as Gold!** He said to tell you that you are going to be on many, many, TV stations and minister to the whole world as you are called to share to the whole world; you will minister to the whole world. We need you here; yep, we need you here! There is much for you to learn here and there are things you will discover here. You have been sent here for a season to this place to learn, but we need your gifts here too." Wayne was so moved he couldn't contain himself and proclaimed, "My God, you are hot fertile ground, so hot I have to sow into this good ground!" With that he fell on his knees muttering that today was his birthday, and this was his birthday present, please take it! He emptied his wallet and even the change in his pockets. Even though Dennis was totally humbled, and we were amazed, we knew the Lord said to receive this precious gift. After we hugged Wayne gave us his phone number and then left the room. The lady who was getting the check walked in and directed us to where the groceries were.

I had gone downstairs to use a phone when we had first gotten to the ministry office just to see how much the deposit for a phone was going to be and where to open an account!

As Dennis and I came out with the groceries, we loaded everything into the van! Getting inside, Dennis opened his wallet to see what Wayne had given to us! Do you think it was a coincidence that it was just a few dollars more than what we needed for the phone deposit?

We drove immediately to the grocery store that took the phone deposit so it could be turned on as soon as possible!

With all we went through, it truly seemed like we had been in a war to move to Texas, but we truly believed it was the right move! The Word says where God sends, He provides; and truly we were provided for! Sometimes Jesus said to go without anything, don't even take an extra pair of shoes, and at other times the disciples were sent out with lots of natural provision! Just goes to show we cannot put God in a box!

Would we have preferred to do things differently? **YES!**

With maturity comes the realization of how little we really know, and how big God is. That's why it pays to lean not on your own understanding and to always trust that where He leads you everything will work out for His glory!

Chapter 36

Trust

TEXAS PROVED TO BE a place of learning. As May approached, Dennis and I were excited about the invitation to share about our faith and the personal relationship available to "Who so ever will".

The boys were being home schooled, and Isaac needed to be flown to California to take his High School Proficiency Exam. Dennis and I continued to fellowship at the ministry, and time and time again our hearts were so broken by the clickishness and selfishness of our dear brothers. Time and time again we were used by the Lord to help widows in their own congregation. You see, this ministry wanted to grow, and kept prophesying that God was sending prophets and apostles and many. Yet there was nothing in place to receive them, or treat them, as we would receive Jesus. God totally opened Dennis and my eyes about how the spirit of religion and mammon had infiltrated this church and so many in America. The same people who were preaching you can't out give God didn't seem to put this into practice in the local church body. Many things were claimed on TV to the whole world that was not lived in their own little local church!

After Dennis and I had been turned out into the cold, within just a few weeks, a world renowned evangelist came through and preached about how God had used a little family to expose his ministry when they were in need of help; and this mega ministry had nothing in place for the poor or the hurting! We couldn't believe it! Because of Dennis' call as a prophet we had gone directly in and asked for a meeting with the pastor of the church. I truly believe we only got it because I mentioned we were going to be ministering on TBN. At the meeting we poured out our hearts, how we had been received, and asked what was in place for the local body? We asked how the "covenant" relationship worked. I now know why the world wants no part of so many Christians. The message was repeated time and time again! Give us your time, your life, your prayers, and your money! In return, your part of the covenant is we will speak words for you! How lame!

The other thing that was so frightening was the way people had been taught to be respecters of persons. The lame, the sick, and the hurting, were not welcome in the front rows where the "anointing was supposed to be the strongest". These precious seats had to be filled by "friends and family", to protect the "anointing". My Bible says devils run at God's presence. I wonder how God ever moves in a supermarket without a 20 foot anointing space! Over and over we saw needs in this congregation, and when asked how to get people help, they were always "prayed for".

During this time the Lord gave me a wonderful analogy. He showed me an auto accident, and asked what do people do when they come upon an accident? Well, they should render immediate first aid; if they need hospitalization to become stable, we do that; and then later, after the person has been tended to, we find out if perhaps an error was made, or how not to be back in the same situation. Then why, when people have financial accidents or marital accidents do we all get sanctified and say, "We'll pray for you". It's because it will cost you something by getting involved! Oh, the things the Lord taught all of us during our year in Texas.

When Dennis and I ended our meeting with the pastor, he ushered us out and word was given that if we had been sent, if there was a call on our lives, we needed to be "POLISHED" by them, to come along side and be like them, to prove ourselves, before they would receive anything from us!

How sad! To think that the God of the Universe wants everybody to be just like you, or they don't have anything to offer?

The longer we stayed we realized how this place was anything but anointed. One service, I remember an old Grandpa "anointed prayer warrior" grabbed Isaac, who had gone for prayer, and kept shoving him to the ground so Isaac would be "slain in the spirit." Three times this misguided man literally shoved Isaac into the carpet on his back. Even though we have had that experience ourselves for real, I must tell you after laughing it off with Isaac, about our over zealous brother, I was so saddened at what my son was seeing. So much flesh!

One week, as we entered into praise and worship, I was so hungry for something of substance that I cried out to God to shut the speaker's mouth if he or she didn't have something directly from Him. For over 35 minutes the pastor's wife stood at the podium with stammering lips and cried, and could not get a word out. Nobody knew what to do, for this wasn't presentable. Over and over the pastor would say He wanted God to arrive, but right when the true anointing started to fall, we had to hurry up and move on with our agendas.

We stayed over four months before the Lord released us, with great heaviness of hearts. We could no longer take fellowship with a people who would stand and group chant

"Money Cometh To Me Now",

when nothing was in place for the widows and orphans. Why weren't they group chanting in such heartfelt glee,

"Money Goeth from Me Now?"

After all, the Lord said it is more blessed to give than receive.

Jesus said the seed in the parables was the most precious thing of all! Teaching that if God's WORD was sown into the GOOD soil of YOUR HEART, you would PRODUCE fruit, 30-60-100 fold. You would be an incredible fruit producer. Didn't God say if I can't trust you with filthy mammon, I can't trust you with the true treasures?

Sincere good people were totally focused on believing God for some earthly thing, instead of hungering for Him and His presence. Like the people of old, they would tromp to the temple to have the priests tell them what to do. Kick now, recite now, fall down now, smile now, and above all, practice confession out of your flesh, not because God told you to believe something, but because we told you to practice words. If you truly think you can drum up results by the flesh, I invite you to go practice at the local hospital! Just walk into someone's room and tell them you know God's plan for their life, when you don't even know how to hear Him. You know what you'll get? Kicked out!

God is never glorified through a hotshot prideful attitude.

What we witnessed was so heartbreaking because we truly believed we saw a lot of sheep being led to a slaughter! You see, faith is so powerful and it is what we live by. Yet, this faith works by LOVE and who among you when seeing your brother in need tells him to "go and be blessed?" God says you are worthless!

If these sheep were ever required to walk like Paul, a life of

Total "SELF SACRIFICE ", they would never make it. Anybody remember the first church and the Covenant God taught? They had to be willing to die for their faith; and the first place they were tested in was would they be selfish with money or did they consider it all God's? Read the book of Acts again, for the first time, and notice how those believers were so anointed, and not one of them had anything that they even considered their own! Then, the anointing was on their lives.

Remember the cross? Where is the preaching of the cross?

A place of CRUCIFIXION!

Remember Jesus said to DIE to YOURSELF?????

Store not up for yourself treasures on earth, but give what you have to charity, and you shall have treasure in heaven?

Even though Dennis and I hadn't meant to, we had been tainted by the gimmee theology in a world that is so hungry for the presence of God. Oh, yes, we understand that in God's presence there is fullness of joy, and everything you could ever want, but the focus is Him, and His presence, not stuff!!!!

The Word says SEEK FIRST THE KINGDOM OF GOD (which is not material) and then He will provide what you need! Jesus said not to care about what you even had for food, or what to drink or wear! And yet, **I was watching the self-proclaimed**

holy priests prancing around in $5,000 suits saying they were dead men! Hardly!

In contrast to that fellowship, and all that we had learned from our "covenant partners", the Lord then sent us to a very humble ministry that met in a storefront. Even though there were outreaches in 28 countries, a handful of simple folks, who loved Jesus, would meet on Thursday nights. What a difference.

Dennis and I had never heard of the fellowship or the ministry. The founder would lead humble little Bible studies once a week. You never would have guessed who might be famous or who wasn't. Unlike the other extreme who paraded their offerings to the alter like some Babylonian practice (or a new marketing scam by mammon), this cowboy had a very unique way of taking offerings. Kind of like Jesus said to: Folks, there's an offering bucket over there if God puts something on your heart. You can put in, and if you need something, you can take out what you need! He was not kidding! I SAW him do that at several rodeos, where he preached to arenas full of people.

How refreshing! During the Bible studies, this humble brother "Ted" would give scriptures to anybody who wanted one, young and old alike! And then when that person read it this precious brother would say, "Well, what does that say to you?" The person would share, and then anyone else with a thought or question was welcomed to give what the precious Holy Spirit had given him or her to share. All were welcomed; and you knew that all were gathered at the feet of Jesus, not a man, or a ministry, but together as the collective body. So simple yet so wonderful! Here this humble man had managed to lift up Jesus and still answer his own phone! No celebrity here!

Some nights we would start singing, and this precious little lady named Estelle would pick up her guitar and sing whatever the Spirit was giving her. Lives were changed, prayers were answered, but only one was lifted up- JESUS!

Time marched on and our family continued to grow. We all learned, like the apostle Paul, to be content wherever God was using us. Peace was on our feet. Some precious friends in California paid for our flight out to California. Dennis and I had the joy of sharing with hurting women later receiving hundreds of letters. We hand wrote each one back praying over every need! What a privilege!

Then yet another surprise came. This precious friend, Ted, invited Dennis and I to share our story on Dallas public broadcasting television

Sharing with Ted

Dennis and I tried all sorts of odd jobs to help the household income, including professional cleaning and delivering phone books. Dennis was still supposed to be taking it easy, but the male ego was just not going to let a widow and his wife support him! We laughed later, thinking how like Nehemiah, we were led to spy out the condition of the church. Is not the mid-west known as the Bible belt? While this education was happening we were literally cleaning houses to help make ends meet! You can bet there was one big house we wanted to help sweep. "It's called the church!" God's answer was "Let's start with YOU first!" That lesson included delivering telephone books for 10 cents apiece, working for a courier service running the Dallas, Fort Worth metro-plex, and also donning a "Merry Maids" T-shirt. Now anyone knows that the likes of Dennis, a Vietnam Veteran, ex Biker, tuff guy wanted to put on a green shirt that said "Merry Maid" in bright yellow and scrub floors with his wife! Wisdom is known by her children; and Dennis and I had the privilege of giving out books, praying for the hurting, and meeting so many hurting, through the vehicle of that job!

Texas, oh Texas...So many memories, the most beautiful lightening storms, electrical ballets that lit up the heavens with splendor. There were tornado's that would literally pass within a few blocks of our house. Yes, we found out 6 people cannot fit in a tub. There is the greatest Tex- Mex food in all of America, and the greatest downtown American City in the nation-Downtown Fort Worth, where you could stroll from an art gallery to an indoor skating rink without any fear of violence. Bicycle riding policemen and strolling officers had made this one of the safest cities in the US. It was wonderful!

After Isaac flew out and passed his test graduating from high school, his friend, Greg, flew out to visit. All of us went to a friend's for a real Texas Bar B Que where I had my hair dyed bright neon yellow, and the boys all rode horses! Israel was so surprised when at the little Bible studies he met the world reigning Bull riding champion, Scott, his precious wife, Angel, and their brand new son, Caden. They were everyday real folks. Scott had invited Israel over to learn to rope a cow; and before long, we had a bale of hay set up in the back yard with Israel in complete cowboy attire, down to his Justin boots, straight from Justin, Texas. Now Isaiah had moved from one great love to another. Burning out on basketball, Isaiah bought his first guitar. Trish had given him her guitar, and then after the boys had made some money working for Rick, they all started investing in their various hobbies. Isaac got his first drum. Meanwhile, Trish's year was an incredible roller coaster, like all of us, of great stretching and great victories. Dennis and I were invited, yet one more time, on an International TV program called Day Star! We were so thrilled at the doors God was opening; and continued to maintain our friendship with Wayne and his wife Barb! As many of the things came to pass that Wayne had prophesied, we made sure to share with him the good news.

In December the Lord had one more surprise for Dennis and I.

We had never met Arthur Blessitt, in person, even though we had talked and met numerous times through e-mails. So after a series of events Dennis and I found ourselves headed to Texarkana on the Texas Arkansas border.

We had obtained permission, from a pastor that was going to be hosting Arthur and Denise, to bring a film crew and tape what Arthur was going to be preaching! Dennis and I were going to the Friday night service; meanwhile Trish and William, the cameraman, were going to be meeting us there the next morning! Now, nothing happens by coincidence, and I just have to share the incredible series of events that led to a wonderful meeting. Dennis and I believed the Spirit had asked us to go film Arthur. So we called and got permission from the hosting Pastor, and then said, "Great, all we need is a cameraman and a camera." A name came to mind, and a man we had met at Bible studies (William) said,

"Why did you wait so long to call? The Lord told me to make myself available to you anytime you needed me."

We can't pay you, but we'll have fun! I said

William said, "Great, I'll be there and I'll even supply the tapes!"

Dennis and I headed out Friday night with just enough money for gas and a room for the night! Driving hours away from Fort Worth we arrived in this Stateline city. We saw the church where we would be going, but up to now, we had no contact with Arthur, and he had no idea we were coming! I had picked up a coupon book with reduced room rates. Dennis and I ignored the book and tried to check into a Motel 6. We were $2 short of the cost of the room so the clerk suggested we find an ATM. Embarrassed, we went to a bank, praying there might be $20 in the bank! Dennis drove up to the ATM, which promptly spit our card out. It didn't say "no money," it simply would not accept our card. So looking at my feet, I was reminded of the coupon booklet! Hey, here's a room that is exactly $2 less than the other one. Speeding across town, we were hurrying, as we didn't want to miss a minute of Arthur's preaching. Dennis pulled into a motel driveway and jumped out. Blowing by the people standing in the front entrance, he cut a quick path to the check-in counter. Dennis was hurrying, as it now was about 20 minutes after what was supposed to be the "starting time". As I followed I couldn't believe my eyes and started laughing. Standing in the doorway, big as life, totally orchestrated by God, was Arthur Blessitt talking with someone.

"Hey Arthur! Hi! It's me Diana! The book, "Product of Love" I was blurting out words so fast as I grabbed on to him for a great big hug!

"Diana, well, what are you doing here? Where is Dennis?" said Arthur grinning from ear to ear.

"He blew right by you in a hurry to go see you!" I said. Meanwhile, Dennis stopped to see what I was carrying on about and quickly realized that Arthur was right there. Do you know the odds of running into Arthur Blessitt in a city the size of Texarkana? As Dennis visited, I realized Denise, Arthur's wife, had walked into the lobby and we shared a quick greeting with her too. Knowing they were supposed to be at this church, we said something to the effect of talk to you later and headed up to our room on the 4th floor.

Going to our room we discovered we had been put right next-door to Arthur's' son, Joshua, whom we dearly loved and had prayed for. Going into our room we hurried to set our things down, not wanting to miss anything!

"Dennis, I wish we had time to tell Arthur about the miracle of how we ended up here, and also, that we want to tape him tomorrow. Oh, well, God will make a way! Coming out of our room we stopped at the elevator, and guess whom came walking out as we tried to get in? You guessed it! Arthur again!

"All right, forgive us," I blurted out, "but we need to talk, if only for 5 minutes."

While sharing how we had ended up at that motel, out of the whole city, Arthur just kept shaking his head and laughing at God's plan. Then we explained that we had a cameraman coming to tape him preaching; and we had not been able to contact him, but was it all right? Graciously, he consented, and after all of us marveled at

God's plan we went our own way. Arthur's message that night was further confirmation of all that the Father had been teaching us in our "Texas University".

"There are no walls" Arthur bellowed and shared story after story about God's grace and mercy during his many years carrying the cross. The love that flowed from this humble follower of Jesus was the healing for our weary wounded hearts. That night after the meeting, everyone met and walked with Arthur, Denise, and the Cross, down Texarkana Stateline road. Right in the middle of the busy street, Arthur suggested we stop and pray. Without hesitation everyone from children to Grandfathers knelt face down at the foot of the cross and prayed for that city. As I closed my eyes, I remember thinking how this felt so right. Young and old, street kids to businessmen, women to little girls everyone belonged at the feet of Jesus. For when one is at the foot of the Cross, nothing else mattered. Time stood still. It didn't matter where you worked, or who you were. It was enough to simply be at the feet of Jesus. It was glorious! Something very special happened to my heart that day, and a new revelation concerning the true meaning of the cross was given to me. You see, when Jesus was lifted up it was so perfect. I think that's what ended up disturbing us the most about most organized ministries. They may not have meant to, but they lifted so much of themselves up! Men in positions of power trying to rule and reign over other men making followers of their doctrines, not followers of Jesus!

Morning came early, and we were able to tape Arthur preaching the next day. A wonderful time was had by all; and meeting precious Arthur and Denise, his son, Joshua, and his wife Nina, was a blessing and an honor!

December came and went, and all of us had feelings of transition again. The whole year we had been in Texas our California house was saved, yet another time, by a set of wonderful circumstances. Renters had been found when Dennis and I had flown out to tape Gavin and Patty's program on marriage, and instead of the house being repossessed; it was sold off to different mortgage companies twice during the year. We had been in touch with the renters, who verbalized the house was too big for them, and that if we ended up coming back to California, they would be happy to leave by the end of February. The new mortgage company heard our full story, and in spite of the lack of payments, they were willing to set up a new payment plan. Where were we going to get the money for them, and the move back to California? Tax return time! Whew! The year had been so bad financially for our family that we received almost $3,400 back! That would be enough to get us back to California.

Meanwhile, Trish had endured many of her own battles that year including the death of her mother, and then had suffered some terrible harassment at her job. Some of the most precious memories cannot be shared since the Lord Jesus says to not let the "left hand know what the right hand is doing when you give." Just suffice it to say, that Dennis, Trish, myself, and our sons, had truly walked out the meaning of the words covenant. At times when we saw needs, we would take our dearest possessions to hock shops to help someone in need. And yet, the Lord often made a way to get the things back out! Our family had the privilege of walking and living out a true New Testament church relationship without pressure and controlling each other. But by prayer and making all needs known to God, the Holy Spirit would speak to one of us if the other had a need!

Getting an offer for an even better job at a hospital in Fresno, California, Trish felt like she to was to continue on with our family back to California.

If I had to sum up our biggest growth at Texas U, as I lovingly call it, it would be that we were delivered completely from following men, and since we had tasted the truth that we are saved by grace through faith, and that not of ourselves, we were not about to go back into any legalistic bondage. We all continued to grow to know God through His son, Jesus, by His Spirit and learned about the greatest experience of all "The Wilderness".

For you see, the first place Jesus went after being baptized was to the wilderness to be totally reliant on God, and to totally defeat the enemy and his ways once and for all in His life. Then, when Jesus had defeated Satan in His own life, He went to spread the Gospel or the "GOOD NEWS". I guess the whole year boiled down to one great word "TRUST".

Chapter 37

Getting To Know You!

Returning to California, we were lighter by one vehicle; Trish still had the Oldsmobile, and we had rented a Penske truck. The joke was we were all so worried about the car making it across country, which was a story in itself.

For four months we had non-stop trouble with Trish's car, and it was acting like the transmission was going if you used overdrive. The good news is that through every break down we had to go to a truck driver neighbor who would help us with mechanics. The Lord had a plan and a purpose as Donna the trucker's wife ended up meeting Jesus through all that was happening; and last we heard her husband was getting baptized and the whole family had been mightily impacted.

After many farewells to close friends and loved ones, we headed across country during a break in the snowstorms and took the shorter northern route. It was perfect weather, and other than chasing all the cats "Christmas kitty" had birthed, the only break down was by the Penske truck! Trish, Isaac, Isaiah and I, rode in the Oldsmobile while wrestling the four cats. Dennis and Israel drove the moving truck with three puppies! Frito Boat, Pork Chop & Spunky were the three little puppies we had decided the boys could have, so our entourage of 13 made quite a site. California here we come! Right back where we started from! Older, wiser, less demanding, and hopefully gentler than before.

Driving up to our big beautiful 2700 square foot home, I couldn't believe all that had been learned and accomplished. We now were a recognized charity organization. We were convinced that a work was waiting in California, and that "there's no place like home". Unpacking that big Penske, there were still a few details to tend to. We now had no stove, or dish washer, and needed to see just what exactly the Lord wanted us to do.

Remember Jackie, Lori's sister? The minute she heard we were back she called. "Honey, now you come pick up some groceries and some hamburger meat. Do you need a stove? I think we have one out at the thrift store, you can just have it, Honey; and by the way, do you need anything else?" Talk about being loved on! Then another call came in and Israel said, "Mom, remember Joel? His mom found out we needed a dish washer and they have one we can have!" On and on everything we needed was provided for! We decided never to worry again how God was going to meet our needs! We knew that for everything there is a season. Trish, Dennis, and I, decided to follow what we believed God was asking of us which was to continue to trust Him for divine intervention and provision while establishing something we had carried in our hearts for close to 20 years.

Dennis and I had seen the horrible spirit of religion parading at it's worst, and yet, we had also tasted real faith and a personal relationship with the One who made us. We, like the saints of old, had seen mammon, and the love of mammon, continually rob widows and orphans while the priests made bigger homes for themselves, and fancier tassels on their clothes. We had learned the difference between a true gift of God that overtakes you when you least expect it, and the "new theology" that promotes love of this world for the goodies' sake. Back to the word we were given so many years ago

"Widows and Orphans."

"True religion in the eyes of God our Father is to visit the widow and orphan in their distress and remain unstained by this world!"

Many, many years ago a vision had overwhelmed me while we were still living on Hall Street: There was a communication's clearinghouse and its purpose was to help people. Time and time again through the years we had seen so many of the organized churches talk a lot, and social agencies might give tangible help, but not in Jesus name, and usually without the tender care someone who is wounded needs. I don't think I can count all the single women we have moved, helped, prayed with, taught and encouraged. So in obedience to God, "Happy Thoughts, Inc. the non-profit was born. It started in Texas, and we were actually incorporated in two states.

So many things happened in our first year back from Texas. Close to $76,000 dollars in direct aid of food, clothes and gifts were given to people. All of this was accomplished with Trish and our little family one-day at a time. At the end of the year we were happy to report less than 12% was touched for overhead! One of the things that had also concerned us about so many of the priests of our day was they want to go to the law to collect a tithe, but then they keep 90% of it for themselves and give out less than 10%.

In Malachi, God taught you have robbed HIM by not building HIS HOUSE first! He also taught He would not dwell in buildings made with human hands but that He was building His temple from LIVING STONES! Oh, yes, Malachi, I agree; we have not built God's house first. The strangers, the widows, and the orphans are told to continually support the priests' high lifestyle while getting very little back that is tangible! Build another house of stone with the widows' money. There will be a day of reckoning. In the old covenant the priests kept 10% and 90% was used to meet the needs of God's people. That is how others saw our love one for another. How have things gotten so mixed up? How much is sown back out to the people of God? And yet God said the world would know Him because of the way we love one another. In word and deed! Faith without works is dead!

Returning to California we had several other special surprises. Walking through an old neighborhood one day Dennis and I ran into an old neighbor. Have you heard what has happened to Sarah? Instantly my heart was tight as this precious Grandma filled Dennis and me in on "Sarah". We had met Sarah when Happy Thoughts, the gift basket company, was first started. When we had moved into the little rental house on Vasser Street it came complete with a precious little neighbor girl named Sarah! She had beautiful blonde hair and a smile that wouldn't quit. This little princess would take my basket making scraps and make me gifts. Little pieces of beads and ribbons were treasures to Sarah, and we quickly fell in love with each other. I couldn't out give Sarah; and her favorite hobby was to make special things for people.

As her grandmother shared what Sarah, now 15, had been through, grief is the only word that can express my sorrow. Trying to be brave for the Grandma, I mentioned please, please tell Sarah, if you see, her that we love her and bring her by. Walking away with Dennis, heading home, I was hit so hard that I thought my heart would burst. Sitting down on a curb I sobbed my eyes out and kept saying, "No, God, not Sarah, no, not Sarah, oh please let her know we love her!" Dennis was considerate of my emotions and tried to help, but words just were not enough. Feeling rejected by everyone and everything, Sarah had been put into the foster care system. All I could see was the beautiful, innocent, little girl I had known; and heart broken is the only word that can describe my sorrow.

Here it was a few months later, and I had been exhausted after a trip to LA with Trish. We had stayed up all night with Joy, a friend of ours, and had gotten home around 9 a.m. Taking a nap (a very rare occurrence) I had just laid down when Dennis came to the steps and said, "Diana, get up, Sarah is here." Coming downstairs, all I could think of was God please give me words to heal her heart! Show me what to say!

There was our little neighbor, Sarah, close to 6 feet tall, still beautifully blonde, but very much a woman, not a 15 year old. As Sarah sat down, within minutes, she was sharing her heart. Crying (something she hadn't done very much as it never did any good), Sarah poured out the sad story about where she had been and where she was going. As she shared about the rejection by her family, Dennis, who had come in and was listening, started looking at me very seriously! With everything in me, my eyes were conveying a message that should have been pretty clear after 22 years of marriage. Dennis asked Sarah to excuse us for a minute and stepping out to an adjoining laundry room said,

"Are you thinking what I think you are thinking?" he inquired

"Well, what is everything we believe worth if when confronted with an orphan, we do nothing?" I responded angrily.

"Hold on," Dennis said and he headed to speak with our sons, while I went back in to talk with Sarah.

You know, these precious sons, Isaac, Isaiah, and Israel had shared their Dad and Mom since they were born. We had the first care home before Isaac was born, and we probably had spent less than a total of three years with our immediate family. Dennis wanted to know their thoughts since we had been helping another woman going through a divorce. She and her son, had stayed with us for a week while looking for a home, and now Trish would be moving with them.

The boys had a golden opportunity for selfishness for their last years as teenagers. Without hesitation all three sons declared that it might not be easy, but they truly believed God was knocking at the door, once again, and gave their unanimous approval.

Dennis arrived back in the room where Sarah and I were waiting and did what my precious husband does best!

"Sarah? How would you like to live with us, for real? Have a real family, no more foster homes?" Sarah's reaction was gratefulness mixed with surprise. She had been through a lot, but through her tears, she told me, "Know what? When I lived down the street from you I always wished I could have you for my parents." Whew! Tears flowed, and then miracle of all miracles happened. To make a long story short, after a few calls, licensing hand delivered a packet to us to fill out; we were licensed in 24 hours, Sarah spent the weekend with us, and was back in our home three days later, exactly one week later. Anyone who knows the foster care system will know what a miracle this was.

Sarah's arrival day was only second to her entrance! At my urging, she playfully bounced into Isaac and Isaiah's room and jumped on the end of Isaac's bed to wake him! Crash. Isaac laid at a perfect slant as his bed was on the floor, one end of the bed crashed through to the ground. Not blinking an eye, Isaac smiled and said there are better ways to wake up, and pretended to fall back asleep right where he was. Welcome complete, the boys now had the fun of learning what the word sister meant! Isaiah came to the rescue; and since all the boys had gotten along with Sarah before, Isaiah and Sarah would sit for hours and talk. Israel had his own special place in Sarah's heart, and her in his, as he dutifully bugged her, but then would share walks to the mall to get crickets for Sarah's lizards and his frog.

During the week we got Sarah, the Lord opened the door for "Happy Thoughts" first transitional home-A place for hurting women to rest and grow, with one on one mentoring. This was not a home for a lot of people to be rushed through, but a home called by God! A refuge! So after almost two years, Trish was now moving in to the transitional home, and our brand new baby girl had arrived. It's funny how God does things. For years Dennis and I thought we were going to have a daughter. Israel was called "Sarah" in the womb for 9 months! Finally, after we decided we must have somehow missed what we thought was one of our hearts' desires, guess what gift arrived? Our Sarah! The delivery was a little later than expected but she certainly could not be any more loved!

Diana and Sarah

As if Sarah's' arrival and the opening of another home, wasn't exciting enough, a call came from TBN. Could Dennis and you please be our guests on the main, live, prime time, Praise the Lord program? Can eagles fly? Butter melt? Birds sing? To understand why this was so special to us, you would have to know our hearts. We want to know God, to know His voice, and to be used effectively by Him for whatever He wants. Twelve years before, when we had taken the manuscript of Product of Love to Paul Crouch, Dennis and I had walked down a little hallway. A tour guide walked by who was telling people, "Oh, that's the Green Room. That's the room where the guests who are going to minister on Praise the Lord wait until it is time for them to come on the air." No sooner had these words left the guides mouth than I heard, what seemed to me, an audible voice that said, "I will send you through those doors to minister world wide someday!"

Here it was over 12 years later and the invitation was here. Knowing I had heard the Father's voice meant more to me than anything in the whole world. Dennis and I both, like Joseph in the bible, had heard some heavy things years ago pertaining to our call, our destiny, and our lives, and like Joseph, it seemed that our paths went farther and farther away from those promises ever being a reality. Yet this was so God could work out His purposes.

Timing is everything; and I am so glad we were not invited on television when we had a 1,2,3 step kick- know it all- attitude! Not that we are done growing by any means! With age hopefully comes some wisdom. While all this was happening, Dennis and I continued to send out newsletters two times a year, help many people who had needs and home schooled the kids, while counting our blessings!

Chapter 38

Happy Thoughts Store

IT WAS IN TEXAS that Dennis and I discovered the Greek and Hebrew meanings for the name Happy Thoughts! To go guide, lead the way, to create, invent, fabricate, to show the way! The meanings were exactly what our calling and lives have been.

As fall quickly passed, December 1999 was around the corner and everyone was busy, with lots of hot dog fund-raisers and preparations for the holidays. January was here and before we knew it, a solid year had passed since we came back to California. Peace had been made, with the current mortgage company yet another time, and Dennis and I continued to look for a storefront. The non-profit was dealing with so many clothes we needed a building. All through the year Dennis and I had been considering the opening a store- a "Happy Thoughts Store." In May, after looking for a whole year, we actually found two stores. These stores were special for several reasons. When we went out to find the stores we didn't even have $100 in the organization.

By Faith! True Faith! Simple Faith! God leads. We follow!

The idea we had was to have two stores connected side by side! Of course, if one is looking for one store with no money, why not look for two? Finding the building, we asked a local ministry to help us with $1,000 to help us get in the door. Even though this had never been done, we were given the OK! The owner of the building then agreed to donate two free months for each store.

I thought, how on earth we were supposed to put a used clothing store connected to a very fancy corporate gift basket store? The design was from on high! Dennis, Trish, Angela, and all the kids, labored away as we did the physical labor to create a very special place. The gently used clothing store advertised 88 cent clothing, and yet, this store was presented like a wonderful boutique. A 20-foot by 12-foot high mural depicted all the beautiful grape vineyards from the valley; as well as, olive and orange orchards. Painted by Sarah, Ivan, Trish and Angela, we actually had farm laborers weep when they realized we were honoring their hard work. In the center of the mural a simple farm worker lifted his hands to heaven while beholding the beauty of the hills and valleys before him.

All the clothing racks in the store were hand made from wood from our friend's old ranch house. Isaac painted walls, Israel and Isaiah built racks for hours on end. Spanish arches were cut in the walls between the two stores, and paintings of bricks and plants adorned the walls. The gift basket store was set up so that all profits, after taxes, were donated to the non-profit! We truly thought this would be a place to welcome whom the bible calls the richest of the richest. The Word says God has chosen those who are poor in the things of this world to be rich in faith. Our perception of the people we served was different than most. The days flew by and as things were needed, one by one, they were donated!

"Trish, we need carpet! Can you call and see if someone needs a tax write off? It's only 950 square feet for that one side." "Oh, now the carpets been found, we need a free installer and some donated glue!" Trish will tell you, after seeing how doors can shut, this was incredible. From donated paint to a $500 scale to weigh cheese and taffy, everything we needed was being donated. We were a businessman's worst nightmare on paper; yet it took less than $300 to open up the clothing side and only about $3,000 worth of product bills for the gift side. The first rent was paid on time, all 30 day bills paid within a week of being due, and when all was said and done close to $40,000 worth of services and items were donated to open the stores. All Glory to God.

The year 2000 ended with a banner figure of very close to $200,000 in tangible food, clothing, and services donated to those in need. Not to mention countless stories of specific changed lives of people who God led by His Spirit to come in to "Happy Thoughts." Thinking they were coming in for clothes or gourmet candy, the Father used some wonderful bait to bring in hurting, hungry people! The presence of God's Holy Spirit in these stores was so strong that total strangers would burst into tears, sharing their hearts, looking for answers to their problems, and we had the joy of directing them to the One with all the answers.

From the homeless to convicts, widows to the cities wealthiest, Happy Thoughts was used to help so many people. There was Laura, from Argentina who came weeks on end and would spend hours combing through clothes, over and over, basking in the most wonderful instrumental praise music. One day looking up from the register I saw to my delight, the Lord had sent another Spanish speaking woman to lead Laura to Jesus, right in Happy Thoughts! Then there was the convict who was going to rob Trish. Desperate because he didn't have any money to buy his son a birthday present he had been casing the store. Trish had obeyed the Lord and greeted him with love and handed him a stack of children's books from "Jesus" because the precious Holy Spirit told her to! Breaking down and weeping, this stranger confessed what he had come for and couldn't believe that someone was freely giving him what he needed; and he got so much more! Trish shared about Jesus before she let him out the door!

We had the privilege of working at a place built for God's Glory!

Chapter 39

Time Is Everything!

JANUARY 2001 LOOKED SO promising… Happy Thoughts had 2 full years' tax receipts and had proven itself a true help to the community with the lowest overhead of any charity around. As an organization we were prime for grants and our hope was that now with proven figures, Trish could submit for grants, and we were on our way. Once again, Arthur Blessitt's prophetic words rang out… **"It's not where everything works out as we may desire."**

Wham! The jolt from the full sized truck ramming our Mazda literally knocked the baseball cap off of Dennis' head. At the same time I felt burning pain shoot through every muscle and ligament from the center of my spine out. Crying out in pain, I turned to see that Israel, who was riding in the back seat, seemed ok, as he had just put his seat belt on a few minutes before. The next six months were a blur of insurance companies, doctors, therapists, drugs, tests, and more tests.

Meanwhile our wonderful Trish covered all the duties she already had, as well as mine, and there were simply not enough hours in the day. Happy Thoughts sent letters to anyone and everyone who had benefited from our years of service explaining about the accident. Not one reply. From local agencies to churches that had used our services for their clients, the only response was one get well card from the local chamber of commerce. **SILENCE**! Amazing how loud silence can be.

Precious Trish didn't have time to write grants, and was realizing between the accident and the drugs, I was having serious memory problems! So much for marketing, grant writing, and any other type of activity to help us. Just keeping up with all the charity's demands, including training troubled youth, took 16 hours a day. Meanwhile our family was having their own challenges.

The boys had grown accustomed to their new sister; and let us just say Sarah's' wounds and issues from her painful past provided opportunities for ALL of us to grow. Dennis had to deal with old Vietnam issues that never really left, a wife who couldn't be physically touched without great pain, a Right-hand who was being driven nuts by my inability to remember what was said, and a 16 year old daughter who was testing, testing, testing!

Farmers' Markets were going twice a week, our charity was running hotdog fundraisers at Wal-Mart and we were home schooling. If this wasn't enough on everybody, we had the opportunity to have a major fundraiser at the annual Fair. I cannot honestly tell you how Happy Thoughts did all these things.

In late May, a word of wisdom from my oldest sister, Chris, was used to turn the tide on the physical battle from the accident. She urged Dennis and I to get to UCLA to see a friend of hers, who she felt was the best in the business and would be able to help. As the good doctor said, "Throw out all these meds, learn the difference between good and bad pain, and change now, or you will be an invalid the rest of your life." This confirmed what I thought I was hearing in my heart as I had digressed to a state where I was taking heavier and heavier pain meds, to no avail, and even picking up a piece of paper shot pain through my back and shoulders. Leaving the Doctors office I had decided no matter what, things had to change.

Driving home that morning towards our hometown I told Dennis what I thought I should do. Detox off of ALL MEDS in the next 3 days! A call from Trish interrupted the conversation! Guess what guys? We just got a $300 dollar gift from so and so. The gift was from some people who Dennis and I respected and loved as being more like Jesus than anyone else on this earth. Weeping at the timing, as there was an urgent bill that had to be paid that day, we marveled at God's faithfulness yet another time. It would take volumes to list every special detail of how, right when we were out of gas, needed food, or had another need, that our loving Heavenly Father would see to it that everything worked out.

Arriving home, I headed upstairs to my bedroom, the room where for over five months I had barely been able to dress myself, and had not been able to simply make a bed. As my feet hit the stairs I heard: "Diana, I want you to spend the next three days bathed in praise music; and I want you to do everything you believed you couldn't do. You can start by scrubbing that filthy bathroom."

You're kidding right? I thought, as I stared at months of film and soap buildup, even though I knew in my knower this was no joke.

Plugging in a Dottie Rambo tape, I will never forget standing in the shower scrubbing and screaming, "It's So Hard to Sing the Blues, When You're Doing So Well!" Tears poured, as every muscle and fiber felt like I was insane and yet somehow it felt better to be doing something to help myself rather than be helpless. Three days later, after coming off of all meds, cleaning my upstairs bed and bath, better than it ever had been before, I awoke feeling so much better. For the first time in close to six months I had my mind back and knew somehow things were turning around!

Heading downstairs and out the front door to feed the cats, I just had to ask! Why God? What has all this been about? I know you could have touched my physical body in a second. You have before. Now, after these three days, I feel so much better. Why Now? Reminding me of yet another conversation about a week before I ended up at UCLA, I started seeing a bigger picture about tests, trials, and learning about ourselves: Laying face down on a therapy table in the dark, tears ran down my cheeks. Frustration was overwhelming as the drugs I was taking no longer gave relief, and the only thing they numbed was my brain. Trying to ignore the pain, the accusation rang out, "God, why won't you heal me? I've done everything I know to do; I've tried to stay cheerful. I'm taking handfuls off these stupid pills, and I really try to keep going, but what are you doing? If I only knew what You are doing," I cried. The response I heard was, "Diana, if I touched you right now, but you missed a divine meeting, would you want me to heal you right now?" Weeping harder, I felt like Peter in the Bible, "You know if there is someone I am supposed to meet or learn from in this process, You know me, I would wait!"

This memory played back as I fed the cats, and I realized a few days later, the appointment for UCLA and the trip to my sister's was confirmed. Pondering all this I then saw even more: Most of us want deeper relationships and more meaningful lives. We love the true stories about the heroes that triumph over impossible obstacles. We want all of this without a price!

One time when I was giving my six-year-old niece a treat from our store she said, "Free?" "YES!" I delightedly exclaimed! "Free!" My older sister, Chris, said, "No, Katie-nothing's free." Nothing is free, as somewhere it cost somebody something! What a revelation. Think about it.

Haven't we all been taught that Jesus is a free gift? Things that are free are special? Quite the contrary,

King David said, "I'll not give to God that which costs me nothing!" Free Gift? Free to you maybe; but somebody has purchased it with a price! It's the price of the gift, the cost that makes it valuable. A widow's mite is 1/128th of a days wages, around 43 cents in today's wages. What a valuable gift if it's all you have.

So many traditions of men woven with religion have twisted our perception about the value of the gift offered by God to join Him eternally. The gift Jesus walked out, as asked by the Father, had a horrendous price. It cost God greatly and it cost Jesus greatly. It is serious to despise such a valuable gift and treat it badly.

You see, my friend, I have learned everything costs something! So, next time you take a "free" item, use a two-for-one coupon, or accept a gift that's been offered freely, do not forget to appreciate and be grateful for how and who provided it for you. Is it possible that sometimes through physical trials a price was paid to touch a life that hadn't been touched any other way, a divine meeting perhaps?

Chapter 40

Transitions

The rest of 2001 for Happy Thoughts as a charity was a resounding social success. We had proven that a faith-based charity could successfully network with government agencies as well as churches and other private charities puling from all of the community's resources to help individuals in literally any area they needed. Financially we ended the year without outstanding debt as a charity and had kept our overhead at less than 12%.

Personally Dennis and I had continued to dig an even deeper hole. There was not enough money to pay even minimum wage salaries so we had not had money to pay our mortgage payment! We all knew in our hearts we were where we were supposed to be. The stores were just not generating enough as "fundraisers" to take care of even 1 minimum wage salary. It seemed every time we caught up, just got a new business lead, or a new promise of support these would disappear into thin air.

In December 2001, a precious friend had given us her

inheritance; she believed so strongly that what we were trying to build for our community was legitimate and needed. This was so hard to receive. The word says all good things come from God! Don't we all feel so proud when we feel responsible for that provision? The question is who really is responsible?

After the friend's gift and some money owed us from the IRS we were able once again to "start over" with the current mortgage company. Whether this was divine intervention and provision due to obedience, or mercy and grace to cover ignorance we weren't sure but knew that in time all will be revealed.

Bible studies once again. Questioning, energetic, spiritually hungry and so pure hearted! Once again the Nickell boys and their sister Sarah would fill the house on Friday nights with friends, potlucks, studies and wonderful times of fellowship. The book "Product of Love" was continuing to touch many and Isaiah had typed the whole story onto the "Happy Thoughts internet site to be enjoyed by anyone.

Christmas 2001 had passed and with spring fast approaching many transitions were going on. Trish was now writing grants left & right while continuing to bring her personal caring touch to people one by one.

I wonder if any of the troubled teens, pregnant moms or even our corporate clients had any idea, or ever remotely suspected the price of the "gift" of Trish's love and service for them. Since none of us took regular salaries, we usually dressed from the "used" clothing store and poured ourselves out to the community without reservation.

The words, "Don't worry about what you eat, drink or wear" became reality and somehow in spit of the challenges we always seemed to be trying to lose weight. Since our agency worked with supplying people in our community with food and clothes as well as other services we never lacked for the basics.

During our years working with disabled I had taken a course on how to assess or analyze potential clients. The purpose was to learn to identify the baseline or starting point so that when you would write objectives or goals they would be attainable. For example if a client couldn't identify a toothbrush you wouldn't ask them to be independently brushing their teeth in a week. You would have a long-term goal of tooth brushing under self-hygiene and depending on the baseline and the client's individual capabilities you might need 6 months and 12 steps or perhaps the goal might need simplified to simply recognizing the tooth brush.

The class had taught me that correct assessments and the ability to recognize the actual baseline was paramount. So what does this have to do with me, you, life? EVERYTHING!

I was discovering that life's challenges were orchestrated to teach me about where I was. My true baseline if you will, in comparison to where I imagined I was. Ouch! Like any one who's ever needed help in any area knows, until you accurately know where you really are at it is impossible to go on to the next step. When Dennis, Trish & I said to God, "Here am I send me" we had no idea what was to come.

If you agreed to be an ambassador or represent someone there is just the possibility that you might think your ready to go long before you really are. There is usually a preparation time. Get the picture? Looking back at our lives we were discovering surprise…surprise…. We seemed to need as much help as those we were helping.

Our Sarah eloped on her 18th birthday with Isaacs' best friend Greg! For over 2 years the kids had been dating and often prayed about the timing of getting married. Should we? Shouldn't we? Pray & Obey was our advice. After all remember Dennis and I had eloped after little more than 3 weeks and had been married over 21 years. As if Sarah's eloping wasn't a big enough change Trish was now headed for Texas. Yeehaw! Laughingly Dennis and I teased Trish and told her you hadn't lived until you've been to Texas twice. We had. Shouldn't everybody?

Another ministry needed help and it was time for our friend to spread her wings and fly. (Or ride as the case may be) Trish was actually born in Dallas, loved horses and was looking forward to a well-deserved change of pace. Here our right hand and best friend was being removed. What Joy! What Sadness! All 3 of us had lived a New Testament covenant relationship and knew that no amount of miles could separate our love one for another. With Sarah married, Trish in Texas and all the boys doing great, we continued to be stretched even more in coming face to face with what we believed.

There is a promise from on high that God will not give you more than you can handle and it is the truth. In the midst of all the tests, financial questions, health issues and more there has always been a continuous flow of things to be grateful for.

Chapter 41

Updates

ISAAC CONTINUED HIS SCHOOLING at the local junior college and with certificates that identified him as a specialist in computer networking; he applied for jobs right and left. Watching Isaac grow has been such a joy for Dennis and me. Being the first-born and the deep thinker, Isaac has lived a totally ordered life in the middle of what appears to be orchestrated chaos.

Our precious laughter that has excelled at everything he put his hand to. Young people! If you would like your heavenly Father to direct your paths, just ask! I will never forget the day Isaac announced, "Mom, I am not going to date. I believe God will show me my future wife." You know what? Isaac did, God did… and Heather did.

Choosing group activities and growing in a personal relationship with God, Isaac learned to hear the direction of the Holy Spirit. When the day came that he realized he had met his future bride to be, he wrote her quite a letter. Several days later, (must've seemed like years) Isaac threw a thumbs up while talking on the phone with Heather.

Several years later after continuing to let patience have it's perfect work Isaac proposed on bended knee to the young lady who had captured his heart. Yes, all you romantics, there are still guys who value faithfulness, guard their hearts and have chosen to live a Godly standard of life in their love lives.

During this time, Isaiah, (our second oldest son) was on his own path of life's learning. Teen years filled with home schooling and basketball culminated after Texas with new loves. Music, Guitar and his computer continue to keep Isaiah busy for hours on end.

Dennis and I have not had preconceived ideas about where our sons' paths might lead. We do believe God has a specific Devine destiny for all three. With Isaiah literally being raised from the dead, it has been exciting to watch his growth. Being the middle child, Isaiah is all heart, and whatever he tries, gets 100% of him mentally, emotionally and physically.

Playing his guitar for hours and hours, pretty soon we realized this was no passing hobby. At the same time, Isaiah poured himself into hours and hours with his computer, and before he could protest, "Happy Thoughts" had its' own web designer. Isaiah has continued his education from home, and became a certified web designer.

Now that Sarah and Trish were gone, Dennis and I were desperately in need of help, and Isaiah and Israel were constantly being called on to help. Angela, (the woman who had lived with Trish and was now in her own home) continued to support Dennis and I in so many ways. After overcoming the challenges of a major back surgery, Angela started teaching and would help Happy Thoughts whenever she could. Recovering from a painful divorce, it seemed there was yet one more special single friend in our lives. Dennis and I have so much gratitude for good friends and simple things like safety for loved ones.

Briiiiiiiiiiiiiiing! Eleven o'clock at night, the ringing phone sounded ominous and Dennis' face went from terror to tense as he listened intently.

"This is the highway patrol, there has been an accident and your son Isaiah was involved."

Time stood still until the next sentence. The officer reported Isaiah was fine, and that we needed to come and pick him up. As he hung up the phone, Dennis reassured me that Isaiah was okay.

The car was totaled, but Isaiah was ok. The drive from our house to where Isaiah was seemed to take forever.

Pulling into the closed gas station's driveway, Dennis and I saw two other wrecked cars, but not ours. Isaiah was standing in the parking lot waiting, and we saw a man sitting in a truck with the front hood smashed. A totaled red hatchback had already been pulled onto the back of a tow truck, and we saw one of the owners of that car.

Overhearing little bits of the story I realized that we were within a few feet of the drunken man who had hit both of the other cars. Taking a deep breath, we hugged Isaiah, got the info on where our totaled car had been towed and we headed home.

While driving down the road with Isaiah the next day, I was concerned that there might be some other after effects from the accident. He had been a little more quiet than usual. Suddenly a big grin broke out on his face as he said,

"I've been thinking what a miracle it was that I wasn't thrown out of the front windshield of the car."

Dennis and I had been told that while Isaiah was driving down the freeway, his car died. Frantically trying to restart it, he knew that he shouldn't leave the car stranded, dead in the middle of the freeway. As speeding cars darted around him, he continued to try to start the car to get it moved to the side of the road. Finally looking in his rearview mirror, he decided he better get the flashers on and get out of there as he knew the car would not start.

Wham! A man who was drunk driving plowed through the red car first, who at the time was already slowing down to avoid hitting Isaiah. Being drunk, the man hadn't noticed the red car slowing and was going so fast that after hitting it at roughly 80+ mph, and throwing the other car across the left lane...he plowed into Isaiah's car. The assessment was he must've still been going way too fast by the time he hit Isaiah. Our station wagon was warped, every window busted out. The only place the car was untouched was exactly where Isaiah had been sitting. Every door was warped shut except the driver's side.

Isaiah continued his story as we drove on.

"Do you realize what saved me? If I had been in the Mazda, I'd be dead. You know I would've been stepping out of the car when he hit me. But because I was in the station wagon, I couldn't find the hazard lights. I prayed, and as I leaned forward to find the switch, I was braced in a perfect position for impact when he hit me."

Isaiah was more thrilled about the sequence of events that had saved him than he was worried about the accident.

By summer 2002 Happy Thoughts was horribly behind in rent. Dennis had just spent another year physically battling all kinds of health problems and with so little help, the store was now open only five days a week. Not one of the grants we submitted were accepted, and the store's owner had done all that he could. God bless Sam. This man had personally paid the price and taken heat from his business partners to help us, but finally was pushed to a place of having to see some money, or close the doors.

As the date grew closer for do or die, it was almost a relief. We had given everything we could, and like Moses, the great patriarch we seemed surrounded by whining, unbelieving, ungrateful people. All Moses knew was that he did his best to do what he was asked and there he was at the Red Sea. Moses enemies were advancing, his relatives misjudging him, and his own people ready to kill him. The very people he was giving his life for. Sound familiar?

Dennis and I played uplifting praise music, warring praise music, and refused to be moved.

D-day, Judgment Day, Day of Reckoning.

It all added up to seeing if what we believed was real. At 4:45, fifteen minutes before closing time, the phone rang.

"Diana, Diana! It's someone on the phone about a grant!" Dennis yelled. He was the most animated I'd ever seen him. The voice on the other end of the phone boomed out,

"How ya doin?"

After ten minutes of conversation, tearfully hanging up the phone, I gave Dennis a thumbs up and called Sam the building owner.

"Sam, guess what?! A businessman who has a charitable foundation will be sending a substantial check over night. Will a payment of $5,000 be okay?"

Laughing, Sam seemed more relieved than me. After none of the grants we had worked so hard on were accepted, this foundation had discovered about us by ordering off of our website. They had literally found us. So with the ability to pay all suppliers up, (and a good chunk on back rents) Dennis and I headed out the door. As he locked the door to head home, Dennis said…

"Okay you old savings and loan, we're not through yet!"

Still drying tears, I truly felt like the Israelites when the daily manna came. God had provided once again, right when it was needed.

Money – M-O-N-E-Y. In the Hebrew, it means

"To become pale, pine after, to fear, desire, be greedy."

In the Greek, money is stated to be, "Something useful or needed." Printed on the currency in our country are the words "IN GOD WE TRUST". Think about it, do we really? Or has America traded this truth for "In money we trust." Money represents provision, independence, position, and identity. What an incredible mirror for revealing so much about our hearts and what we trust in.

Jesus said, "Seek first the kingdom. (His Kingdom) Seek the place where God your Father is in charge. Where He is ruling and reigning and all that you need will be added to you.

That is His promise of provision.

Why did Jesus say it is impossible to serve two masters? And then specifically identify two choices. Will we serve God or serve Mammon? The definition of the word Mammon is "Confidence, Wealth Personified, and Avarice Deified. "**The question is who and what do you put your trust in? Where is your confidence?**

Dennis & I were in the midst of an incredible learning time face to face with what we believed and whom we trusted in. We were discovering as lifes challenges came people lived what they believe.

In the book Product of Love we had shared about many of the wonderful experiences as simple followers of Jesus. We didn't share much about the daily battles thinking that to focus on that would be negative. **Yes & No!**

Here we were summer of 2002 and finally after 31 years Dennis was face to face with his old enemy Vietnam yet once again.

Chapter 42

Face to Face

"DIANA," MY LITTLE SISTER Pauline began, "Paul has a friend who has discovered that there is help for Veterans like Dennis. Have you guys ever checked into the V.A.?"

The sacred subject! The source of so many of our family's painful moments. Carefully I responded, "Well, you know when Dennis had the heart attack? We checked into some things and came out with mixed emotions. The man from the V.A. indicated that retro compensation wasn't available and then started talking about how Dennis would have to be seen by a psychiatrist. Dennis wasn't even ready to talk to anyone about Vietnam, especially anyone connected with the military. "Finally," I added, "We thought somehow it would be doing God a disservice to talk about what was still wrong when He has helped us so much."

The conversation went on and after encouragement and offers of help I hung up the phone! Around this same time within a three-week period that Dennis and I were selling our "Happy Thoughts" gourmet products at Farmers market, it seemed like Veteran after

Veteran would end up at our booth, telling Dennis their story and sharing how they finally had some relief after receiving help from the V.A. Dennis had started wearing a ball-cap with the words "Vietnam Veteran" on it, with some patches representing units he had been with in Vietnam. Many times this same hat had been used to draw hurting men, still wounded from the war and Dennis would share his story of how God had helped him. Even a congressman, I had spoken with once had asked why with Dennis' service record and physical problems, he hadn't been to the V.A.

One afternoon, in Happy Thoughts, after 24 years of marriage, incredible struggles and victories, I shared with Dennis, something I had learned from several of life's experiences, and most recently from my auto accident.

"Honey, remember when I told you the most painful emotional day after the accident, was when I faced the fact it had really hurt me? As long as I plugged along and acted like it was no big deal, it seemed like things were okay. But one day, I realized that

Due to someone else's actions I had been victimized and hurt. Helpless was how I felt and anger welled up as I admitted to myself I had seriously been hurt physically and emotionally. That accident had not only caused me pain, it robbed me of months of my life. I had become addicted to painkillers. I suffered. Dennis suffered, and yes friends and family suffered. Happy Thoughts suffered. I discovered in life that yes, the joy of the Lord is your strength, but there is a time to be angry, and a time to grieve! Until I had faced the truth of the cost to me, and to my loved ones, I couldn't go through the steps of truly trusting God and forgiving those who had hurt me."

Buried wounds! Dennis listened and reluctantly allowed the first serious conversation about Vietnam and his wounds since we had been married! Agreeing to one V.A. office visit, and no more, my husband started down a path that ultimately would lead to much needed healing. Busy, busy with Happy Thoughts, the fall of 2002 was yet another season of education of what people think they need and what they really need. The stores were not pulling their own weight and still we were busy helping many.

We realized that most people shopping at our stores wanted something for nothing. We had tried to raise prices to pay the bills, but still we were the cheapest thrift store in town. Instead of everything being 88 cents like when we first opened, some of our prices had been raised. I remember the time a lady in a Mercedes was so proud of herself for refusing to pay the full price for what she bought. She wanted the article of clothing she was buying for 88 cents NOT $1.88. Many of our customers would bag the savings and head to a restaurant nearby to drop more on lunch than Dennis or I made in several days. Now sometimes, the people we intended to serve did benefit. The older Spanish woman in the wheelchair was happily having the children she was with run 88-cent clothing to the register. Carefully picking out the clothes, she was having the greatest time and yet I could see she was in an old push wheelchair, and dressed in used clothing herself. Moved by the scene, I asked the children with her, who all the clothes were for? Come to find out, she was widowed and lived in a farm labor camp. As children of neighbors would visit her, and offer to help with housework, etc., she would always send them home with a new piece of clothing. Mysteriously, the register rang some clothes at 50 cents and some just slipped through.

The wealthy woman was so proud she had saved a dollar at our expense and undoubtedly is one of the poorest creatures on earth. The Spanish grandma in the wheelchair will be rich all the days of her life. My mother has a favorite Dolly Parton song: "The Coat of Many Colors." The lyrics are so true. A person is only poor if they choose to see themselves that way.

True riches are carried in the heart.

Chapter 43

Freedoms Cost

THE BUILDING OUR HAPPY Thoughts stores are in is going to be sold and torn down, according to the newspaper report. **What?!**

So the part of our Happy Thoughts ministry dedicated to helping the community was coming to a close! Was this an answer to prayer? Dennis and I did not want to "give up the ship" so to speak, even though more often than not the income was simply not enough. Closing doors was no longer the threat of humiliation, but perhaps a message of "Job well done!" and on to a new assignment.

Meanwhile the V.A. visit had proved to start the long overdue healing process for my wonderful husband. P.T.S.D. Agent Orange. Diabetes. Heart Disease. Hypothyroidism. High blood pressure. These are the words that identified the battlefields for Dennis now. Dennis had faced his worse fears, including pride. To face the truth, he was only human, and had been horribly violated. No amount of pride, drugs, denial, or violence could change the fact that an idealistic 18 year old had joined the army to avenge the death of a friend. No longer his own man, he had become the "property" of the U.S. government and was subject to their bidding. Vietnam had left him a 20-year-old drug addicted paranoid schizophrenic with a destination of Palo Alto Mental Institution. The price that was paid by Dennis for service to his country was as real as the veterans who had come back physically crippled and maimed. As Dennis acknowledged the cost an even deeper root came to light. He had not only come back totally incapable of leading a "normal" life, he had added guilt to the equation. Dennis blamed himself. Helplessness was the most frustrating feeling, as he didn't understand why he couldn't get rid of all the problems. Some men had died in Vietnam while others came home with the visible proof of their sacrifices with missing limbs and all sorts of other issues. The VA in Fresno has these words etched above the entrance,

"Here is a place where the price of freedom can be seen". It reminds me of the Cross of Jesus! You couldn't see Dennis wounds. No one even knew what PTSD was. Even the public had turned against these young men who had been so brave. The very public enjoying the freedoms to disagree because of others sacrifices.

Finally after 31 years in the writing down of what he had been through in Nam for the VA, Dennis perception changed and so did mine. Sometimes we fight battles that seem single faceted and very easy to deal with and sometimes a battle might be as complex as all the issues a person might deal with who's been in a major accident. Vietnam had been the catalyst to produce battles in the spirit, soul and body and trying to deal with only one aspect was not enough. The book Product of Love had focused on the awesome changes that had occurred as a result of Dennis spiritual growth. This did not mean there were not daily mental and physical challenges to be overcome. We decided there's no shame in admitting that there are battles.

How healing an understanding word can be.

"Dennis, anyone who was 18 and went through what you did would have serious issues, this was not your fault," the shrink said

The 2 psychiatrists confirmed and showed in real every-day words what Dennis still struggled with, how every day is an incredible challenge and now we really understood what a miracle his life is. The fact that Dennis has been given the grace to deal with such extreme challenges without drugs and alcohol now, seemed to mystify the Drs.

"Well what do you do? How are you doing this without drugs etc? were their questions.

"I've learned that no matter how badly my mind freaks out, or how bad a fear attack is, it will pass" Dennis replied. What he didn't share was that what he had focused on, as his example of what should be "healthy, or normal" was based on his relationship with Jesus. Even though the mark was often missed he prayed and asked God for His Grace for these situations that seemed so overwhelming.

You see we hadn't shared in Product of Love about the daily battles for him and our family. We did not write about the daily struggles our family faced and how we lived a lifestyle of looking at all the good things and not the bad. From the beginning of our marriage it quickly became evident that even though certain areas had truly changed Dennis still was incredibly challenged. Yes Dennis went from screaming 6 and 8 times a night to just a few. But the panic attacks and startle responses have never completely gone away. Yes we had all the joys and true underlying peace that comes from knowing God and yet all of this was accomplished with much effort. The Apostle Paul's words fight the good fight of faith come to mind! Faith is a struggle, a fight! We realized that with only sharing what God had accomplished a picture of a perfect family might have been painted. Oh, what a wrong perception. The God we serve and His Gospel is based on GRACE!

The VA tests provided info to Dennis and I about how his natural mind literally still freezes when he is faced with situations his mind perceives as authoritative, new, threatening or hostile. Sounds simple as for most folks it takes pretty big triggers to make us think something hostile is happening. For many veterans the invasion of a simple unexpected phone ringing is a reason to feel violated. Someone voicing a different opinion is the same as calling you stupid and all authority figures are there to harm you. We now understood why so few veterans stayed married and why so many are still roaming the streets today!

As the psychiatrist asked Dennis to remember 3 simple objects over a very short period of time we finally understood why he had never been able to hold down a job where he wasn't self employed. Between people thinking he was stupid from the way his memory worked, which was then compounded by the brain freezing in situations he felt threatened in, we had some understanding of why our family had gone through many of the trials we did.

Looking through work records and medical records, the VA psychiatrist probed. A pattern, of life challenging daily experiences were revealed. Fear attacks, interrupted sleep, and perceptions of every day events he experienced were constantly affected by his time in Nam. Social Security records showed an inability to hold down a simple normal job. The records also showed in spite of all these challenges he kept trying.

The medical Dr confirmed the connection between Vietnam and the heart attack. To give you an idea of the pain still involved Dennis blood pressure read 180 over 110 when he sat through the VA physical After going home to a "safe" environment and some deep breathing Dennis blood pressure dropped to 140 over 80.

Shame and guilt and the burdens Dennis never should have carried started being realized and dealt with.

The Cost of Freedom! His service to his country had come at a dear price and so few understood and even fewer ever said thanks. Veterans were spat on, heckled and misjudged adding insult to injury.

On the 4th of July 1998 in Texas a precious South Vietnamese man named Linh Vo met Dennis. Giving him an autographed copy of his book "Dear Daddy" we now had another view of Vietnam.

"Papa San! Papas San, you GI's are my Papa Sans. Thank God for You. I was on the first airlift out of Saigon as the country was being over run by communists. They overtook my families' village and I had a split second decision as a university student in the city whether to jump on a helicopter to freedom or stay. I was in the first arrivals to Camp Pendleton. This book "Dear Daddy" is dedicated to all you Gi's my Papa Sans!

"I AM THE CHILD YOU WERE FIGHTING FOR"

The gratitude poured from this precious gifted poet was more than I could take. He was one of the oppressed that had been rescued and the gratitude was unmistakable.

With his wife Monique, Linh had built a life in the United States. Blessed with a daughter Tam, and two sons, Tan and Trung, Linh Vo and his family has experienced freedom first hand. As a nation we worry about becoming involved in other nations problems but as brothers in the family of man isn't it heroic to want to help the oppressed? All we knew is many Veterans need to hear Linh's perspective on America and Vietnam. So much gratitude for Freedom!

Chapter 44

Justice, Mercy & It's a Wonderful Life

NOW WITH THE STORES closed and Dennis battling physically I finished paperwork for Happy Thoughts knowing Israels' 17th birthday was fast approaching. Israel "our baby". The bible refers to physical Israel as the "apple of Gods eye" and our 3rd son has endeared himself to so many. The family spitfire who seemed most like a cross between his Grandpa Hershey & Dennis combined. When I think of Israel I think of him skateboarding down a set of stairs oblivious to the danger while giving a war hoop or skiing straight down the mountain with arms wide open in what we referred to as "the Jesus position".

Israel went to the local college for a semester at the age of 16 after graduating home school and quickly decided he was much more serious about his guitar and band. Israel had reassured me that he knew birthdays were not about stuff but Dennis and I were wondering how we were going to be able to give him a special gift. One morning while taking a walk Dennis brought up an unusual thing he had seen in the paper. There was this ad that said, "Volkswagen for sale. $3500 or will trade for truck." You know Israel and I have been talking for years about how fun it would be to get a little Volkswagen to work on together."

"No way" I exclaimed, "Why don't we check it out?" We had a truck that we were not using nearly as much as when the stores were open. By now Dennis was getting really excited and suggested that we run this idea by Isaac. Since we had no regular steady income, were pouring ourselves into working on the new book and a

screenplay about Dennis life, it seemed nuts to give away the one asset we had. After hearing about the ad Isaac suggested we check it out, as we didn't know even what kind of truck the guy wanted and thought if he really wanted to do a deal with our truck why not? The bright orange Volkswagen was any kids dream complete with a chromed tail pipe that made it sound like a Harley. After calling home so the brothers would keep Israel away from the front windows Dennis drove up and parked the new little car in the driveway. Going into the house he called out to Israel to please come help him wash the car. Israel mumbled as he wasn't in the mood for chores and as he walked outside and saw this adorable bright orange VW bug he yelled

"WHAT? What is this?"

"Happy Birthday son" Dennis said tossing him the keys. Isaacs' dimples were showing and Isaiah enjoyed the moment as well. Laughing our whole family continued to watch Israels reaction as he just kept shaking his head!

What a joy. Right in the middle of another time of total trust and faith we had the joy of giving such a gift to one of our sons. For Dennis, who remembered Isaac's 16th birthday with no home and only a lemon meringue pie, things were looking better.

What happened next was and is truly amazing.

AUGUST 8TH was the date on the letter from the VA stating they finally had recognized the challenges Dennis now faced as a direct result of his service to his country. The letter stated that they would be sending him a pension and compensation payment the rest of his days. Not only that but all of his family qualified for schooling, our medical needs would be covered and he would never owe taxes on his home again! We even were given life insurance!

The question we are left with will only be answered by time Were these wonderful provisions for Dennis and our family justice for trying to live a sacrificial life in answer to the call of God? Or is it simply His mercy for some pure hearted over zealous children who desperately needed help? You decide!

Our thoughts?

"It's a Wonderful Life following JESUS!"

Chapter 45

Save Us from Ourselves

WHY OH WHY, WERE we naïve enough to think that as we headed into the second half of our lives, that somehow, we had arrived or at least earned the right to take a break from the types of afflictions and tests that seemed so "bountiful" when Dennis and I were younger?

With "Happy Thoughts" closed and our eyes set on a "time" of reflection and rest, we had no idea the fiery trial that was ahead. Five years have passed since Dennis and I thought we had finished writing our true stories of pursuing God. As life hit us square in the face yet another time, we realized our journey was far from complete.

Here Dennis and I were given the greatest gift that we had always asked of God! TIME! Back in the days when we were working 7 days a week and doing so much we always thought if God could just give us more time…we would "show Him" how much more we could accomplish for Him! Right! Ouch! Talk about an invitation for a new fire to reveal what truth is!

Oh, God had been faithful and done absolutely everything Dennis and I so faithfully shared. Our focus was on sharing the good news that we as simple followers of Jesus felt was so important. Years of serving others and becoming so busy had bred familiarity and contempt. Once again…and somewhat, sadly… we had forgotten the basics. Sometimes focusing on everyone and everything other than our own lives is an escape in itself. Think about it. How many people have you met who are gonna save the world while their own lives leave so much to be desired?

One of our favorite get-a-ways was to go to "gatherings" where a prophetic musician from South Africa "soothed our weary souls" with incredible worship music. It left us more in heaven than on earth. This man sang love songs and songs of great joy. Warring songs that sounded like marching armies were sung, and so many more. "Send us the fire…send us the rain…we're ready", were words to one of the songs.

Oh my! Little did we know how badly we needed a fresh fire to make room for more growth. Once again… we could say, had we known what the invitation for more "growth" in the Lord would bring, I am almost certain we would have said, "No thanks, Lord."

Of course I am sure you can appreciate the joke in the words, "No… and Lord!" God must laugh when we say, "Lord and No!" Missionaries for Jesus! Super Christians! OverComers! Heck we had our claim to fame…We had a book! Shared on international platforms about our wonderful relationship with our heavenly Father! Life was certain and nothing could shake our faith!

Long ago, I had survived an attempted murder and Dennis was the victorious warrior that old wounds from Vietnam could not defeat!

Right! Weren't we the chosen who were guaranteed success now that we were both over 50 and so smart? OK! So maybe we had become overly familiar, less than humble and a bit judgmental. You think? You mean we were not perfect yet? Here we were very sincere…and most assuredly… sincerely primed some new growth.

Like the fires in the national parks…fresh fires often remove useless old dead wood. And like the droughts that proceeded the hottest fires, our lives had become paper dragons, and form without substance. We were parched dry land, a tinder box waiting to be ignited. Originally firefighters tried to stop forest fires until a discovery was made. Fires were actually good in the long run for the forest. Many seeds and nutrients were buried in the earth at the feet of the giant trees and only the combination of the ash from the fires and the clearing out of the "old" allowed the "new growth" to begin. Our lives had accumulated lots of useless, dry kindling and as followers we had invited God to reveal Himself to us… and through us…We were ripe for fresh fire.

Meanwhile our friend William from Texas called and offered a gift that was straight from the heart! This was the same brother who had freely filmed Arthur Blessitt for us in Texarkana. He had a Texas accent second to none and I think the phone conversation went something like this!

"Dinnis? I know this man in Port Arthur who can heel ya! If yu and Dina can git out here… I'll payee for yuuu to see hum."

Precious William went on to explain that when he was a young man, doctors had told him he was very ill and was going to need to have his colon removed. There was nothing he could do about it! Well after visiting this man, who believed in healing naturally as well as divine, William was healed. Learning that so many battles people fight physically are self-induced, whether on purpose or through ignorance, this brother had made it his business to help others find out they didn't have to stay sick!

Remember the scripture that says "We die for lack of knowledge?"

William had read a book, years before, named "Sugar Blues,"that exposed how refined white sugar was so deadly for our bodies. William offered to fly us to Texas to see his special doctor hoping he could help Dennis get well.

Knowing that the years of fighting health problems had worn on Dennis, the offer sounded good. It was hard for Dennis to receive and finally after almost a year he decided he was willing to try anything. Here we were the "faith people" who had boxed God in and demanded instant answers.

We were about to find out the difference between faith, grace and responsibility. Remembering an inspiring faith teacher who said, "Only an idiot would bang his thumb with a hammer while he asked God for healing," I had to smile. I knew that there probably were lessons to be learned when we had a responsibility in our own healing.

So who wouldn't always like an easy answer?

Flying to Houston, Texas, Dennis and I drove several hours to the small city of Port Arthur. Looking for the address Dennis groaned when he saw the humble clinic that was located behind an old gas station.

Great! Flying half way across the United States, we walked into a building that was more reminiscent of a bad veterinary clinic than a marvel of modern science. Trying to be positive, I snapped at Dennis to stop going by what he saw. Meanwhile I prayed we both weren't totally out of our minds.

Walking into the little reception area, I could see it was simple and clean. A few Christmas cards decorated the plain walls. A woman handed us some forms to fill out even though we had previously sent the longest questionnaires I had ever seen in my life. Informing us the "process" included blood tests, that wouldn't be done for at least a day, we were invited to take a seat. The older light fixtures gave a soft glow to the wood-paneled walls, and I felt at peace about where we were. Then the most amazing thing happened that we had ever experienced from a doctor before or since.

A gentleman who we had heard was in his mid seventies strode into the room. His natural, jet-black hair and the incredible shape he was in made him appear to be in his early 50's. Vibrant, positive and laughing, he loosened us both up. He then announced due to our coming so far and his wanting to truly help Dennis and I reach optimal health, he closed the clinic doors to walk-ins. He declared he had purposely not scheduled anyone else that day so that we had his undivided attention.

As this man shared his own stories and educated us on how eager our bodies are to be well, he gave us tons of literature with the latest holistic approaches to healing. Trained as a Doctor of Osteopathy, he was approaching illness from a kinetic understanding that believed all of our bodily systems are so interactive you must treat the whole person.

Explaining that America was about the only nation that had the idea you didn't need to clean your own body from time to time this doctor ran tests that we had never heard of. After taking great care to review our medical histories, he proceeded to explain what he was going to do and why he believed it was the best course of action.

Never had either of us had anyone so thorough or gifted help us with our health. This man believed in healing. William had informed us that one time he asked this good doctor if there was anyone he couldn't heal. The doctor's reply? "If they had breath he believed they could be healed." With the dozens of friends William had taken to this man, he said the only ones who didn't keep their success were those who decided not to do what the doctor said.

The doctor taught us about our need to "detoxify" our bodies from years of all the environmental stressors, and poor nutrition. In Dennis' case, exposure to Agent Orange in Vietnam, was also identified as a factor. We heard things that made sense physically and spiritually.

Jesus said to bring every thought captive to the obedience of the mind of Christ, guard your heart and to remain unstained from the contamination of this world.

Sounds like a remedy for all the mental "stress" people complain about in this modern age. Well here we were hearing how the same truths applied to healing the physical body.

This man spoke healing from the moment we arrived and his only question was how best to achieve it. This was a far cry from so many "modern" doctors who simply treat symptoms and write prescriptions for chemicals that mask those symptoms. Dennis and I left that night laughing and rejoicing in the good news that he could be well and whole. It might not have been instant but it still was good news.

There was one small catch. Now there would be the doing, not just the hearing and self discipline was not a strong point for either one of us.Many people will testify to the fact that the number one issue in America is health and medical care. Maybe many of us had become like the idiot banging his thumb with a hammer while begging God to heal him.

After three days, Dennis and I flew home with literally close to 100 bottles of nutrients to detoxify, heal, and rebuild our bodies. I am not kidding. We had literally our largest suitcase filled with all of these different herbs and tinctures and capsules and lots and lots of instructions.

The regime included taking liquid drops on an empty stomach before you even got out of bed, to measuring and taking nutrients before, during and after meals throughout the day. Some nutrition needed to be taken alone and some with water. Some were to be taken with milk and some were to be stirred into a very expensive clay type of mud that needed to be mixed and spread onto the bottoms of our feet and left on for 15 minutes before being removed.

What a bunch of work! Now we knew for sure why lazy people would much rather take a pill and cover the problem. This seemed like really hard work. I was starting to get suspicious that God had a plan in taking us through all of these gymnastics.

We had been warned that when we started detoxifying, often the body would feel very sick as toxins were leaving the body and our dear friend William must have told us a dozen times to make sure to finish what we started and not to give up.

This reminds me how sometimes we think it's better to let issues be buried than to deal with them because bringing them up can hurt. There is always a cost associated with growth. Timing is everything and miraculously as Dennis and I did what the good doctor said, we both felt better.

Knowing we couldn't be flying back and forth to Texas for follow-ups, I contacted the company who made the bioactive nutritional products we were using and asked if they knew anyone in California who used the same products. This search led us to a very gifted physician who Dennis and I now respect and love as family.

Leaving a message with a secretary I requested that if it was at all possible, I needed this doctor to call me. I had no idea how I would pay him. All I knew was that Dennis needed to finish the process he started. To my surprise, later that evening, I received a call from "Jorge."

Visiting for close to an hour, he agreed to see Dennis and that we could barter down the road. I could hardly believe it. He was kind, warm and personable, asked lots of questions and didn't seem in a hurry.

Riding the Harley to Santa Monica to meet Jorge, Dennis was still a bit put off that he had to be part of his own healing. Many a lesser man would have given up and I continued to be the cheering section, pep squad and instigator. We continued to take this battle for Dennis health personally and seriously.

Pulling up to a very nice office I was looking forward to meeting this man, while Dennis still struggled with the whole issue of being such a center of attention.

We both were from the old school of "take two aspirin and keep going" thinking that if we were just full of enough "faith," all the issues would disappear. I guess we were just starting to truly learn that our bodies have been designed with warning signs for a reason. In our exuberance we had become spiritual snots and wanted to tell God how He had to work. I'm sure no one else reading this has ever been as presumptuous.

To admit we need someone's help is not a very comfortable place to be. So there we were, Dennis and I like the odd couple, me so excited to meet Jorge and Dennis wishing he was at home in front of a good ballgame.

Dr. Moreno strode into the office with a huge grin and eyes twinkling. Attractive and athletic he exuded health. Heading straight for Dennis with right-hand extended, this man had a confident and friendly air about him that made even my husband relax. Visiting away I couldn't help but notice I felt like we were all old friends. Laughter and stories filled the air. This physician had made sure to set aside close to three hours for our first visit and once again we realized we were in the presence of someone who was obviously in their God given calling.

Dr "George" as Dennis affectionately dubbed Jorge, was a D.O. who just happened to be a brother in the Lord. This brother with a knack all of his own managed to treat Dennis from a holistic perspective that included addressing issues spirit, soul and body.

Love and gentleness permeated this man and before leaving Dennis was compelled to share with Jorge, that never had he ever met someone with more peace and he was truly happy to have met him.

After several more visits I noticed that the screaming panic attacks seemed to lesson considerably. When we were first married sometimes Dennis would awaken us both by screaming and after about three or four visits to Dr. Moreno over a six month period, these episodes dramatically decreased. Sometimes Dennis would actually go several weeks without any screaming to awaken us at all.

I remember reading as the soul prospers, your health will. I also have always believed "a merry heart does good, like a medicine."

Going through all these battles and revelations in the middle of a society that wants quick fixes, blame and excuses I wondered why everyone seemed to have forgotten simple truths I was raised with like "Garbage in...Garbage out," and "What a man sows he will reap."

We now had no doubt! Much of Dennis ongoing issues were self induced whether through ignorance, laziness, or complete disobedience. Yes he had a much rougher road to health, due to all the physical and mental challenges associated with Vietnam, but the truth was, he could be well. As hard as it would be to get well, years of being ill had not been easy either.

Preparing to leave, Dennis and I noticed a beautiful picture hanging on the wall. Staring at us was Jorge with his beautiful wife and family. I couldn't help but notice, they all were the picture of happiness and vibrant health.

What a concept! If you are going to engage in a battle for your health, try finding someone who practices what they preach and is successful

Chapter 46

Time

THE AMERICAN HERITAGE DICTIONARY defines "time" as events that occur in an irreversible succession from the past through the present to the future. Having more time is what we believed we really needed.

With a set monthly income and the "Happy Thoughts" stores closed, Dennis and I had been given the very gift that we thought would enable us to pursue our hearts desires without feeling stretched and pulled in so many directions. We had finished home-schooling our youngest son Israel and even thought a break from offering Bible studies was in order.

A book in the Bible, Malachi, says that God is not happy with those who were more concerned about building their own "houses" instead of "God's house" From the beginning we believed that God's house is built with "living stones" as Jesus said…in other words, we are talking about people! Dennis and I had spent years of our time sacrificially investing literally everything we had into others lives. Our time, our resources, and even where we worked, were always decided upon with one goal. We wanted to share Jesus, follow His leading, no matter how crazy it appeared, and that was what our lives were all about. We sincerely believe Jesus heart is for the widows and orphans, the poor and the down and out. If anyone ever felt like they were building "God's house" first,

Dennis and I did. Now the marching orders were to take a good look at "our own home."

I think of Arthur Blessitt's words when meeting Yassar Arafat, "It is one fanatic to another," That totally describes my husband and I.

We were clueless that our own "house" was in such need of attention and I am not just talking about our physical home.

There is only so much time in a day and in our zeal to live a "servants" life we had not taken time for many of our own basic needs as husband and wife. Our physical bodies needed attention, our physical house was in disrepair…and more importantly, in time, we were to find out even our spiritual and mental "houses" were in much need.

We had finally started to feel some relief with the small but steady income from the VA pension but we continued to battle with the VA process and fought through numerous appeals.

During the first few months Happy Thoughts was closed Dennis and I tried to work on some home projects. It seemed that with ongoing physical battles and exhaustion he really needed some space. I have heard "steel sharpens steel," yet this was horrible. The years of feeling like he was always the "helper" had left him humiliated and wounded. Wanting help on projects and yet honestly feeling like any suggestions were "telling him what to do" I realized how badly Dennis needed some space. Not getting along very well when working on projects, I encouraged Dennis to take on solo projects where he needed little assistance and focused on the rest of the new changes happening in our family.

Isaiah like Isaac had chosen not to date and often hung out with friends in groups. Two sisters that were also home-schooled started stopping by to visit "Zay" on a regular basis. April and Heather were the lovely ladies who glided in and out of our front door. One day I remember in particular the one sister had an extra sparkle in her eye and her hair seemed to be styled with some extra curls. I thought, "Am I seeing what I think I'm seeing?" The next thing I knew our incredible son Isaiah shared the news that he knew Heather was "the one!" That's right…like his older brother Isaac who married a Heather, who became a nurse, Isaiah became engaged to a Heather who also wanted to be a nurse. Two Heathers, who both loved caring for others…double blessings. Dennis and I jokingly offered to help our third son, Israel, find a Heather since that seemed to be the way to go, and He assured us he didn't need help. It became a family joke whenever we were out about where he would meet a young single named "Heather." Dennis and I would make sure to tell Israel about it. Ok, so he didn't need our help and finally we decided to let well enough alone.

Wanting to really surprise Isaiah and Heather with a great honeymoon trip I discovered I actually could make money going to school. Deciding it was a great way to make some money, finish some unfinished goals in life and give Dennis some space, I enrolled in the local junior college. Going back to school was a real turning point for Dennis and our relationship as it was going to take a lot of time.

TIME! Our understanding of this word will greatly influence how we live and what we choose to believe about what is important.

In an article written by Ronnie Littlejohn a professor of Philosophy, Belmont University, Nashville, Tennessee entitled, "The Hebrew Concept of Time" he states…

"Our perception of the passage of time can change with the blink of an eye. Time stands still; time flies. Time drags on. Where did the time go? I just need a little more time! We had a great time! If only I had the time."

There is a growing sense in America that we are losing time. How can we take back control over time? Possibly paying attention to the Hebraic concept of time might be a way for us to regain control. For example, we sometimes notice the difference between spending too much time making a living (paid employment, household chores, and personal maintenance) and not taking time for living. But for the Hebrews, the way we live (making a living) is time itself.

We may only choose how we live or how we "time." So, we must be careful how we live.

One of our major problems in America is that we are too busy spending time on unimportant things and events and we have become too busy for the truly important, but not necessarily urgent, matters in life. For example, while conversing with a loved one, we will quickly answer the cell phone and spend several minutes on the call even though the call may be totally unimportant. The perceived urgency of a ringing phone overrides the more important activity that does not have a need for urgency attached. When we engage in this kind of behavior, we are showing what we think really matters. We could improve life if we changed our paradigm of time. But how can we?

"Time" for the Hebrew people, was about effort and achievement. People do things. They write, play, travel, sleep, dream, perform ceremonies, go to war, and pray. God does things too. Time consists of the story of these events, and it has no existence beyond these. To make the most of time probably meant something like living your life so that others mark their lives and tell their stories in reference to your actions. In the Hebrew mind, the real question is not, "What is the best use of my time right now?" but rather, "What is the best use of my life right now?"

Wow! Here Dennis and I were convinced that what we needed was more "time" for life to be more meaningful. Here our whole word of our testimony was already about events, meaningful events. Is there possibly a key here that we weren't seeing yet?

Remember that life is about the journey…not just the destination?

"A word to the wise ain't necessary--it's the stupid ones who need the advice." ~ Bill Cosby ...

Yep! I just wish some of us didn't need to grow by experiences instead of listening. Dennis and I both had buried our lives into everything and everyone else and we both were in for an education.

Chapter 47

Changes

REMOVING SOME OLD TILE in the kitchen revealed several old layers of tile underneath where who ever had done the work before us had not taken the care to do a thorough job. We also discovered the reason the tile had water damage was far more involved than originally thought. Upon removing each layer and getting closer to the root of the problem we found the cause turned out to be a slow long term leak coming from the plumbing behind the kitchen sink.

Now that we discovered the real reason for the damage our simple tile job included having to replace rotted sheetrock hidden behind the sink as well as cabinetry that had molded and was probably a considerable health hazard.

Like our lives…anything we notice on the surface is simply a reflection of something else unseen that cannot be taken care of as long as we continue to stay superficial. And just like our kitchen renovation often we are afraid of the true cost of getting to the real root of the problem. It seems God in His infinite mercy and wisdom patiently teaches us step by step. My father, Ivan, in his later years started comparing peoples' lives to an onion, which is designed with layer after layer. His life analogy was that each time a new layer was peeled off yet another new unique layer was revealed.It is with us, as my father said.

Excitedly picturing what classes I would take at the local college I had no idea how complicated such a simple idea could be. Trying to sign up for "fun" classes, I discovered that to receive the VA funds for school, I actually had to have a "goal." This quite honestly was not how I was accustomed to thinking as our lives had been spent pretty much lived in the moment.

All the classes that I was interested in were not what I needed to take to finish getting my liberal arts degree. The thought of an eight-to-five was not appealing to me and I really thought I was supposed to be in school. So after facing the disappointment of having to take classes I didn't think I was even interested in, I found myself signing up for Nutrition, Child Development, and English One.

I remember my mother explaining to me, why some things just are the way they are. You don't always understand at the time how valuable or important they are. I think the subject matter was why I should memorize my times tables. I was not sure I believed that at the time but being a kid, there was not a whole lot I could do about it.

Years later while sitting in Mrs. Marinellis college English class, we would be in the middle of memorizing basic "English grammar rules." Then along would come an "exception", something that totally broke all the rules and Renee would laugh and say,"This is what is known as a GET OVER IT!" Explaining… she taught us sometimes there are things that appear to have no rhyme or reason and it is just the way it is and no amount of trying to understand it would help! Talk about a life lesson! As the school semester went on I discovered that every class I was "forced" to take turned out to be incredibly important and meaningful.

As the non-threatening "Grandma" in the classes I was amazed at the number of hurting, searching young people who would seek me out and feel free to pour out their heart breaking trials and simply wanted to know someone cared.

Taking a nutrition class, I found great parallel between how our spirits, minds, and bodies have been made to work. Two things seemed to be so obvious. God who made us is incredibly into detail. Everything that is done affects someone else. Over the years

I had been criticized by some for my love and attention to details, whether planning a meal or simply sharing a thought. Smiling I realized the same God who could touch us with the simplest thing also was a designer who incorporated a love for fantastic detail. I also marveled at the way our physical bodies are so dependent on all the other parts to work well. Working together, what a concept!

Yes, even the Child Development class was interesting and with grandchildren not to far off I had to laugh at the stories and things that I learned.

Meanwhile, Dennis was coming face to face with himself! Insecurities that had been conveniently buried began to surface. The very slow down and "time" we had prayed for was now here.

For the first time in twenty-six years of marriage we were not joined at the hip twenty-four hours a day. Fifty-three years old, along with years of serious medical challenges wore on his mind and body.

Chapter 48

Let the Games Begin

LIKE ROME DURING THE days of the apostle Paul, America, seems consumed with games of entertainment and competition. Maybe that is why, in his letter to Corinth, Paul compared the challenges faced in this life to running a competitive race.

First Corinthians, verse nine, chapter twenty-five says;

"And everyone contending exercises self-control in all things; they truly, therefore, in order to take a decaying crown, but we, an undecaying one."

The American Heritage Dictionary defines the word contend this way:

To strive in opposition or against difficulties; struggle: *armies contending for control of strategic territory*

and; To compete, as in a race; to vie

I always thought the point of games was for happiness…rest and relaxation. As a woman I hated the cruel childhood memories of competition where someone is ahead at the expense of someone else. What pride, ego, and puffed-up humanity deem as winning and the measure of success, has always been incredibly offensive to me.

Years ago I was listening to a tape that my mom had given me where the speaker was trying to point out some of the gender relational and social differences between men and women. When most women are given a compliment they immediately try to even the playing field to show they don't consider themselves "better" than the person giving the compliment.

"You look great! Is that a new dress?" The reply often has an explanation like "Yes, but I bought it on sale!" It's called making the playing field equal.

Little did I realize that "opposition, difficulties and struggle were actually the true meaning behind "games and contending" Dennis and I had forgotten some of the basics from our first experiences as brand new followers of Jesus. If our minds, hearts and souls were the battlefields then armies contending for control of strategic territory" would be a good way to describe what was happening in our lives.

Taking summer classes I continued to pay the price for the years I was in college and basically took all the fun classes I wanted. I had lots of units, but not the right ones for a degree, or a transfer, so I continued to take all the required courses I had dodged in my younger days.

Occasionally I would try to help Dennis with a project for our home but the simplest tasks would end with him being frustrated and me in tears. The blindness to much of our own dysfunction that had seemed to help us stay focused on everything but our problems for so many years, simply wasn't there. Dennis clearly resented needing help. Everything made him feel stupid and exposed. I suffered with lots of rejection and was grateful that our daily activities gave us some space.

The news that Isaac and Heather were expecting our first grandchild was only made sweeter when we heard our precious Sarah was expecting as well.

Signing up for more classes I continued to be amazed at how many spiritual truths I was hearing taught. We have a major lack of communication. Many are under the impression that because they spoke words, their message is understood and received or refused.

Mamma Lori taught Dennis and I years ago that the question of the ages was going to revolve around the question, "Hath God said?"

Here at the local college as I took a class in business communications, I found myself wanting to demand that everyone I know should have to take this class. The instructor, a fantastic teacher named Lucy, inspired everyone. First we looked at the different kinds of communication such as verbal and non-verbal. I had to laugh thinking about how even though what we say and how we say it, is so important, what we actually do with our lives speaks louder than any words.

My mother used to say "Your actions are speaking so loud…I can't hear what you are saying."

Next the most refreshing news was that the business world in general wanted simplicity, not hype. When I was in high school, teachers taught that formality and big words were important for business communications and here I was being taught that now clear concise meaningful thought was appreciated. Over the years one of the biggest turn-offs to Dennis and I, when we listened to some Christians teach or preach, was that they were not themselves. One day I was watching this grown man, strut all around a stage, using Elizabethan English, and talking at an extra loud volume. I wondered if this was how he talked to his family at home…It seemed so put on and I honestly could not focus on the message he was trying to share due to all the affectations. Why do people think that if they start to talk to God, or about Him, they need to put on airs? This is the sort of poor communication that has been such a stumbling block in sharing the "good news."

Thrilled about all I was learning about communicating, I tried to share with Dennis who was by now not enthusiastic, about hearing how we could grow. My husband was well on the way down a path of self discovery that was not a pretty picture. Every devil in hell must have been sent to speak into the ear of this man who had already faced so many challenges. While he was feeling insecure and old, I was starting to be awakened to the fact that we were young and might have half of our lives left.

Time after time, I would try to talk about what was going on in my heart and mind and as Dennis was in the process of shutting down I was awakening and went to the only place I knew to go.

"Honey, I am so spiritually hungry. I want to go visit Mamma Lori for two weeks." And in January that's exactly what I did. As a matter of fact, I think it turned out to be closer to three weeks. Dennis was invited but declined and thought maybe a break would be good for us.

Arriving in Oklahoma, Lori's son Greg picked me up at the airport. Pouring my heart out about how badly I needed rest, Greg got a funny look and said, "Well Sis, listen to this." The most heavenly music with words about "rest" filled the air and I cried like a baby. It was like these songs had been written for me and I felt like I had entered into a sacred and holy time of rest.

Checking out of the "world" so to speak, the next few weeks were spent at the feet of Jesus. If you have never totally shut out all distractions and just fellowshipped with the Lord, you have missed an incredible opportunity. Sitting on a fold out sofa in the living room of mammas humble mobile home, I renewed my spirit, soul and body. Often waking in the wee hours of the night, I would softly play the special worship songs that I had first been greeted with on my arrival. Opening the word I would take communion and reflecting on all that Jesus had done for our little family, I found myself weeping and thanking God. "If you never did another thing for Dennis and I, we have already been so blessed," I would pray.

Mamma Lori's nest was so warm and cozy and if time could have stood still I would have stayed forever. We would awaken when we felt like it, read, study, visited and enjoyed the pure presence of the Lord. Peace like a river flowed and time stood still. Every few days, Mamma would put some homemade soup or stew on the stove and then we read, studied, and focused on Jesus. I added a daily walk to thank God for my health and would talk with no one, focusing on whatever I felt led toward. One morning in particular, I remember telling Jesus that I loved him so much I would walk through anything he wanted me to and that no matter what…I swore like Peter the apostle did, to never let selfishness rule in my life. Little did I know the incredible fires that were to come. I truly believe now I was granted this wonderful time of preparation for what was to come.

Chapter 49

Family

GRATITUDE FOR FAMILY HAS inspired Dennis and I when the rest of life has become challenging. The wonderful things that were happening to, and for, our precious children helped us to stay focused on what we felt was most important.

The birth of our first grandson Evan was only made sweeter by the realization that there was something very special about his birth date. Isaac and Heather had kept Evan's name a secret until he was born and it wasn't until a few weeks later we discovered quite a surprise. Evans name is Welsh and Irish for "young warrior."

Before Evan had arrived I had been teasing Heather about how Isaac had been born circumcised and I wondered if there might be anything extra special about this first grandchild's birth. Standing in the kitchen several weeks after Evan was born Dennis realized that his first grandson was born on the third month, the sixteenth day and that his name "Evan" is the Welsh name for "John." So there we had it. Evans' special secret. His birth name and date he was born symbolized "John 3:16,"the most recognized scripture in the bible.

"For God so loved the world, that He gave his only begotten son, so that whosoever believes in Him should not perish but have eternal life."

Our precious children Isaac and Heather who had played the song "Show you Love," by Jars of Clay, as the theme song

at their wedding during a slide show, had not left a dry eye in the house.

Part of the words seemed prophetic, and as anyone who knows Isaac and Heather will attest, they have such an incredible calling to reveal and reflect a kingdom family.

"Speak - and say the words that no one else will ever say

Love - love like the world we know is over in a day I'm gonna show you love in every language I'm gonna speak with words that need no form I'm gonna give you what you never had before"

Now years later even the birth of their first child is a reminder of the "good news" and their precious family truly reflects the picture of love.

In the fall yet another happy memory was made. Unlike his brother Isaacs heartfelt traditional proposal, Isaiah's proposal was unique too, and how should we say…with much dramatic flair! Taking Heather to Disneyland in Anaheim Isaiah proposed at the top of the "Splash Mountain" ride. Yep! Right before the steepest drop, my awesome son whipped out a ring and asked his future bride if she wanted to "take the plunge." Happy and shocked, Heather and Isaiah became officially engaged.

I had watched through the years as my middle son faced tests and challenges without ever giving up. With spring flying by and the wedding approaching, Isaiah who had been an independent web designer was desperate to have a steady income before he actually said "I do".

"Mom, I know there is a wedding set, but I am not getting married if I don't have a steady income."

"Well son, God put on your heart all that you have planned and I think you need to shut everything down and seek Him for help. You have done everything you know, so stop and go to the mountains and wait to hear from him"

You know sometimes we get so busy handling our own lives we forget we have a loving God who is just waiting for us to trust Him. Isaiah headed for the mountains the next day and he truly just stopped to smell the roses. Calling several times, as he wasn't hearing anything specific, I encouraged him to enjoy the scenery and know that whether he felt anything or not, I believed with all my heart things would change and God would honor his humility at asking for divine guidance.

Late that day when Isaiah returned, he shared he hadn't gotten any great big revelations, but felt at peace. Within a few days he had a thought to check back on a job he had looked at almost a year before that was actually in our town and was right up his alley.

To Isaiah's amazement, the job was still listed as open on the internet and he called immediately. First he was told that the company thought that it had found someone already, but they would send someone to meet with Isaiah anyway. Well, the meeting went so good that the next thing Isaiah knew was that he now had an appointment with the owner "Cass." Wouldn't you know it! Isaiah ended up hired locally with the most successful web design company who just happened to be believers, and even allowed him the time off for a honeymoon even though he was new.

The more we saw Heather the more we knew what a treasure Isaiah had found. So Isaiah's Heather Marie, now joined Isaac's Heather Dawn making our family more complete. I knew I couldn't have asked for sweeter girls for the boys.

Our middle son Isaiah, was the comedian, the musician, the graphic artist and the consummate basketball player. Our Isaiah who has his mother's dramatic flair, and will pull out a hysterical impersonation at just the right moment. One moment we had Jim Carrey as "Ace Ventura" and the next Dustin Hoffman as "Hook" was in the room. Isaiah has his mother's gift for demonstrative joy. Our home was constantly lit by his humor and presence!

One day, while I was working on schoolwork, Isaiah gave me one of the greatest gifts I have ever received. "Mom, I need you to pick out a special song for the mother and son dance we are having at our wedding." I don't know if my son knows how much his mother likes to dance but the honor of his asking was such an incredible gift.

How could I possibly share what was in my heart without falling totally apart?

Memories of triumphs and tears filled my heart and I was hoping it wouldn't hurt as bad since Isaiah was the second son to leave home.My selfish side hurt so bad as it seems a twisted irony that after you pour all your love, passion and heart into someone your reward for a job well done is to lose a part of yourself. Oweee!

Searching through songs that had been written from sons to mothers, I couldn't find hardly any written from mothers to sons and then of all things, I remembered a song by Rod Stewert, "Forever Young" Listening to the words I couldn't believe what I was hearing.

> May the good Lord be with you down every road
> you roam,
> And may sunshine and happiness
> Surround you when you're far from home.
> May you grow to be proud, dignified, and true,
> And do unto others as you'd have done to you.
> Be courageous and be brave,
> And in my heart you'll always stay
> Forever young (Forever young)
> Forever young (Forever young)

The words would be literally a blessing, they would speak my hopes for my precious Isaiah and I wept like a baby. I literally had to listen to it for months before I thought I could possibly hear it without falling apart. The wedding had some last minute challenges and yet sailing through them I found myself dancing with my son in a moment of privilege and great emotion. As the song ended six-foot tall Zay leaned forward and with a chuckle whispered…hold tight mom and making me feel like a school girl again he smoothly whisked me off my feet and twirled around several times with the biggest grin on his face.

Giving is truly more fun than receiving and the joy Dennis and I had sending the kids on a dream honeymoon, was great. A full week, in Florida, at Disney World. Becoming like "little children" was the ticket to a memorable get-away for Isaiah and Heather.

Dennis and I have never had a traditional Honeymoon, and somehow it seemed so special to be able to give our kids something we hadn't experienced. Heather had not been out of central California and with some shopping on the internet, the kids even were able to stay in one of the actual Disney Resorts on their Honeymoon!

The rest of the summer flew by and August 17th our precious Sarah and Greg gave birth to a beautiful baby girl, Mykayla. With the biggest eyes I had ever seen, we had an absolute blast picking out some awesome baby girl things. The circle was complete and Sarah who had always wanted to be a mother had her own real life princess. Now Evan would have a little cousin to play with and the girl count in our family was gaining ground. Hooray. I'm not saying I felt alone all those years until Sarah joined our family, but after being raised with two sisters and no brothers, all the years of testosterone had made me forget what being a girl was until Sarah joined us. Now with both Heathers and Mykayla, the official family count was boys six and girls five.

The fall flew by and while Dennis continued to work on projects on the house I took more classes. Since Isaiah and Heather were married our home was quieter and Israel actually had just Mom and Dad all to himself! For years our home was the hub of activity. Over the years along with Sarah and Trish joining our family we also had shared our home with a few others. Each time we opened our hearts and our doors to share what we had, everyone grew.

One of our more memorable moments was when we had been joined by a funny young man that Isaiah had met. Zeb was from Kentucky! Red haired, lanky and the first straight man I ever met in my life who thought it was cool to wear nail polish, black nail polish! Zeb has an incredible sense of humor and my fondest memory was one night when several other people in the living room had started to argue, the next thing we knew, Zeb came to the rescue, galloping through the living room wearing an Indiana

Jones hat and riding a broom like a stick horse. Having everyone's attention the whole room busted up after he announced that since we were all acting like children, he wanted to join in. Wow! What a gift. Realizing he had some unfinished business back home in Kentucky, Zeb headed home a little older and wiser from his travels and promised to stay in touch.

Now, Israel...aka "Buck"...was enjoying the lime light as he played guitar in several bands. Farewell Seasons was the name of the band he and some friends formed that played local venues for several years. Dennis and I watched and helped as all the boys grew in life and through the experiences they were all having. Then as the name implied Farewell Seasons was ready for some changes and the name of the new band was "Shelby Snapshot".

Heading for 20 our youngest son was enjoying life to the fullest and perhaps a little too much. A picture of his dad, this son was going to learn by the school Arthur Blessitt affectionately calls "University Street."

Dennis was comfortable working on our physical house, and yet for some reason, any mention of talking about our relationship as man and wife, what was important and even what the future held caused outbursts and punishing silence.

The message was clear. Don't talk about anything of substance. The years in Terra Bella where we shared our hearts, hopes and dreams were far from us. Sharing times of fellowship were not for Dennis anymore and we started growing farther and farther apart. I was starving for true intimacy and it seemed everything I did was wrong.

Taking classes yet one more semester at the local college Dennis and I continued to grow farther apart. No amount of good things happening for our children could erase the pain of feeling so alone even though we lived in the same house.

Chapter 50

The Accuser

It was already January again and I couldn't believe it had been a whole year since I had been at Lori's. The promises I had made with all of my heart to Jesus about slowing down and taking time to make sure my priorities were in order, were really sincere. Life and challenges had once again started wheels in motion that seemed impossible to change. Memories of basking in great peace had quickly faded as demands on my time from school and family helped the stability that came through busyness.

Dennis continued to grow angrier, with everything and anything. The disturbing thing was I was always to blame. We all have issues and my husband truly is a warrior who had overcome so much, and still…this was different. If I didn't know better I would have thought we were back in the days before he had asked the Lord to lead his life. Cutting words would slip out and there seemed to be no restraint when it came to anything in his life.

Israel was still at home and even though we had not had anyone living with us for over six months, Dennis was verbalizing his need to be alone. For the past year there were some relational things happening that were not making any sense. My husband kept saying he needed to be alone with me, but he never wanted to interact relationally. When we did have time to spend together he wanted to stare at TV. He didn't want to visit, date or talk.

Forgotten was the word about "enjoying" our son Israel's final years at home and concentrating on our marriage. Dennis would have reoccurring dreams about Terra Bella, the place of total surrender to God where we had experienced so many great things and yet if I mentioned prayer, studying the word, or having bible studies I was greeted with hostility.

Terra Bella was a training ground and a place of simplicity where our sensitivity toward wanting to spend our lives about our heavenly Father's business was a reality. When Dennis had been delivered of alcohol and cigarettes he had studied the word daily. The prayer "Thy will be done on earth as it is in heaven" was what ruled our life choices. We were not kidding. Lori used to say, "Honey... if it wouldn't belong in your heavenly home, why would you want it here?" Fellowshipping, bible studies, and listening to teaching tapes daily was "The Way" of our lives. We embraced teaching from the whole body of Christ! Thanks to TBN, we listened to true stories about Gods love and we never cared what denomination or "pedigree" the speaker was. We had been honestly overjoyed when God would bring someone to our home, whether it was simply for physical food, or encouragement, we were motivated totally out of wanting to let our "light" shine. We truly wanted to reflect "Jesus" in us.

For several years after closing "Happy Thoughts" my sweetheart kept saying that all we needed was to get away. I was finally realizing, no matter how long or far we went, it never solved the problem. My husband had been on more "get aways" than Doans has pills, so to speak. We got away together, apart, sideways...he went by himself, three days, sometimes a week. True we had never taken two weeks to Fiji as a honeymoon, but if getting away would solve the problem, I knew it should have worked already.

Hmmmmm! Let's think! Burn out, woundedness, lack of word, isolation, poor health and a legion from hell! My knight in shining armor was losing it and there was nothing I could do. Isolating himself he was determined to make it through this battle on his own.

Trusting God to handle what was going on I tried to steer clear and hid by focusing on my precious son Israel who was still at home and under my schooling. I noticed Dennis was not as prone to say mean things when others were around and I was grateful that my littlest treasure was still in the house. Bringing home lots of his friends I continued to offer our home as a place where Israel's friends were welcome. My son had shared over the years how it meant so much to him, to have a place to bring friends and hang out.

Over the years Dennis and I had absolutely loved our children's friends. Back in Terra Bella, Dennis had even given a prophetic word to me about my call to "mothering many sons" and how the streets would be filled with those who I would be used to lead to Jesus. All the boy's friends, homeschoolers and then some could be found eating mom's tacos and homemade dishes. Neighborhood kids were welcome and our home was the center of activity, and I loved it. I was totally convinced that my staying sane was to focus on people who wanted my love and joy and I had decided I could not join Dennis in this depression. I truly don't believe any of the kids knew how devastating this all was and I continued to try to hide all the dysfunction.

Walking on egg shells, making excuses and trying to cover for my husband's foul moods, I continued being the consummate enabler, oblivious to what so many were seeing. Over the years I had been trained well and due to major rejection issues thought it was my job to make sure peace reigned in our home. That meant keeping Dennis happy no matter what.

My best friend was in such pain and like Adam ,the first man… in the beginning…Dennis seemed to think I was the source now of all his problems. Blame, anger, and isolation were his friends and the accuser of the brethren was constantly speaking in his ear. Exhausted, confused, and miserable, anything Dennis heard in his ear he believed.

Chapter 51

The Gift of Jake

AFTER TAKING MORE CLASSES I became convinced that God had a special plan for my schooling. In simple faith I tried to make some sense of putting one foot in front of the other. I often wonderd why I was doing what I was doing, and yet I was sure I was where I was supposed to be. I truly wish I could share some formula about how I was hearing God so clearly...yet all I knew was I seemed propelled from event to event and there was great comfort in feeling useful.

Dennis and I were invited to Evans first birthday party where Isaac and Heather had the most wonderful surprise. After Evan opened all his gifts, Isaac handed a small little box to Evan and proudly said that this was from him and Heather. As Evan lifted a little t-shirt out of the box, the cloth fell open and we realized it said something. "I'm a big brother!" I think I started screaming and laughing and the whole room was filled with people clapping and saying, "Congratulations!" Here in the midst of my own trials, was one more reminder of how much Dennis and I both had to battle for as a couple, and as parents. Ask anyone from split families, holidays, birthdays, and special days, are never the same after a family is split apart with their parents divorce. Here in our faces was the reality that our children were being blessed and needed us now more than ever.

One day Israel walked into the house and told me about a new friend he had made that he wanted me to meet. Israel made friends easily. Some he told us about and some he didn't but this was different. "You need to meet him mom. Jakes mother died of cancer and it really messed him up. He went through a time where he was partying and mad at God, but he's better now and he's awesome."

Israel has always been a great judge of character. He may not always follow his own advice but when it comes to his ability to hear the Holy Spirit he has always been very keen.

Little did Israel know I had been praying for God to send someone who truly loved the Lord. Not perfect...just sincere like Israel. My son had lots of friends but some of the closest were off on the journeys that so many of us take when we are young. I prayed and prayed that God would send one with a great sensitivity to the Spirit of God. Suffering from a broken heart and wondering what he truly believed in, Israel had been venturing out into his own tests and trials. I knew those he chose as friends would have great impact on his life. God was perking up my ears to this "Jake" and a short time later Israel had yet one more story. While going to school at the local college, Jake had moved into Visalia and the boys were hanging out more and more. One night the boys went to the coast and this new friend poured his heart out to Israel. My son shared how meaningful it was to him that Jake had opened up and trusted him. All I could think about was the profound relationship in the Bible of Jonathon and David. I was so grateful for this new friend that sensed what a good man Israel is. In spite of the spiritual warfare with Dennis and I, the answers to prayer in these other areas of life helped my sanity.

One day Israel busted through the door. "Mom, this is Jake!" The young man that greeted me had the most contagious genuine smile. Eyes that reflected brokenness and pain could not drown out a childlike exuberance. Tall, over six feet, and obviously of Scandinavian heritage, Jake stuck out his hand with great respect but didn't seem to mind the motherly hug that came quite naturally.

Over the next few weeks, Jake came and went often and then one day as Jake left after visiting, an incredible thing happened. I was told, "I would like you to be Jakes mother on earth. He will be your son. His mother has come to me and asked that someone special can be there. He is carrying so much pain. I am restoring both of you"

At the same time I was hearing all of this I was hit with such pain and love and joy that my knees literally buckled. In my heart I felt like a mother when she has just given birth and yet I had never heard of such a thing. Wanting to make sure this was from God I didn't say anything to anyone for weeks and continued to pray. "Lord, where does your word say people in heaven can talk to you about people on earth?" I felt so stupid as I was reminded that Jesus is in heaven talking with the Father about us daily! Lazarus was talking with God requesting that he go tell certain people how to avoid the torment he was experiencing....Hmmmm.

Then about a week later, while doing laundry I said ok Lord! And where is it in the word that you could give someone a second mother? As soon as I thought the question I saw in a vision, the cross. Jesus looked down from the cross and said, "Woman behold your son.... And to John he said... "Behold your mother."

I burst into tears so ashamed, I was repeatedly questioning what I knew was truly the Lord. Only God and God alone could know what it meant to me to be entrusted with another son. I had suffered loss by choosing to abort some of my own children many years before. Now our family included not only our three sons, it also included precious Sarah, her hubby Greg, both daughter's-inlaw "Heather Marie and Heather Dawn, and now our new son "Jake" as well!

Talking with Dennis I told him what had happened and what I had heard. In-spite of the horrendous warfare Dennis was fighting he shared how he trusted Jake, and was moved in his heart in a special way towards this young man. Giving Jake a copy of our book "Breaking Chains," Dennis wanted to support this young man in any way he could. I was free to share with Jake how much God loved him and that his mother in heaven was thinking of him and even more... so was Jesus!

One day Dennis, Israel, Jake and I were downtown. I believed the Lord said to share "now" with Jake what He had shown me.

To my amazement in response to what I was saying, smiling... Jake said, "I know, God already told me!" What a response! What awesome confirmation! Not in my wildest dreams while praying for a great friend for my son did I ever imagine what the Lord had in mind.

One night during a family dinner I shared with all of my children what God had done and a little awkwardly perhaps, my attempts to convey to my precious treasures that Jake was assigned by God to our family. I couldn't have been any prouder than if he had just been physically birthed. I seemed to be the only one totally blind to the age and size of this "new baby." Once again my children, including Sarah, gave a hearty welcome to our new "gift,"

Jake is talented with lots of construction skills and has a beautiful way of sharing his ideas. When I saw him work with Dennis, I was amazed by how well they worked together. Here I was taking all these communication classes and somehow after years of watching Dennis get so frustrated when working with others, he was spending hours with Jake on projects without any problem. I realized there was much I could learn from watching the two of them interact. I had picked up habits that were hurting Dennis and it had never occurred to me. For so many years I had been asked to be the "technical" part of the project. Knowing how quickly Dennis would get frustrated when dealing with new things, I had started communicating in a way that was very hurtful. I sincerely did not even think about my delivery and thought I was doing Dennis a favor by being "brief" and not wanting to be questioned!

One day in particular Dennis and Jake were working together when I was in the room and Dennis pretty forcefully was telling Jake how they were going to "do this next step" of the project. My eyes met with Jake's and we both knew that what Dennis was proposing wouldn't work. Had it been me I would have shortly said "no, you need to do this or that," which would have led to an argument, and further hurt. The way this son handled it was, "I had an idea too, but let's try yours first and if it doesn't work, I was thinking maybe we could..." and then Jake explained his idea. Do you know that Dennis got totally quiet and said, "Why don't we try your idea first?"

Standing there flabbergasted all I could think of was all the hurt feelings we both had suffered during projects. Some of this was partially due to the "habit" I had gotten into of mowing over him to get to the bottom line, to save us both time and energy! Wow! Granted, he also had gotten into a habit of not wanting to "listen or hear" and had his own issues, but I knew now more than ever that our new family addition was being used by God in some amazing ways.

Israel and baby brother Jake

Chapter 52

"The Trish"

As all the challenges were happening with Dennis and I, our precious best friend Trish, was in God's "University Street" as well. Having been in Texas for several years, Trish found out as we did that life was throwing her some surprises and found herself in a horrible relationship.

Married to a man who had put on quite a front, to her horror she eventually found he had been unfaithful and had been so calloused as to have numerous relationships all at one time. The worst part was that the emotional and mental abuse she had received kept her wondering if she was just imagining things, or truly to be blamed for all of his unhappiness.

Angela, Dennis and I had flown out to Trish's wedding to meet this man and we knew something was very wrong. Trish had asked Dennis to "give her away" and I was maid of honor. My precious friend absolutely glowed and looked stunning. I was to find out a year later that on her wedding night she had been taken home to an apartment that was literally knee high in trash. Our Trish, trying to look on the bright side, decided this man just needed some help. We serve a God who says, "I will never leave you or forsake you"... and we had to support our friend no matter what we were thinking. What do you do when someone you love is set on a course you profoundly disagree with? We decided that God was in charge, so we supported her, trusting that if what we were sensing was real, there must be some bigger life lesson happening here.

The enemy isolated our friend and before long I would get calls where Trish was literally whispering, so her husband would not hear her, and tell her to hang up. He didn't want her talking with others and was very controlling. Heartbroken we watched as our friend who deserved and needed so much tender care had been snared by loneliness and conned.

There is such stigma about broken marriages since it is a covenant with God, and yet we also are told the Holy Spirit will depart when He is not wanted. Once a precious relative to me announced she and her husband were getting divorced. As my heart was being torn at the news, tears filled my eyes and I was filled with sadness. I clearly heard…"Stop. Don't grieve. They (and the Spirit said their names) have decided not to grow together…but they will grow!" Whoever heard of such a thing? Is it possible that in our zeal to please God like the Pharisees of old we have become legalistic hardened and condemning those who Jesus forgives? Is it possible to make the institution of marriage an idol? Didn't our precious Lord say I want mercy…Not Sacrifice?

If the Holy Spirit cannot operate in an abusive strife filled relationship not centered in Christ do you really think he cares more about a piece of paper and promises to men? Mamma Lori said years ago, "Honey, He even has to fill you with the hunger for Him, you can't just make that happen!" A covenant isn't broken by mere words… It is broken by your actions. To keep a charade going for legalistic doctrine and appearances sake can be sick! Our friend spent two years making sure that she was not easily walking away or giving up. On her second wedding anniversary she discovered her husband was being unfaithful again. He was literally online on the computer with another woman while talking to her over the phone about the anniversary card she had given him that morning... that did it!

Answering the phone, I wept with my friend as she shared her discovery of a few minutes before. The pain she was having transcended the distance and moaning I literally had to hand Dennis the phone. Once again, the heart of the man I so admire, came to the forefront while forgetting his own challenges. "Trish, you hear me? Come Home! We love you! Pack your car and let us know when you are on the road. You don't need anything. Don't worry about a thing."

As Trish headed out, the Lord, her true loving husband gave me specific instructions. "Reserve Trish a room in (and the Lord named a town). The best, and make sure it has a spa. She is emotionally and mentally exhausted and fragile. Order her flowers and a gift basket and include what I tell you on the card! "Great!" Didn't God know how tight financially we were until our next check came in? "How?" I asked. A picture of the "trip rewards card" flashed and I had to wonder. When Dennis was going back and forth to all the doctor. visits with Jorge in Santa Monica, I had signed up on line for a membership card that gave you points whenever you stayed at certain motels. Calling the phone number on the card I discovered that over the two years, we had racked up just enough points to get Trish the room. Since it was midweek the desk clerk was even willing to upgrade the room to include the "spa room" when I asked. What a God we serve!

Upon arrival at the motel, the desk clerk; who was in on the surprise, acted like we had paid for a regular room. Later Trish shared how words could not ever express what she found. Miraculously sleeping despite all of the pain, she found the strength to walk the hard, lonely painful days ahead.

With Trish enroute we had several days to prepare, so we scrambled to do all that was placed in our hearts. Dennis carefully painted the back bedroom and after that we headed out to a yard sale to find a matching wing chair and reading stand. Moving in a bed, we even bought new sheets and pillow cases to match the comforter. Only God knows how He orchestrated this and finding the matching mauve wing chair we put lavender highlights throughout the room.

When my mother heard that Trish was coming home she offered the perfect lamp for reading and a few other odds and ends. Completely decorated down to silk flowers across the top of the curtains next we filled the private bathroom with a giant gift basket filled with bath goodies that had pictures of the ocean. Our friend absolutely loves the ocean so even a special new shower curtain with Tahitian bungalows was hung with great love. Yet something was still missing. Going to a local farmers market Dennis and I bought a dainty lavender bird cage complete with a gorgeous sky blue parakeet.

Remember the vision I was given in the prayer room of TBN? Here was a little bird that was broken and bound that we were going to be caring for. Our heartfelt, honest prayer was that our little wounded warrior would be set totally free. Complete with candles, two dozen fresh roses, a welcome home card and even a mini fridge stocked with the finest health foods we added the final touches. A very special Teddy Bear waited patiently sitting in the middle of her bed holding the "welcome home card" in his paws.

Trish arrived at our house and we were so happy to see her home again. Our wonderful friend was very close to a complete physical and mental breakdown from the abuse and here in a place of true covenant…her final cares were removed. "Trish," Dennis excitedly said, "You are here to rest, and you are to rest. Completely! We recently had an increase in cash flow and the Lord has said to meet all your needs, and bills, and give you spending money for three months." Seeing the love and care that had been poured out on Gods behalf, Trish wept. My prayer was that she would see how her heavenly husband, Jesus wanted her treated, so she would never believe she deserved abusive treatment ever again.

I am sharing this to say although appearing like King David, in the Bible when one moment he was so high on God and the next he was in the depths of despair, even his own torment couldn't stop Dennis from sharing all that he had with a true covenant friend. The book of Acts was in action and instead of some gratuitous, manipulative farce, we both felt like we were privileged, to have been chosen…to be God's hands extended to his wife…"Trish"

I was thrilled for some long overdue female company and we were able to give Trish the gift of a safe haven and nest. Not in my wildest dreams could I ever think I myself would be needful of one of those in the not so far away future.

The healing that was accomplished during the summer was unprecedented. I know the great video in heaven has it all recorded for recall at will, let's just say we saw God miraculously wipe away years of stress and pain.

Once when precious Jan Crouch could not be any lower in despair and depression, God asked her to help someone hurting when she truly believed she had nothing to give. Answering yes with her actions in spite of her own pain, she did and it became a turning point in her own healing. How many times when our own crises threatened to swallow us up, did Dennis and I find common ground helping someone else who was hurting.

Now with plenty of diversions, Dennis and I were at least civil and with focusing on everyone but ourselves there was the faint hint of "Terra Bella" in the air.

Precious, beautiful Trish

Chapter 53

"Reroofing and Repairing"

WITH ISRAEL AND TRISH both in the house it seemed to help Dennis be on his best behavior when they were around. Wondering what on earth was happening in the bigger picture, Dennis and I refinanced our home and planned to reroof the house in the summer. Jake, Israel, Trish, and even William from Texas were all part of the plan.

Meanwhile Trish and I were both catching up on some badly needed girl time. Through the late spring yet again the Lord tried to use our new son Jake in a very special way. As Trish and I both were awaking up to the fact that it was ok to be individuals, we both realized we had seen enough TV and wanted to live life, not watch it.

Jumping at the invitation to play tennis, walk the track and tackle the enemy of laziness and apathy, Trish and I both couldn't get enough of mothering Jake and getting in shape at the same time. It seemed for Trish and me that when life got rough we never would take care of ourselves, using our partners as an excuse for our choices. To say that the Lord was using Jake to encourage us to come out of our shells was putting it mildly.

Spiritually it felt so good to pour out again to Trish and to Jake. I was realizing I had another good 30 years or so and I didn't want to spend it watching life go by. Trying to be sensitive to what Dennis was going through, Trish and I would invite my husband everywhere but he was not having any of it. Dennis was at a point where like King Saul and King David, one moment he thought God had sent Jake. The next, whispering evil voices would tell Dennis that his wife was out of her mind, all of our problems were simply because his 53 year old wife didn't want to settle down and she was going through "the change."

Dennis seemed oblivious that during this time, he was the one who had just experienced several years of rest and projects and was bored to tears. The delay of some of our dreams seemed to be catching up with this Veteran and even though the world had freed him from a normal job, God was not releasing him from his "call" in life. Dennis wasn't sure anymore what that call was or if he wanted any part of it.

William couldn't arrive until the end of May to re-roof the house and in central California the temperature was heating up and so were the emotions. Isn't it funny how what is inside boils up to the top when great heat is applied. As the heat soared, Dennis and William did not see eye to eye. Meanwhile faithful Jake was helping between working several jobs and even Trish and I were wearing out from trying to be "roofers." Israel helped when he could but it seemed that Dennis and William were now left with the majority of the work. In spite of the underlying frustrations I now look back and remember some of the events of that time with great humor. Just try to picture Trish and I up on our roof tearing off shingles. The neighbors were now convinced our family was nuts. Here were a couple of women both close to 50, roofing a house,

One day William dropped one of the nail pullers down inside the attic of the roof. Since I was in the house getting water, the guys thought I should go into the attic from the inside to retrieve the tool we needed to help remove the shingles. Jake said, "Mom, when working construction we would put baby powder on ourselves before going into an attic to protect us from the insulation." Sure! Laughing, I now pictured myself looking like "Poppin Fresh," the Pillsbury dough boy or even better, like "Mr. Staypuffed" the marshmallow man in the movie "Ghost Busters." Not quite sure that I wasn't falling for some joke on me, I found some baby powder and covered myself from head to toe. Poking my head out the front door, I announced to everyone on the roof that I was now ready for the great excursion into the attic.

Before I could turn around I saw the nail puller I was supposed to retrieve thrown down in front of me on the lawn and everyone on the roof had a great laugh as they had figured out a way to retrieve the tool without the need for me to go into the attic. This started a running joke between my new son and I and on more than one occasion when in our home he would be the recipient of a "baby powder" prank when least expecting it.

Our dream to provide extra income for all and save money was turning into a race to finish the roof project before we all died from heat prostration. The electric company decided to double their rates that very month. We literally had the roof off and a one month electric bill of over seven hundred dollars added to the pressures of the job.

Jake accepted a job working at a hay ranch in Nevada for the rest of the summer, and to my surprise I found myself crying my eyes out at the thought of this new son being gone for the whole summer. "Don't cry, I'll be back for school. I think this is a good opportunity." I heard the words but they didn't seem to help the hole in my heart. It seemed while Dennis wanted nothing to do with the ordinary nurturing that wives and mothers so long to give, God had provided a new son who really had needed some Godly mothering. It felt good to know I was being of use with Trish and Jake since, my best friend, Dennis, was such an unhappy camper.

Our friend Greg, (mamma Loris' son), arrived in the middle of the reroofing and once again I was hopeful that he would be used by God to help Dennis somehow. My husband's heart showed through as he threw Greg the keys to his Harley motorcycle and told him feel free to use it whenever he wanted while he was in California. He knew Greg loved to ride and I was elated that the two were spending time together. Greg was one of the very few that Dennis had ever considered a friend and I knew he also could give me some insight about what was happening.

The more Dennis sensed that change was in the air he would struggle more and more even though the old ways of doing things were just not working anymore. The freer I became from enabling destructive behavior by simply putting up with abuse, the more Dennis tried to manifest "control." Barking orders and demands, my honey seemed oblivious that people were noticing. It seemed like the years of covering some very dysfunctional areas were now catching up and I was waking up to the fact that I couldn't just ignore what was happening any more. When others I trusted lovingly confirmed that my best friend was way off base, it helped me to understand that I was indeed seeing and experiencing things that were not okay. I still was a long way from realizing the price we were going to have to pay to grow and often the voices whispering to me were full of blame and accusation.

To add to everything else, Trish and I were getting in shape and now that too was a source of anger and jealousy for Dennis. If I could sum up the analogy during the re-roofing time…it would be that like our rotten roof, the enemy was attacking my husband's mind every way he could. There was worn out, rotten thinking that needed to be replaced. Like our roof, years of storms had made their mark and the roof that was supposed to offer protection and safety needed replacing. Isn't it remarkable how often the natural is a reflection of the spiritual in our lives?

While visiting, Greg had noticed the verbal abuse and anger that would slip through in the middle of daily activities and asked me how long this had been happening. Sharing that I had been noticing discontent for quite some time I asked our dear friend if there wasn't something he could do. Sadly he shared that after praying he believed that Dennis was going to have to hit bottom, like he himself had so many years before, and prayer was the only thing to do.

Great! Wonderful! Meanwhile the Lord continued to ask me to trust Him and do daily what He said and refuse to be "bullied" or controlled by the demons that were trying to destroy my husband. "Let your light shine. Stay busy about my business and don't lose your joy!" were my marching orders. As Dennis continued being oppressed with wanting to hide in the "cave" so to speak, I was being directed to fight with everything in me the lie from hell the enemy was selling Dennis. He was verbalizing that our lives were over and we were destined for 40 hours a week of TV, lots of food and conversations about how old we were. Meanwhile I was hearing the exact opposite.

The very joy I was having in staying active, busy and serving others seemed to further aggravate my honey. In the middle of this, knowing how the enemy works, I was given yet another task that would make me need to choose whether to obey what I knew was right or would just keep peace. Through the years at different times for very special occasions, Dennis and I had actually given loved ones special pieces of jewelry to commemorate a "word from the Lord" or a very significant decision they had made. Years before when our sons were of age to know right from wrong, they had vowed to God to give Him their whole lives. We commemorated this event by giving them very special rings that reminded them who they truly "belonged" to since rings are given to symbolize commitment. One time Dennis had been led by God to give our dear friend Trish a very special necklace that was a reminder of a promise from God concerning how much He loved her. On more than one occasion we provided rings to young people as we felt led, to be a tangible reminder of a very special event.

When I believed God said to also buy Jake a specific keepsake to be a physical sign of God's restoration and love for him I knew it was not unusual. I also knew that with all that was attacking Dennis, surely there would be false accusation from the devil as well as jealousy.

My own husband had prophesied that I would be the mother to many "sons" years before but that was a different place and time. I never could tell what kind of reaction I was going to get from Dennis. I prayed and cried and hoped for wisdom of how to navigate the waters of being faithful to my new call to be a real mother to Jake, knowing he deserved our best, and yet so aware of the warfare over my husband.

Greg was still visiting and so after purchasing the very special "Mizpah" necklace, I sat down with Dennis, Trish and Greg to share what I knew I had heard. Both our friends who knew about our giving and supporting in the past were adamant that I was to obey God and I explained to Dennis that the reason I was sharing with him and our friends, was that I didn't want the enemy to have any room to pervert, torment or misconstrue my actions. I whole heartedly wanted Dennis to be a part of this wonderful gift and wanted his support and blessing. With less than the greatest enthusiasm, he basically said whatever.I was glad whether he received it or not, that I had shared with our friends and they gave total support.

I still stand amazed at how God is so detailed and when we follow our hearts in the littlest of actions the most profound truths can be revealed. At the time, I had no idea the fullness of the word, "Mizpah" and why I had been asked to share this special gift with Jake. All I knew is I believed with all my heart that there was a very special bond that was holy, and important to God between us. I was to be his mothers hands extended on this earth.

The "Mizpah" which is a circle that has two halves, one to be kept by the giver, and one to be kept by the recipient. When I gave Jake the gift I had not researched the word, the fullness of the meaning or anything about it. I simply told Jake that this was from God, and that he needed to see what the fullness was. In general I relayed that at times in our lives, dad and I had given such gifts when prompted by the spirit and I hoped it was a reminder of God's faithfulness. I expressed that dad and I both were so blessed to have him in our lives and would be praying for him while he was in Nevada! So with that, Jake looked a little embarrassed and said okay.

What happened next confirmed that this was no accident and that if I had searched for a special meaningful gift I couldn't have done better. I discovered that in Genesis thirty-one verse forty-five; that "<u>JACOB</u>" made a memorial, with his father-in-law called "Mizpah" and said, "Let Yahweh act as watchman between us today, when we are no longer in sight of each other." Next the father-in-law advised Jacob on his days to come and told him not to ill-treat his daughters or marry others!

So here in the Bible was a story of "Jacob," which is actually the true root of the name "Jake," and how Jacob made a memorial to God called "Mizpah" where a beloved older relative asked God to watch over them when they were out of sight one from another. Truly Jake's mother in heaven is simply out of sight from him.

The other thing that was so heavy was that in mothering and parenting Jake, I had given him the most wonderful book that my son Israel had shared with me called "Innocence Lost, Hope Regained". It is a compilation by author, Richie Lambeth, of short stories, true stories of how different people of various backgrounds and beliefs had lost their innocence and the outcomes of these experiences. I do not know a single person who has held a brand new innocent baby and not thought about what on earth has happened to rob us all of our purity and innocence.

Giving this book about innocence lost, to Jake, I had very passionately shared about why God wanted purity and innocence and how to walk a meaningful life regarding relationships. As a woman and mom, I had shared with my new son that true love, thinks of far more than a fleshy self-satisfying moment. Far from an angry legalistic kill joy, my understanding of Gods reasons for being monogamous and pure was because He who created the purest form of Love, knew the cost to our hearts and souls of sharing intimacy with more than our true soul mate hand-picked by God! Sharing about the pain of abortions, rejections, suicidal bouts and so much more, I shared my own true story hoping that God would encourage Jake to live a life that would be patient and kind and yes, even think about the fact that every young lady he would meet, actually had been created to be respected, cherished and protected by honorable men. Wow! Here in the same place of the Bible it talked about Jacob. Mizpah, was the admonition to be pure and careful.

Last but not least, after even more study, I discovered that Mizpah, with numerous different sites in the Old Testament was a place where the prophet Samuel took all of Israel to repent for all disobedience to God as well as being a place of safety among other things. Yes, my new precious son was honestly heartbroken over some of the choices he had made while hurting so badly over his mother. Yet again, God had directed him to the good news that there was a place of healing and forgiveness.

The joys of discovering all these things helped me to put one foot after the other and try to focus on all that I saw that was good, in-spite of the daily challenges. I think the hardest part was so missing the true closeness with Dennis. Like the roof that was being repaired, the structure of our marriage revealed much was lacking and we were in the middle of a painful and long process.

I was starting to discover just how important not being isolated is and how incredibly helpful having true friends are when being tested and tried. As the house repairs came to an end, William shared that in spite of all of our differences he had come to the realization that as pretty as California was, in observing our love for our family, he realized he wanted to stay in Texas to be near his own children.

Now that is the greatest testimony to the power of God. In a time when Dennis and I had never been more messed up personally; somehow, someone saw something good. It just goes to show you that truly God can use who He wants and it always is about His goodness. The message is always about Jesus.

Trish and I had both taken summer school and when Trish finished some classes that were super accelerated she beamed like a kid getting their first "A." It was so good to see our friend start to heal and blossom. She had been so gracious and even though she knew things were really bothering Dennis she continued to support us both. At times she confessed to wanting to strangle him and yet she believed like I did with all of my heart, that God was actually behind the discontent and that there was nothing anyone could do but weather the storm.

To Dennis and I, Trish looked so much better and was getting back on her feet. What came next made our friend feel totally betrayed. Dennis had no more to give and honestly believed the Lord had directed him to tell Trish that it was time for her to go. I was so torn and yet remembering years before how he had ended up falling over with a heart attack from the cost his body pays with all the mental garbage, I felt like I was being called out on the carpet by God.

I was losing my marriage, losing my joy, and my spouse said I am telling you, Trish has had over three months and God will open a door. He must! God has said, "It is time for her to go" Dennis was exploding as he was talking, stressed to the max and explaining that he knew he was losing it, and felt like there was no place to be private. The truth was, Trish is very insightful, can read Dennis like a book and the last few weeks had taken to heading straight to her bedroom when at home so she wouldn't come between Dennis and I. Later she told me that she honestly thought it would cause Dennis to be nicer to me, but I was feeling guilty that the quality of life had changed from wonderful fellowship to where my friend was feeling as if she had to hide. The truth was, my dear friend was in our home by divine appointment to help us walk through this incredible time of testing, just as much as we were there to help her!

Praying for wisdom, I realized deep in my heart, I had to trust God with my friend, and support my husband. I didn't agree but knew he didn't know what else to do. He was feeling skinned alive and having an audience watch was just too much.

One morning Dennis shared with Trish in the kitchen that it was time to start looking for another place. I just stood there and tried to say that God would open a door, but it was very obvious Trish was incredibly crushed. It was as if, having the total three months, all the tenderness and love put into her little nest, and our wonderful times of friendship, all counted for nothing. It just simply devastated her and there was nothing to do but pray. Within a few days she shared that her old job in Texas had offered her a job back and that with no other doors out here opening, she would take door number one.

We asked if she was sure, and yet the damage had been done. Rejection had come on top of rejection and our best friend was not going to hang around where she knew she was not wanted. The hardest part was knowing, I would not have made the same choice. I totally enjoyed her company and I hadn't heard from the Lord the direction that Dennis was adamant about. Sometimes in life things are just hard and I hoped that someday God would show Trish that once again Dennis was honestly trying to do what he thought was right. Trish was his spiritual child who he has wept over in his heart probably more than anyone he knows, and here he was drowning in depression, doubt, jealousy and a whole host of other things that had him screaming to drive everyone away. Little did anyone know that Trish was simply the first in what ended up being a mass exodus from the house so that Dennis could experience being totally alone. Perhaps it was God, no matter how painful!

Chapter 54

"Tried by Fire"

MAMMA LORI SO MANY years before had written the following verse in the front of a wonderful Bible she had given to Dennis and I.

First Peter

"That the testing of your faith,
being more precious than gold that perishes,
and having been tested through fire,
may be found
to praise,
and honor,
and glory
in the revelation
of Jesus Christ.
(Heritage bible translation)

A good coach knows how to bring far more out of a person than they ever even thought was possible for themselves. Untapped potential…greatness…excellence. The next 18 months of our lives it would be fair to say, my husband and I were stretched far more than we could ever have imagined.

Looking back now it is plain to see why we needed the testing and fiery trial. How else is real life revealed? My uncle Lonnie once laughed and said "It is where the rubber meets the road, that you find out what someone really believes." Truly it is when gold gets totally melted that all of the impurities show.

It was the middle of August and temperatures often over one hundred degrees ushered in Jake's return to Visalia and the start of school. With Trish's departure, and our twenty-eighth wedding anniversary coming up, I tried to hang on to the non-stop roller coaster that I couldn't get off of. Having Israel still at home and lots of company, I was hoping for a miracle. Dennis became more and more verbally abusive and the meaner he got, the more determined I became to "fix" whatever was wrong.

Trying to make the best of the horrible year, I decided to totally spoil Dennis for our Anniversary. Remembering how when we first met, Dennis had romantically lit a bunch of candles to impress me, gave me an idea! Shopping at a local Marshalls, I found the most wonderful line of candles that individually each had a little leather tie and a little square bronze medallion hanging on each candle. The medallions had the Japanese sign for words like "happiness," "peace," etc. They came in various sizes and I decided that I was going to buy not one, or two… but twenty-eight, one for every year we had been married. Next I went to a little store in town called "La Passione" and spent a small fortune on the most beautiful negligee I had ever seen. Inside I honestly didn't even know if Dennis would even be talking to me when the day came but I was choosing to do everything I could to try to let Dennis know I needed him and wanted to work things out. Reserving a cabin getaway 30 miles away in a little mountain community known as Three Rivers, I also made arrangements to spend the morning on a rented house boat just a few miles away. As the day arrived, while Dennis and I were enjoying the houseboat at the lake, Israel snuck up to the cabin and filled the room with over 28 candles (one for every year we had been married). He brought a CD player complete with a custom recorded CD of all of our favorite music we had shared, my specially bought negligee, heels, sparkling cider, and a black silk robe I bought for Dennis. My precious son even sprinkled rose petals in the room and later kidded me about the fact that he felt a little awkward. In spite of that, Israel even left a beautiful card from him to us and it meant the world to both Dennis and I.

A few days before our anniversary, Dennis got mad about something and ended up yelling that he wanted a divorce! Still undaunted, I let things cool for a few days and when it came to a day before our anniversary my husband half-heartedly said something to the effect of, "So you want to do anything on our anniversary?" I couldn't comprehend that Dennis really didn't understand how mind bending all of this was, and no matter how I tried to bury the pain, I felt like a kicked dog that would cower when ever its master came around. Remembering Terra Bella where unconditional love had broken my husband before, I tried to continue to ignore the cutting, heart breaking behavior of a few days earlier and said, "Sure, let's go ahead and celebrate."

The weekend getaway was better than I expected and we talked for the first time in a long time. We talked about our children and blessings and tried to figure out what on earth had been going on with us. The next morning sitting over-looking the beautiful mountain scenery my husband had Jake on his heart. At one point Israel had mentioned that he wanted to help his friend out and wished he could live with us! In-spite of the battles within, Dennis asked me if I wanted Jake to live with us! I was honest and said, "Yes!" I had seen the way this young man touched our family and I wanted to honor Israel's place in our home as well, by opening our home up to someone he cared about. I honestly believed that when Dennis was giving what he could it helped him stay in touch with the man of Terra Bella who wanted to share Jesus in word and deed. The man who loves Jesus. All I knew was that for several years before Trish came, being alone with just Israel and I, had not solved any of Dennis's problems. I also knew that often giving was a response to challenges that seemed to accompany divine intervention!

Arriving home, Dennis took a copy of our true story, "Breaking Chains" and told me to call Jake up and invite him over. I did and when Jake read what Dennis had written in the inscription to him, he looked moved! Dennis told Jake, he had seen his character and thought a lot of him and wanted to help him out. Prophetically, Dennis also wrote that he hoped Jake could handle Dennis's issues. Little did any of us know what was to come. Inviting Jake to officially move in, I felt a breath of fresh air and it seemed maybe Dennis hadn't forgotten everything that we had learned.

After Jake moved in, I was enjoying mothering someone who was so appreciative and Dennis seemed to be feeling good about himself. Both Israel and Jake were gone a lot with school and work and I couldn't have been happier with those areas of my life. Having fun in school and finishing the requirements to transfer to a university made me feel alive and worthwhile. For the first time, I had taken horse-back riding, something I had wanted to do for over 30 years. Asking Dennis to take the class with me, he laughed and let me know, it wasn't even a remote possibility. Clearly communication was still often not happening and I started verbalizing a need to go to counseling, a marriage seminar, or anything for help. I was starting to realize that it seemed life with Dennis was okay as long as everything was his way, his timing, and what he wanted! His life seemed to consist of health battles, oldies but goodies, and a desire to watch lots and lots of TV.

I couldn't understand how he could be satisfied with that routine, and yet I still tried to be understanding. Sitting in the parking lot of the local junior college, I listened to Jack Johnson singing about "Banana Pancakes" and love. Class was over and I was preparing to go home when I burst into tears and realized my heart was broken. No, worse than broken, I literally had no desire to have any relationship with Dennis what so ever. As the simple words conveyed the songs message I wondered what had happened to my girlhood dreams of love and happiness. Literal blinders were lifted and what I saw was horrible. Literally gasping for air, my mind screamed to God questions right and left. What was going on? Why was I so blind? Where had I been?

All I can tell you is that I knew as deeply as I know my own name, this was not just an emotional female moment brought on by the passing of time. I knew, that I knew, that I knew, I had been given a glimpse of reality and it was devastating. Still questioning, asking the Holy Spirit, the "comforter," "My God, what on earth was wrong with me? I know you are the one who holds my heart in your hand. I love you. What is wrong with my heart concerning Dennis and his towards me?" What I heard next was direct and clear and straight from God.

"I have hardened your heart! It is not the enemy. Just like I said in my word it was Me that hardened Pharaoh's heart for My purposes, and I have hardened yours. There are areas in your relationship with Dennis that are not pleasing to me and you will not deal with them unless I allow this pain."

Evidently for years, our heavenly Father had supernaturally "covered" some incredible dysfunction while Dennis and I focused on all the wonderful things that were happening with our children, our friends, and the true story of how Jesus has so impacted our lives.

"Change of Life?" Yes! Absolutely! With all of our hearts, Dennis and I want to share the true story of how real Jesus is and that when invited, He longs to teach us the ways of His Father and the real kingdom, the kingdom of the one true God! We as his children, are to grow from glory to glory and **be** a living revelation of His love for the world.

In the area of respect, and God's idea for marriage, ours evidently needed growth and until we saw where we truly were at, we couldn't be helped. If you don't believe there is a problem, you cannot be helped and now, I was forced into facing the fact, both Dennis and I were really messed up relationally and the years of dysfunction had now taken effect. Family and friends could clearly see all this dysfunction and now it seemed the time had arrived for home improvements.

Weeping harder as the words to more songs seemed to point out much that was missing, I just couldn't get past the pain of realizing, I could not fake, cover or fix what was happening in my heart. Slowly driving home, I tried to fight the horrible pain.

The Spirit of God continued to reveal much over the next several days and I was told that Dennis was wrestling God Himself and there was nothing, I could do to fix this situation! After the initial shock I decided to write a letter, sharing what was going on inside and hoped that Dennis would see this crises as an opportunity to grow, not fall apart! As I poured out six pages of exhortation, I could not believe what I was seeing.

I was a first-class enabler and had unknowingly done every classic move to play into horrible dysfunction. No wonder Dennis and I needed to grow, while we were telling the world how free we were, there was this glaring fact, that for people who claimed to have it so together, we still were carrying lots and lots of garbage. We were hurting others as well as ourselves. It's true only God is perfect, yet excuses seem empty when staring into a mirror of goodness and love.

Even an idiot wants to remove a splinter from his own foot. Now, Dennis and I were about to enter into a process that would honestly have us wondering if we would survive.

> The Wikipedia , free encyclopedia defines "***Process***" as movement. "A naturally occurring, or designed sequence of, "changes of attributes, of a system or object".

Dennis and I were ready to have some changes!

If God wanted us to go through a fire to reveal what needed to be removed, then so be it! My only prayer was that we would survive the process, and that we wouldn't hurt others in the process.

Writing this incredible love letter to Dennis, I actually thought God would do an instant change. I thought my heart would be restored and all would be well. Right!...No, wrong! I had written down and chronicled what I saw as the true state of affairs, so that Dennis could digest, pray and think before he reacted. One of the side effects related to being a war veteran was exploding at anything unforeseen and thinking later, so I truly believed it would be wisdom to write a letter rather than try to communicate verbally when I knew my husband was bound to be defensive.

Rage, anger, and total disbelief, might partly paint a picture of Dennis' reaction to receiving my letter of love! It didn't matter, that I was so heartbroken, or that I had honestly said I was truly excited for God to teach us how to love and respect each other. All Dennis saw was communication that said he had done something wrong, and that was not ok! Throwing the offending message back at me, it was clear, he totally believed I was trying to hurt him. Declaring that nothing was wrong, Dennis yelled that obviously I was crazy, going through the change and I was going to kill him with all of this nonsense. In his words, "We are fine!"

Change, communication, and help, were all filthy words to Dennis and the fact that his wife was now confronting him added even more fuel to the fire.

In my original letter there was not even the suggestion that I wanted anything but restoration and God's will, and for us to grow as a couple to be more like Jesus! My husband's wounded pride responded with denial, accusation and anger. How could this be? Hadn't we ministered worldwide about how to save your marriage? Now, it seemed I didn't even know this angry man who was furious at the "light" that had revealed some darkness!

As God continued to lift blinders, I couldn't believe what I was discovering about myself. The hardest part was the realization as I cried out to God, "Why did you show me this?" I was happier when I was stupid, and blind! Seeing reality was harsh and no amount of wishful thinking could change what I knew in my heart. I didn't know from moment to moment which Dennis I was going to get.

There had been a great cost, being the wife of a "wounded warrior" and I was now honestly suffering literally from secondary PTSD myself. Years of being kept at arm's length from my closest friend had left neediness, loneliness and a totally broken heart! Exhausted from being the enemy, I had fought, and stood and battled for over 26 years with and for Dennis. Now that I needed him, I was accused of wanting to hurt him. It was if all the years of being there for him meant nothing and I thought I would go out of my mind. The Lord reminded me, "Dennis is wrestling me not you".

One Friday afternoon, shortly after giving Dennis the letter he verbally told be off about something and told me to get out. So I decided I was going to go visit my friend Joy.

Years before, we had made a wonderful friend who worked for TBN and knew what a pure heart this wonderful lady had. Totally out of character, I packed a few things without saying a word to Dennis, and decided to drive three hours away for the weekend!

Calling once I was on the road, I left a message for Dennis and then called my girl friend. Thankfully, Joy answered with a warm hello! Asking if she wanted company I laughed and said I was actually on the way! Simply taking a trip to visit a friend was incredibly liberating. Thinking as I headed south, I sensed the weekend needed to be spent in some girl time and anything that was not religious.

A whirlwind weekend included the Long Beach Aquarium, lunch at Bubba Gumps and shopping to boot! Laughing and enjoying female companionship I couldn't help but realize how few and far between good healthy relationships with some girl friends were. It was so good to spend time with someone who loved to laugh and we both felt like school girls gone crazy! Before leaving town, Joy took me to one of her favorite restaurants and there where you would least expect it, after several days of totally letting our hair down, we ended up having an incredible time of fellowship with the Spirit of God. We barely could eat, due to the tears and revelation that was shared between the two of us!

Joy who is incredibly sensitive to the moving of the Spirit of God, handed me a page from a workbook of a precious man named Dave Mick. In a nutshell, I was reading an explanation about how wounded people who don't deal with wounds will develop insecurity and allow fear to become a driver in their lives. The fear of being wounded even more, will allow pride and other deceptions to take control of our lives in areas where we should trust God. Truthfully, whenever control and manipulation are running anyone, God has been left out of the equation.

Relating to all the wounds Dennis and I both had been through in life, I remember him angrily exclaiming on more than one occasion, that he would never trust anybody including me! What I was reading seemed to validate what I was walking through with Dennis and the issue of feeling like I was always held at arms length.

Next Joy gave me some Joyce Meyer CDs. Starting the drive home I looked forward to the "manna" from heaven. As this lady taught I knew she was speaking directly to me! Boy was I naïve. Here I was constantly pointing the way to Jesus, wanting to be the "answer" for my husband, and I had already been told, that for whatever reason, Dennis was in the middle of a wrestling match! Great, He was struggling with God and every time he turned around, I was saying, "Go to God!" Wonderful!

After the wonderful time with Joy and listening to words of encouragement, I was ready to take on all of hell! That was until a few weeks later. I was now walking a path of loneliness I never would have imagined. I wanted so badly to protect our sons and our daughters, but through the years we had invested so much in them spiritually, that they honestly were our closest friends. I felt like God was saying, don't isolate, cry out for help, and yet Isaac, Isaiah and Israel could only bare to hear so much! Dad kept telling the boys mom was "just going through the change," and yet they really didn't know how dark it had gotten behind closed doors. Dennis was now using the word divorce on a regular basis and often demanded that I get out of "his house." All of this was done when no one was at home, so in the beginning Israel and Jake were spared the worst. I could not bare to hear the word divorce and I continued to give Dennis special cards, write letters and tried to communicate in every way I knew how. I was totally exhausted from being the enemy, not being trusted and I needed my husband to allow me into his heart.

The more I tried to communicate, the meaner Dennis became. I must have been pushing every button without meaning to, but for the first time, I was speaking up about the horrible things he would say. I started suggesting that Dennis needed to "go to the mountain" like he used to, to seek God, but he was so insecure he thought I was simply trying to get rid of him. Dennis' biggest battle was denial and mine was to stop trying to "help" the situation.

Chapter 55

"Friendly Fire"

Do you really think
Anyone cares
That the fire that burns…. is friendly?

Hearts and body parts
Pieces of promises
Are all being blown away
I need you to see
The power you have over me

I know you didn't mean to
But the outcomes just the same
You lean over me, and cry from the truth
You've done it once again

Searing, Burning, Pain I can't control
Someone save me

You didn't mean to do…
You didn't mean to say….
The words that shot like fire, through my soul today

Hearts and body parts
Pieces of promises
Are all being blown away
I need you to see
The power you have over me

I know you didn't mean to
But the outcomes just the same
You lean over me, and cry from the truth
You've done it once again

Kneeling in blood like a child with toys
You cry out to God above
Breathe, Get up, you scream through your pain
I think I've killed my love

THE WORDS FLOWED LIKE a river and I continued to be amazed at how the Lord used creativity to help keep me sane. "Friendly Fire", was my daily existence and it was time to admit it…expose it… and deal with it. Writing yet one more letter of encouragement to Dennis I included the words to let him know the condition of our relationship.

Whether writing words to a new song, cooking home-cooked meals for the boys and their friends, or encouraging Israel and Jake to keep playing their guitars, every day was a step into the twilight zone. I never had any idea what I would be facing. I was so grateful the boys were around to pray for us and add some balance to the home front. Yet mixed with that gratitude was the most horrible guilt that I wanted my sons to be in a place of love and support and they were surrounded by a war zone.

One moment my husband would say he wanted to try to understand, and the next I was informed everyone was telling him I just had hormone problems so he felt totally justified in his behavior. At these times I offered to go to counseling if he truly thought I had a problem, but Dennis would not consider it! There was no way he wanted to talk to any stranger when he was already feeling so betrayed. In his mind, the fact that I was admitting we needed help, meant I was now even more of an enemy than before! Meanwhile, God was getting ready to free me from old rejections while the person I had trusted the most with my heart was going after me with a vengeance.

One afternoon my husband was angry once again and I begged him to calm down. The next thing I knew, he announced he was divorcing me, and would never be back. Coldly packing his special suitcase that fit on his Harley, I continued to follow him around the house trying to talk some sense into him. Frankly I was so tired from all the fighting and hearing the word "divorce" continued to batter my heart even more. I honestly was surprised that I could even feel pain. I just wanted some peace and knew inside I had no power to fix what was wrong. Following Dennis to his motorcycle I continued to tell him he simply needed a break, and that God could fix this mess. Telling me no matter what else, I had been a great mother to his children, He climbed on his bike and told me I would probably never see him again as the devil would probably kill him if he didn't do it himself!

Walking into the house, again my first thought was gratefulness to God that the boys hadn't seen Dennis saying all these hateful things. My heart still seemed more concerned at how others might be hurt by his behavior. For months I had been covering, making calls, making excuses and trying not to let anyone know that our home was a war zone. I had quite a well developed habit of thinking it was my job to apologize for Dennis and explain how he didn't really mean to do the things that he did.

All of that was about to change. That evening, I decided to go visit both sons, who worked at different Starbucks. I knew I could sit home and worry, or try to believe that in a few days Dennis would figure out he really didn't want to be away from home and hopefully me. He had already taken off several other times by now but it had never lasted more than a few hours, and I honestly was ready for a few days rest.

Going upstairs into my bedroom I pulled out a pair of jeans I was particularly proud of. The weight I had lost had allowed me for the first time in years to feel good about the clothes I was wearing. The more angry and jealous Dennis became, the more I decided to ignore him and continue to try to take good care of myself. Later I discovered this played into insecurities he was already fighting, no matter how I tried, nothing I did was ok. While everyone else commented on how great I looked, Dennis was critical, accusing me of wanting to have people stare at me for all the wrong reasons. One day as I headed out the door to school I had on a new outfit and was told that I had no business looking nice unless he was there. I could not believe what I was hearing!

Well I was about to have an epiphany and it was a moment that was incredibly freeing. As I pulled on these pants I looked longingly at a pair of boots I had only worn one time for Trish's wedding. Along with all the other "restrictions" I had been told not to ever wear shoes that made me as tall, or taller than my husband.

Deciding I needed to feel "special"…a "girl thing" I decided to wear these boots. As I sat on the bed to put them on, I pulled one boot on after the other. Just as I was zipping up the second boot, I heard the roar of a Harley motorcycle and without even thinking, immediately started to change my clothes so my husband wouldn't get mad. My first thought was that I would be in trouble if Dennis saw me wearing high heels. I found myself literally shaking so badly, I couldn't get the boots off and then my son Isaiah knocked on the door.

Taking a deep breath, I heard the bike keep going, and headed downstairs to let my son in the door. Asking my son if I looked ok, he answered without having a clue how badly I needed his approval. Rejection would try to rear it's ugly head, after all, my husband had just said he was leaving me for good again. I felt so unloved! Isaiah laughingly told me that I looked great. "Mom, since you lost weight you have been dressing differently, but I think it's nice." Assuring me I didn't look "hoochie," my son gave me a great big hug and said goodbye as I ran out the door deciding not to change.

After visiting Israel awhile, I headed out to where Jake worked and happened to arrive just as he got his break! "Hey mom, I'm walking over to McDonalds for a bite, wanna come?" "Sure", I responded happily. Walking across the parking lot we laughed and talked about Jake's work, and how his friends were doing. Stepping inside McDonalds all of a sudden it was like blinders were lifted off of my eyes and I literally saw myself falling apart at the thought that my clothing might "displease" my husband!

My God! Hear Dennis had just told me for the umpteenth time that he was leaving me, hated me, wanted a divorce and had been horrible emotionally abusive and my reaction? Fear that I might do something that wouldn't please him! Talk about control and manipulation! I saw red and gasping, I couldn't believe what I was seeing. There is a thing called righteous indignation, and I think this may have been that. All I can tell you is I was so angry and for the first time saw how clearly I had been enabling very unhealthy control and knew that the same demons who had been trying to control Dennis had been doing a pretty fair job of manipulating me as well.

I could not take anymore. Remembering how I used to enjoy a Heineken beer occasionally when I was younger, I stopped off at a Seven Eleven to pick up what my sons refer to as a "forty!" That means not small, not twelve ounces. Dennis had left again telling me he was leaving forever, and I knew Jake and Buck were at work. I think I'll have a pretzel, some beer and sharp cheese! Come to think of it, I was ticked now about everything it seemed. Here I was often not being honest about what I would like, always thinking of Dennis.

Something had always bothered me about the way we would pride ourselves over the fact that we "didn't drink," as if that made us better than someone else. I remember hearing Dennis say one time to someone that if he allowed himself one drink he would be drunk for ten years. Thinking all of this through I thought, that's not freedom! Now if God himself had said to Dennis, "Don't drink" then Dennis shouldn't drink. But not because he a man full of the Holy Spirit thought he was incapable of stopping. I think if our society diagnosis one more form of selfishness as a "disease" I will absolutely scream!

Yes, anything that is done to excess is harmful and you invite demonic influence, oppression and then possession. There is a path there however and a condition of the heart that is way deeper than those surface actions! So I had decided, I was sick and tired of feeling responsible for being a guiding light for a man who was now constantly treating me like dung! His choices were his, he was wrestling God, and I was going to enjoy a beer! I did and it was good! I even felt a little less judgmental of many who I had judged.

Two days later when Dennis called to say hello he made the mistake of starting the conversation by saying, "Oh, I suppose your having a lot of fun." No apology. No remorse. No, How are you? The phone call literally started with accusation. The truth was that a bunch of Israel's friends had spent the night to keep me company, and we had all prayed for Dennis and I continued to speak that he was going to be fine, and I was sure he just needed a break.

With the accusation I literally started yelling at the phone and told him in no uncertain terms that I was the angriest I had ever been in my entire life. I told Dennis that if he wanted to let demons of depression, anger, and manipulation control his life, that was up to him, but I was not going to entertain any of that! On top of that I informed him of what I had been shown about demons controlling and manipulating. I screamed into the phone that I would never ever be controlled like that again, and as long as I was satisfied that what I was wearing was fine, I would wear what I wanted, including high heels… "click," the phone was hung up by Dennis.

The next call two days later was from a humbler man, who said he didn't know why he was riding around in circles and he thought we could work out what ever differences we had at home together! "Come on home," I said without hesitation, I think we can work this out to too.

Chapter 56

"The Gifts"

As the fall progressed, there was a small glimmer of hope in an incredibly dark place! Isaiah had encouraged Dennis and I to go to a "Family Life" weekend marriage conference for quite some time and Dennis committed to going. I was ecstatic and with the hope that admitting we needed help was meaningful, I looked forward to one of my dreams.

I honestly had come to a point that if Dennis hadn't agreed to go, I believed our marriage was over. Up to now, I had a basket filled with wonderful love letters to Dennis, awesome books given to me, and him as gifts, and lots of cards that encouraged we could come through this trial, and what had he given? One or two cards, basically saying thanks for not giving up on him.

Driving towards Monterey, Dennis was acting upset and the knot in my stomach grew as I realized something was very wrong. Confessing that he was honestly furious about missing a big playoff football game, I stared straight ahead in shock. Pictures of my hope-full, smiling faced boys, waving goodbye as we headed off, ran through my brain and the thought of this weekend being less than a brand new beginning literally made me feel sick.

The mother instinct, wanted so badly, to protect my children from any pain and things kept happening way beyond my control, and they were getting hurt!

So this was the big effort to save our marriage. I had just battled months, still felt totally betrayed, wounded and dead inside. I had allowed myself some hope that Dennis truly was struggling and not some selfish monster. Now on the road, to the very first effort in over 28 years of marriage to invest in us, he was "pissed-off "about missing a football game.

Wow! Excuse me. Silly, silly, thoughtless, Diana. I hadn't planned trying to save our marriage around a football game.

My husband went on to share that I should simply be grateful that he was showing up, since he was sure I was the problem! Yep, all I needed were some hormone shots and that would take care of all of his abusive treatment, the years of not dealing with all the dysfunction from the PTSD, and almost no communication the last three years.

He honestly believed that junk. I guess I was discovering he had come more to appease me than for anything else. So much for the dream get away. Arriving, we unpacked while Dennis asked what we had to go to that night and what the schedule was. I was starting to feel like the only reason he was here was because it included a "date-night" and he was hoping to get "lucky." I know that's a horrible thing to say about a married couple, but I finally was owning up to the fact it was too destructive for me to try to fake wanting to have any physical contact with Dennis.

We were not friends. We were not having any communication, and usually after a particularly abusive emotional episode, Dennis would want to reaffirm his claim on me by getting physical and I just couldn't do it anymore. For the first time in our marriage, I allowed myself the right of not feeling responsible for Dennis's happiness at the expense of my own soul.

I had heard of women who had used emotions and their bodies to manipulate and punish their husbands so for years, I had bent over backwards to make sure that no matter what was happening in my heart, I took care of making my husband happy. I am not kidding...after all... in Terra Bella I had learned that love never fails. I can honestly say there were times when my heart was so broken from unkind words, I would beg God to get them out of my head, and when they wouldn't leave, I would make love to my husband anyway even though I literally would feel raped.

You see, I was now seeing how dishonest I had been, in trying to please Dennis, and he had unknowingly become an idol. If truth was to prevail, it was time to get honest and real about every area of our marriage. I guess the question is, what is real love? I was finally realizing true love would trust God, and I needed to let Dennis know how I was doing whether he wanted to hear it or not.

These truths were hitting my hero at the core of his masculinity and yet I was literally sickened at the thought of going from hearing the word divorce one moment, and then being told I should be "in the mood" the next, because he was a man with "needs."

It never occurred to me that Dennis wouldn't have wanted me to be with him when I didn't want to be. I was so busy trying to make the way smooth, and do Gods job, I had taken a vulnerable wounded friend and had helped make him think his happiness was the ultimate goal!

Where in the word does it say that? Where did Jesus say, "Follow me and your life will be a bed of roses?" It doesn't!

So here we were at the very start of a process called communication and God was demanding honesty from me. Honesty with the man who's approval I wanted more than anything in the whole world. And all of my disclosures were causing us both, great pain. I never thought of myself as a dishonest person and yet here the Lord was showing me I had been horribly dishonest in the most intimate area of trust.

Hoping for the best, I ignored Dennis' grumbling and we found ourselves sitting in the Friday evening conference laughing our heads off. The speakers were great and as they handed us the work booklet for the weekend I was thrilled. "Weekend to Remember" was the title on the manual." These people spoke my language and everything in the booklet addressed the issues both Dennis and I were discovering. Opening it I saw the first two sessions focused on:

Five Threats to Oneness

- The first threat is difficulty to adjustments,

- the second threat is for couples to enter marriage based on performance,
- the third threat is failing to anticipate selfishness,
- the fourth threat is our response to trials
- the fifth threat is affairs whether they be family, or career, or activities, or love.

...and the results of not knowing how to deal with these? ISOLATION ! Hadn't I been trying to tell Dennis that we had been through many adjustments and calls in our lives and he had just retreated into isolation? Yes his call as a prophet demanded seasons of isolation, but wounds and challenges had turned seasons into years and he now was wanting isolation from even his own wife and children! He was threatened by my going to school, growing older, and our children leaving home. His reaction to these events was a textbook response of trying to fight change as if change was a dirty word.

This conference was designed so that after teaching, we were given a time to individually write down our responses to what we had heard answering some very hard but necessary questions. Then as couples we were to come together and share. Then finally, in the back of the book, there was a place for making a specific plan of action since the point of the whole conference is to do something different. It taught us how to apply what we had learned..

I was so ready to solve our greatest problems and wipe away what was standing in between us. I just could not imagine that Dennis was not ready. So imagine it! We went to the sessions the first two days and even though we never one time made a specific plan of action, I told myself that simply hearing these people was better than nothing.

Saturday was date night and much to our surprise Dennis discovered that the game he had been so concerned about was actually going to be on. Knowing that it was our date night, he laughed about finding out and then said he was willing to humor me and go on a date instead of watching the game he wanted to see. After getting dressed up in a brand new outfit, my husband actually noticed and said how nice I looked. He even complimented the little black high heels I was wearing.

Strolling along the Cannery Row, I had envisioned a dinner at my favorite seafood place, Bubba Gumps, but as we walked along I noticed across the road, a Pizzeria with a giant big screen with guess what on it? The Game...Dennis hadn't noticed and pausing for a moment, I knew I had an opportunity to give him a truly unexpected gift.

Weren't we both struggling with so much and trying to survive this process? Taking Dennis's hand I steered him over to the restaurant, and seeing the big screen he looked surprised. "What? I thought we were going to get a special dinner at Bubba's"? Batting my eyes at him I said, "I'm in the mood for football, and laid a big long kiss on him!" Grinning from ear to ear like a little kid, my sweetheart discovered that the game they were showing was the one he wanted to watch, so ordering from the menu, we both curled into the booth to watch the whole game. Slipping my leg over his under the table cloth in the booth, I continued to surprise my husband with a clear sign of a promising evening, and snuggling closer, the message was clear.

Truce.*
"*a respite especially from a disagreeable or painful state or action"

The rest of the evening was wonderful and after an intimate evening once again, "faith was the substance of things hoped for... the evidence...of things unseen.

Chapter 57

"Highway to Hell"

IT ONLY TOOK TWO days for Dennis to make it abundantly clear he had no intention, of discussing any problems, making any plans, praying together, or anything else. Once again, our views of what had been accomplished were incredibly different. My husband thought it was miraculous that he had done me the "favor" of even showing up for the seminar. He felt that was worth him being left alone for another six months. After all, we didn't have any problems and I simply needed more hormones. On the other hand, I wanted to be on the same page and was tired of the roller coaster ride! The conference for me was a last ditch effort to see if he even wanted to address the fact that we needed help.

I didn't like the answer I got when only two short days after coming home I tried to pick up our special books and broached the subject of actually communicating about our marriage, maybe finish all the parts we hadn't, etc. Screaming divorce from the top of his lungs, I was assured that he had no intention of counseling, working on anything, and I better well like it or get the hell out! I was ruining his life by bringing up these problems and his solution was to ignore them and they all would go away!

With Christmas only a month away, I was told to put on a charade for the "kids sake." We would talk about how we were going to end this once and for all after the holiday! Because if I didn't hide all this from the kids, I was the worst mom in the world!

Nice. Convinced now that I was living with Dr. Jekyl, Mr Hyde, I decided to simply do just that. Thumbing my nose in the devils face, I bought all of the married kids presents from the conference aimed at keeping the romance in their marriage and spent my time making the house extra nice for Christmas.

Taking a job at a local Applebees restaurant, I decided to get out of the house even more and simply stay away from the "friendly fire." The less I was around, the less I could be emotionally bruised. There was always a host of hurting people who really seemed to appreciate the love and joy that God had given me to share with this world. Dennis wasn't wanting anything to do with his wife and her gifts, so by golly, I continued to look for opportunities to try to be a shining light for Jesus!

Spending New Year's Eve away from Dennis I awoke in the mountains to a new day and the smell of fresh fallen snow. I remember it as if it was yesterday and the sunlight was so bright. Ice crystals glistened and a soft wind pushed new snow off the tips of the evergreen branches that had been freshly coated the night before.

Walking towards the lodge where I could get a cup of coffee, I was hit with such sadness that Dennis wasn't there to share such a serene, peaceful, magical moment. As I walked I talked with God and realized that taking the job at Applebees had not helped what Dennis was going through. He was crying out for help with his words and actions and I was adding so much busyness that I was convincing him I didn't need him at all! That really was not my original intention. I was constantly trying to check my heart and make sure that my choices were following Jesus, not being mean or spiteful.

Arriving at the lodge I called Dennis and let him know that I was going to quit Applebees as I knew it upset him and I knew how much stretching we both were doing. I told him as soon as I was home from the mountains, I was going to tuck in and watch the football games with him. He didn't really react like I thought he would, but I was determined to show support in any way I could without being dishonest .

With January started, I waited to see if Dennis was serious about separating, or if he was just venting yet again. Classes at the local college started up and one day on campus I discovered that there was a part-time job in the counselor's office. Begrudgingly I took the job, as we needed the financial help and working 20 hours a week helped me to try to hang in there for Israel and Jake. At the time I accepted the offer I had no idea what was ahead and had pictured one of my own personal worst nightmares, a boring office job,

All of my grown children were struggling through this horrible, horrible time of testing and refining. Israel and Jake knew that things were bad between Dennis and I but thankfully, they were at work and school a lot. Dennis spent a lot of his time at home either parked in front of the TV, or by himself upstairs in the bedroom, where no one would bother him.

Israel was talking about possibly moving out in the fall and Jake was taking about moving away in June so I was determined to outlast both the boys! I felt so responsible for offering Israel and Jake a warm home, and there was no way I was going to strand them. Running from school to work, and home to cook meals, I simply tried to lay low, leave Dennis alone, and put up with his foul moods. He was now really angry that I wasn't romantically inclined, and I was determined to be 100% honest and fake nothing!

As my birthday approached, once again my husband exploded over something and informed me that I would be celebrating it "alone." You know…when the going gets tough…the tough get going. Israel just happened to be in a band that was going to be leading praise and worship up in the mountains at a Christian camp, so I decided to try to make the best of the occasion. Calling a young lady who I had adopted like a daughter, I also made plans to go from the church camp over to the coast for a few days.

I was starting to spread my wings and it was very empowering when it came to where I went and what I did. Everything had always been around Dennis. His syndrome, his health, his moods, his need to be kept busy! I somehow had become probably the biggest stumbling block to the very growth God was wanting. As blinders continued to be lifted I still had trouble believing how blind I had been. Friends and family were brutally honest and suggested that I had helped make this mess and encouraged me to do what I needed to for peace, yet never was giving up an option from any of them.

Preparing to leave Visalia to drive to the mountains, I decided I wanted to celebrate my birthday with a very special drink. After all, here I was celebrating my birthday by myself. So heading into the local Albertsons, I bought some Mikes' Hard Lemonaide, or maybe it was Jose Cuervo's pre-bottled Margaritas! God knows! As I was checking out, there stood my beautiful daughter in-law followed by my son Isaac! Saying something about how I was headed out of town, I could have sworn, I saw a look of surprise on Heather's face. Mercifully neither one of them said anything, and yet I could hardly help wondering what my children would think about seeing their mother buying alcohol after all the years we had preached against having any at all!

Fire was revealing a lot about Dennis and I, and all I knew was that I continued to try to pray and follow what I felt at peace with deep in my heart. After spending an awesome night, where Israel was, I gave my son a new guitar to celebrate my birthday. Son, I really want to honor God, and hurt the enemy bad. Please use this acoustic to play praises to God. You see, trust even in the midst of the storm, somehow in spite of all the warfare there were glimpses of the kingdom, and the one who was refining Dennis and I. According to scripture, offering a sacrifice of praise when you can not understand how on earth anything is going to workout is one of the highest gifts of faith and trust you can give God!

Think about it! What do you really believe? Has God carved you in the palm of His hand as Isaiah 49:16 says? Do we as Gods children honestly believe anything that He says? Why do you thing worry is considered a sin? Our whole nation has majored on worry! We are going to do Gods job and protect you, fend for you, feed you, teach you, yes, according to the actions of most, we don't even need a Holy Spirit anymore.

Scripture says that we actually only need the Holy Spirit to teach us. But no, like the religious men of old, we want to be taught by men, and blame them for our problems. We often keep God at arms length, and go our own way! Some say God is dead! Is He?

Trusting God again, I felt better, but, Dennis felt even more threatened and didn't know how to cope. He was still at a stage wanting to blame me for all of his issues and I was not accepting that any longer. Not only that, I decided to start living life, and if he wanted to stay isolated, and depressed, that was his choice. I was meeting many hurting women at my new job at the college, and had a bunch of Israel's friends who really loved having an extra mom, so I decided to pray and obey. I can say from the bottom of my heart I never purposefully tried to hurt Dennis and I simply stopped enabling all the dysfunction!

Through the spring, the kids and I went to a destruction derby, rode bicycles, walked the track, played tennis, rode horses, and more. I literally invited Dennis everywhere I went, but he would usually say "No" right off the bat, and if he said "maybe," he always managed to explode before the event came up and then would pout if I went anyway. I took my first riding class and absolutely loved it. I started playing guitar and wrote several songs that helped my heart through this incredibly hard time. Having received my AA in December, I now was working on transfer units and an AS at the local college.

Working at the school turned out to be an absolutely divine assignment and several precious ladies prayed with me through some days where it felt like my heart was being pulled apart piece by piece. One of the most memorable days was when a little lady named Alma, arrived in the counselors' office to see a friend Sylvia who worked there. Sylvia had called me into her office and she sensed that things were not well on the home front. Arriving Alma handed me a white daisy and mentioned that the Lord was specific she was to give it to me. After a wonderful time with the ladies, I hurried home to see what a "white daisy" stood for. "Innocence," bursting into tears, I literally got on my knees to thank God. He knew how many mouths were falsely accusing. No one, not even the boys had any idea the true picture behind the scenes and that truly, no matter how many times I heard I was hated, or stupid, or to blame, I kept trying to believe that what I heard from the beginning was the truth. Dennis was wrestling God, and I was catching the fall out. It seemed like whenever there was a really important test, that would be a day that Dennis would end up screaming at me and it is a miracle, I made it through school.

Sometimes, I would go to the local Save Mart and buy carrots to take with me to feed the horses, at the Ag farm. Carrots were not all that I bought! Sometimes, I would chug a few beers or some other brew and after getting a warm tingling feeling, the pain that was crushing my heart would subside a little! Taking a breath, I would feed the horses, and try to convince myself that everything was really all right, and I was just too sensitive. All I can say for myself is that God is the judge and my intention was never to harm anyone.

I held myself to such a legalistic standard for so many years. I had embraced a life of celebrating dead works. It was my badge of maturity. Now I understood that honesty, humility, and allowing myself to be needy or weak actually allowed people to approach me more easily.

Through the fire, God used all of my children, and even their friends to be the hands of God, and love when I needed it most. For years we had been in the highways and byways solo for Jesus, and now I was seeing how important the body of Christ is. I cannot imagine having gone through this alone. That was probably the hardest thing for me to understand. From the beginning, God had confirmed to Dennis that I wasn't crazy.

One time when things had gotten so bad that I had literally slept downstairs in my son Israel's room, my angry husband told us all off, and then went to bed. The next morning, I was awakened softly, by a humbler man with a cup of coffee in his hand, literally in tears. "I have been up all night in pain I cannot even describe. God told me that He was allowing me to feel a little of the pain you have been in. I am so ashamed," he confessed. He promised to try to get to the bottom of what was going on in his heart.

I was so grateful for those times of supernatural confirmation, because if Dennis was not listening to me, maybe he would pay attention to God. On another occasion when I was suffering from extreme torment, I begged Dennis to go for a ride and talk to God. Coming home many hours later, Dennis said, "God told me He has hardened your heart and when it is time, He will melt it like butter."

Looking very troubled, my husband also said "God sternly warned me to stop treating you the way I have been or I will lose you."

These occasions of communication from Dennis were the beacons of hope that helped me to know that I was not crazy! I was not simply some hormonal woman, needing lots of attention. God repeatedly would tell Dennis directly what I was saying in cards, and letters. What a relief…for a few days…and then things would return to the way they were before.

Confused I would ask Dennis, what had happened? When I would try to remind him, that he himself had said God had spoken, he would angrily tell me I was going to make him drop dead from high blood pressure and leave him alone. So there it was! One moment one thing, and the next, something else! Somehow between the trips to feed the horses, prayer without ceasing, learning to focus on Jesus, and Jesus alone, slowly I grew and tried to believe God would not give me more than I could handle.

With the school year wrapping up, Jake was moving up north to spend a season, with his friend Ryan and I had a feeling things were going to get worse not better. Talking with Israel and his new friend Jaime, I told them I had heard that Yosemite needed stable hands, and trail guides. You received, room, board and pay! With us needing money and Dennis still refusing to get any kind of help, it sounded like a great opportunity for us to get some space. To say the idea wasn't accepted by my spouse is putting it mildly.

On top of everything else, the last year my father's health had declined dramatically and it was heartbreaking as he made some choices that certainly didn't help his health. The feeling of abandonment I was dealing with was incredible. I couldn't go to anyone anymore and I needed to get away from the oppression and depression. Three months working in a National Park, sounded like a wonderful break. Standing my ground, I let Dennis know that since he wouldn't get help, or go anywhere, something had to give. I was going no matter what.

Wanting to break the insanity of doing the same thing over and over and expecting a different outcome, I continued to search for answers that would allow growth without giving up all together!

Chapter 58

"Breaking the Bread"

JESUS, TOOK THE BREAD, then He blessed it, then HE BROKE IT, representing what would happen to "His body" so that it could be distributed to the masses! Arthur Blessitt, once asked God what on He was doing with Him, and he heard, "Grinding you to powder Arthur, so I can blow you where I will!"

It is so easy to talk to someone about their cross, it is another to deal with your own. Not one person on planet earth has a totally carefree existence, and yet somehow we all try to escape the inevitable.

Phrases like "liquid gold," "refiners fire," and all the stories of suffering in the Biblical stories, always portray a loving, benevolent God who says He will never leave us or forsake us, while exhorting us to "endure to the end." These are not words of retirement, and ease!

Surely, Dennis and I were in the process of being broken to be useful for even greater purposes, despite our weakness, and humanity. Like Abraham offering Isaac, all I could do was take one step after another in pursuit of peace, joy and freedom. A wonderful young man named Jason Upton came to our town for a three-day conference and it seemed as if every song, every word, had been hand picked to speak to my heart. Songs that spoke about trusting God, even an ongoing theme about "letting go" ran through the conference worship songs.

I had a husband not sure of what he believed even though he was hearing from God that I was not crazy and that what I was trying to tell him was the truth. He refused to change anything, and just kept saying, something would change. One day he was saying he would stop the emotional abuse, and the next was back to screaming get out of "His house".

I needed to get out of harms way as physically I was so ill I had literally dropped over sixty pounds in less than three months. I could not physically stand to eat, as the moment I was upset I would vomit, unable to handle anything on my stomach. Old demons of bulimia and anorexia tried to ad to the stress and pressure of all the rejection!

One day while enjoying the riding class at the Ag farm, the teacher had announced job openings for the tourist season in Yosemite working with their stables. The thought of spending some peaceful time with the beauty of a national park, and horses, and get paid for it seemed great. Housing was provided, and food was very little, so here was my answer to getting some space for Dennis and I while we worked things out. Making some much needed money and getting a break from each other, all made perfect sense to me. The man I married seemed unable to protect, or even care about the side effects of all this dysfunction and I was hoping that a temporary break was what the doctor. ordered. Letting Dennis know that I was going to take a summer job in Yosemite with or without his approval, I continued to try to communicate that it made perfect sense!

With Jake moving for sure, and Israel and his best friend Jamie not heading to the coast until August, I encouraged Israel and Jamie to come to Yosemite with me. Calling ahead, I spoke with a kind man named J.R. who gave us great favor and hired all three of us. Wrapping up my job at the local college and finishing the spring semester of school, I packed my car to head to the new job at Yosemite. Jamie and Israel had actually headed up a week before I was finished at the college, and I looked forward to some much needed rest from the war-zone at home.

Most of the drive to Yosemite was absolutely wonderful. Resting in a place of trusting God totally to work out all of our problems, I took some deep breaths. Dennis was angry that I was going and was fighting losing what he saw as any control over his life or mine. I had purposely turned off my cell phone and played some awesome worship songs enjoying the beauty of the ride to the park. Getting closer to Yosemite, I checked the cell phone and I saw what appeared to be literally seven or eight calls from Dennis.

Listening I sat through, the first that said, "hey, sorry, I was such a creep. Maybe, you'r right, this break will be good for us, call me!" When I hadn't called back within a few minutes, the next call was accusing, saying I didn't want to hear from him, and by the last call, he was literally screaming, demanding, I call him immediately, or else! Accusations were made that I had not set him up with information to pay the bills while I was gone, etc. and he was going to call our sons to help him since I was so mean!

I had left total instructions, lists, and more, and had constantly reiterated that I could not emotionally take any more stress! So literally the day I was on the road the badgering continued. Convinced all the more, that for Dennis to start treating me with some respect, I needed to stop the enabling, I waited until I was parked, and called Dennis, assuring him that I was fine, and was not abandoning him. I then told him I would call in a few weeks, have a nice break!

I was going to be sharing a cabin with some younger nice, girls, and I had hoped selfishly for a cabin to myself! I was told it was impossible and then after totally unpacking into the tiny cabin that held four, I spotted an empty cabin that no one seemed to know about. The office in charge of handing out cabin assignments allowed me to move into it, so after moving all of my stuff yet again, finally I had arrived. I wasn't to start work for one more day, as I had to attend a "safety" training seminar, and taking my time I turned my little cabin into a warm nest!

Guitar, harmonica, paints, CD player, you name it, I was ready to call this little cabin home. I couldn't help but notice it seemed like most of the people who worked for the stables had an affinity for beer and late night bonfires. Israel and Jamie were worried as they had actually been placed into accommodations into different locations in the park and had heard that "the stables" cabins belonged to the party crowd!

In the few short days they had been there Israel and Jamie had already gained the approval of the stable bosses and on their day off had managed to go rock climbing with a man who had taught professional rock climbing at another National Park! The kids were having fun riding their bicycles all over the Yosemite Valley floor. Even though they were not entirely fond of the hard, hard work, like troopers they were working away and meeting new people.

Less than a week after arriving, my body gave out. A few months before, I had been in an emergency room twice due to severe head aches that caused vomiting that led to dehydration. Here I was in Yosemite with a severe migraine and the nausea was starting. I tried repeatedly to call Israel and Jaime, and since their phones were turned off, I faced the only option, driving home. There is no hospital in Yosemite, and there was no way I was going to be airlifted out the next morning. Praying for strength, I drove all the way back to Visalia, and arriving home, Dennis greeted me with concern saying I never should have gone.

Trying to explain what was happening physically, I headed to the downstairs back bedroom where I had moved and tried to fall asleep. By that evening our home was a warzone once again. By the following day I had an offer to stay with my wonderful sister Chris and her family in Southern California while I went to our wonderful Dr. Moreno, and tried to find out what on earth was wrong with my body.

Calls flew back and forth to the kids, and Dennis seemed oblivious to the fact that this was a situation where I needed support. One moment he was yelling, and we both decided, it would be better for me to go through this without him, than to have him constantly losing it. For whatever reason, my husband did not have anything to give in this hour of need.

Hiding out in a bungalow overlooking the Santa Monica basin, I couldn't help but marvel at Gods provision yet again. I actually was walking through the apointments with the doctors with peace, and one day I even took a wonderful drive up the coastal highway from Santa Monica to Malibu! It seemed God was continuing to unwrap one layer of this onion at a time, and the ongoing revelations were sometimes almost more than I could bare.

The day I took the drive to Malibu, I was faced with yet another startling discovery. Stopping at a Starbucks, I noticed a very handsome, black man who exuded friendliness. Smiling, he asked for my order, and I realized I was uncomfortable looking into his eyes. Taking a heart check, I questioned God whether I was embarrassed because he was very attractive, or was I having a problem, when I realized something even sadder. The last year had left such wounds, that I was not comfortable looking into anyone's eyes deeply! There were only a very few who I trusted and I was carrying the scars of dysfunction in a new way. It had nothing to do with him, or his race, or attractiveness, or my heart! I was simply so wounded that I literally shied away from the light in fear. My God, this was almost the most shattering of all. I who had carried an absolute gift of joy, was afraid to look another person in the eyes. I noticed the next few days that often when in public I avoided eye contact like the plague! What was happening to me?

While staying with my sister Chris, she kindly confirmed, that I was completely responsible for my part of being an enabler and that any time I was ready to stop it…I could! What I love about Chris is her ability to get straight to the point. With all tests finished, I kissed, Chris, and her whole family goodbye, assuring them I would take care of myself, and thanked them for the warm hospitality!

Preliminary test showed a good possibility of cancer and upon hearing the news precious Israel and Jamie flew home to be there when I returned from the tests. I can honestly say after all the years of supporting others through physical trials; there is nothing so lonely as facing serious bad news by yourself. There is nothing colder than being alone, in a strange doctor's office where a total stranger tells you it appears you have cancer, a potentially fatal disease. I can honestly tell you that with Jesus, I was not afraid. As much as I personally hate sickness, I had honestly told God that no matter where he wanted me to walk, if it would help my precious husband I was willing. I am not kidding. I was not afraid. I don't believe God ever sends sickness on anyone, and yet I know often our own actions and insistence on our own ways, may lead us into trials that we seem to learn from that include walking through some sort of illness or health challenge. I absolutely believe my God is the Healer, and that His perfect will is that we continue to pray thy will be done on earth as it is in heaven AND BELIEVE IT!

After lots of tests, and a week at my sister's, I headed home with news of several physical challenges, but we still had to wait for the blood work for several more days to let us know whether cancer was included in the list. Arriving home, I remember finding a card, welcoming me home, and in it my husband swore to try to be calm, and not attack, and yet in less than one day, he found himself losing it still. Finally the news came. NO CANCER! All Glory to God! If stress affects cells, it is truly God's grace that we received such a report. Dennis was relieved while also saying he would have been furious if the result had been any other, and all I knew was that I was so grateful.

Continuing to live downstairs, I had finally set some parameters for my own sanity. Israel was getting ready to move to the coast with his friend Jamie, and I decided that I would just live downstairs while Dennis came to the end of himself. All the anger, rage and stress was taking a tole and I honestly didn't think he could keep up this struggle much longer.

Debbie, a mighty prayer warrior who works with a friend of ours, had less than delicately, told me I really had some major issues and needed to "Let go". Let Go? Let Go of what? Myself? Dennis? Marriage? Control? What? How? When? Faithfully handing me a printout about letting go, Debbie gently said what needed to be said! I had to confront the demons, and I had to get on with whatever God was doing in my life! True trust! It seemed for the next three months every church I visited, every speaker I listened to, on and on the messages were always about letting go.

It was inconceivable to me that after a cancer scare, Dennis still was refusing to talk, communicate or deal with all this mess. After talking with Debbie I went and bought a giant bottle of Tequila and headed to my Dad's empty house to lay by the pool and think about all that was said. After doing yard work all day and totally downing the entire bottle over about six hours, I headed home to let my husband have it with both barrels! To say he was in shock was putting it mildly. I cut loose in a way that I never had, and he actually apologized and was nice for a couple of days.

"You don't love me! I shrieked! You don't even know me! You are not my friend! You keep saying you want me here and then do everything you can to drive me away!" I actually thought that I had gotten through. I screamed at him the way he had at me for years when he was upset and he genuinely seemed shocked." You've been living in a television for years, and want to die! What are you still doing here? You think God is done using us?" I declared how sick and tired I was of all the lies, false accusation, and how dare he think that he had any right ever to treat me in any way that was less than what God had destined for me as his daughter and bride. You need to find out what you believe I bellowed louder! I honestly cannot believe someone didn't call the police, as quite this was not! For a good half hour I unloaded and for the first time I ever remember, Dennis was speechless! Repentance was in the camp but it only lasted for a day or two!

One Sunday, going to church with Isaiah and Heather, I heard the same word again! "Let Go"...At the front of this church stands a big wooden cross. By the cross, is a basket holding a hammer, nails, paper and pencils. After the service and taking communion, I fell literally on my face, at the foot of the cross. Oh my God! What a different place it seemed, than when Dennis and I had together knelt at the foot of a cross in Texarkana. Sobbing so hard, I could barely write...there at the cross, I wrote my husbands name, the word covenant, marriage, and literally nailed the tear stained, folded up, piece of paper to the cross.

Accompanied by my middle son and his wife! Isaiah, the son raised from the dead!

. Where oh, where had my husband gone?

Chapter 59

"Letting Go"

TRYING ONE LAST TIME to find a temporary solution to our need to find some space, I looked for jobs at resorts. Hearing from a hunter's retreat in Colorado, I was promised, room, board, and at least $200 a day in tips from waiting tables.

I had repeatedly begged Dennis to go visit Mamma Lori, or her son Greg, find a campground to camp in for a week, anything, but since this awful time had begun, even though I had heard he was wrestling God, I kept hoping that we wouldn't have to formally separate, or move away from each other.

The home front was just to volatile and no matter what I did to avoid warfare it was coming down the hallway, and seeking me out. How I ever finished one class let alone passed with a high GPA can only be credited to God helping me to learn to focus no matter how bad the warfare was at home.

Packing the truck yet one more time, I noticed Dennis kept accusing me of leaving him. More often than not, he was yelling at me to get out of his house, and yet when I made plans to get a break, he was angrier yet. By now I realized that I honestly believed I was dealing with more than Dennis.

Driving to Colorado, I spent the night in the truck in Primm Nevada. There is an oasis of sorts, where you can buy a prime rib dinner for $6.95 and the rooms are only $19.95. The owners are so sure you will drop lots of money gambling, so everything is very cheap! Spending a day in Primm, I rested, and sadly listened to a group in one of the casinos, sing all the best Motown love songs that Dennis and I used to enjoy together.

I still tried to picture God restoring my heart, but by now all I could see was accusation, anger and jealousy from the man who I had once shared so much with.

Continuing on to the resort, I pulled into the front office! I was given a tour by the woman who had hired me, and anxious to get unpacked, I was escorted from the million dollar lodge to a broken down laundry room, hidden by some pine trees. Now this was incredible. Here some one had placed an old mobile that they had covered the sides with in fake logs hidden by some trees. There was a door on each end of this little building and I could see there was no lock on the door I was walking into. In the middle of this "building" was a commercial washer, a few dryers, junk, old food, and a poorly built table that was supposed to hold towels and wash cloths that the "maids" were supposed to wash. To the right was a room, with a twin bed sized stained mattress, no dresser, and carpet with holes in it. Completing my new "apartment" were the three windows that had glass broken out of with old torn sheets hung across to help keep out the soon coming fall rains. It was mid August and the temporary job was supposed to last until November. To get to the only bathroom, one had to go to the other end of this mobile and knock on a door to another bedroom, asking its occupants if you could please use the toilet. There was no shower and the young couple shacking up in the other end were so stoned that my first night there, they forgot to unlock the door, So I literally had to pee in a plastic trash can!

Staring at all of this, once again I hit me knees and asked God what on earth He was doing with me! I am willing I cried out! If there is a soul here who needs you, I don't care, many have had less! But this was not that!

"GO"!... Oh my God NO! Exhausted I called Dennis weeping and told him what I had been greeted with! "I knew you weren't supposed to go", he proclaimed. "Come home where you are loved." Right, loved one moment until the other Dennis showed up! Be that as it may, my insides were absolutely churning and packing in the wee hours of the morning, I drove away without so much as a goodbye! That woman knew what she did! She thought I would be unable to afford the gas home! God forgive her, I have.

Heading home on the freeway, I had a meltdown, and finally could take no more. Dennis had called and screaming at him, at God, and continuing to cry out why? I fought off strong suicidal thoughts! What did God want from me?

Wasn't I trying to give Dennis the space he needed? I physically and mentally could not take the roller coaster anymore. My sons didn't want to be in the middle and my mother and sisters were not exactly objective with the pain they had seen me in. Worst of all, my 82 year-old father, my hero was dying. Suffering from one ailment after another, he was on the journey of his body and mind shutting down and not once through this horrible ordeal had I ever mentioned to Him that Dennis and I were having any problems.

For the last three years of his life, my precious Father would watch Monday night football with Dennis and they had made quite a friendship. Dennis enjoyed the father he had not had for many years, and Dad enjoyed a son, after having three daughters. There was no way in his failing state I would have troubled him with something he could do nothing about.

So here I was up against a wall, and absolutely shattered. Dennis tried to say a few words of encouragement, but talk had become cheap. Promising to go to a counselor, and swearing we would do whatever it took, Dennis shared that he couldn't believe how heart broken he was after I drove away, and he realized I wasn't kidding. He thought I would be gone for three to four months and he had hit his knees yet again, calling out to God.

Hanging up from Dennis I called Trish, and asked her to pray, and cried, and cried, and cried! Driving a fourteen hour day, I made it back to Prim, an deciding that I might as well take a breath, I stopped by for another prime rib dinner, and a room for the night to get some good sleep after the long drive there and back! I arrived home the next day and Dennis kindly helped unpacked the truck and made an appointment to request a counselor from the VA. I called my poor children who had tried to be supportive through this whole crazy summer. They chose only to welcome me back with open arms.

I could not explain why all the tests, why all the doors would seem to close when Dennis would call out to God. I could guess but only will time reveal what was flesh, and what was spirit! All I know is I felt like the prophets of old when they gave the word of the Lord, and then God did something else and they were left looking very stupid.

I know it seems hard to understand but my only hope and faith, that I was not totally insane, was the truth. That from the beginning, I know, that I know, that I know, what God said to me, and like Job, I am very aware how all of this appears. But to the best of my ability, my heart all along was to try to be led by the Spirit of God, and I did not want to give up hope that there actually was a triumphant end to this nightmare.

Hadn't I repeatedly let go? What was I missing? With school starting yet again, I signed up for classes and found that if I worked hard by the end of spring, I could have yet another degree. The VA counselor finally called, and Dennis headed out the door to face one of his worst fears. Why on earth would someone so wounded willingly expose himself to someone else who couldn't possibly understand what he has walked through?

We were both desperate for help, I frankly didn't care how the help came, I simply wanted Dennis to suggest anything, anything at all, just as long as we did something different! How on earth can anyone think you can change nothing and expect different results, and yet we have a bankrupt nation that has fattened itself off of the poor, taken advantage of the ignorant, and when the recent financial crises hit, those in power gave more money to the same people in charge of making the initial mess. They were surprised that nothing has changed! Maybe more than just my husband and I have been fooled at times! Well after a few visits to the counselor, Dennis quit and he still was not honestly ready to change anything. Lashing out yet again, I could barely believe what the last year had held. Neither was willing to give up, and yet deep down I knew this trial was still not done! My husband had realized this past year how little he truly knew about his wife's heart and at one point was willing to even take a horse back riding class with me. When he went he really did enjoy himself, but the struggle inside surfaced and he would punish me by quitting the things he had committed to. Our lives had been so wrapped up in him that when people would ask me how I was, I immediately went to talk about Dennis. I had become a non-entity.

Surprises of all surprises in the midst of the storm, yet another gift from on high! Micah's first birthday was approaching and few had forgotten how cleverly Isaac and Heather had announced her pregnancy at Evans birthday party. Now a year had passed, and the family was gathered at Isaac and Heather's. After opening presents, Isaac smiling announced, "and this is Micah's gift from Heather, and I." As Micah tore the paper off of the last package, a magnetic toy for the refrigerator was revealed, and at the same time, a book fell onto the floor that had been tucked in with the toy. Smiling extra big, Isaac held up the book which was a Bernstein's Bear book entitled? AND BABY MAKES FIVE!

Here in the midst of our worst trials, God faithfully continued to bless and protect our family. Isaac and Heather were pregnant with their third child, an answer to prayer. Deciding not to find out whether the new baby was a boy or a girl, we all were in for an exciting spring! Looking at Dennis I wondered if this would be a wake up call of some kind.

The news was a little ray of light and hope in the midst of a very dark time for us as parents. Overjoyed I just could not picture our family separated, and was sure that perhaps God would use this to change my husband's heart.

Thanksgiving had come and gone, and Dennis had stayed home and gotten drunk instead of going to the family dinner! By this time I was honestly not surprised at much of anything. I felt numb most of the time.

Getting up the next morning, I was walking down the hallway to the kitchen when Dennis came from the other direction. The presence on my husband was an old familiar for I recognized and standing my ground I braced myself for what I sensed was coming. "You ruined Thanksgiving, now you've ruined Christmas, and we are not going to have any lights this year"! Intimidating and pointing a finger in my face, there was no apology and I was repeatedly told that there would be no Christmas this year! I remember thinking, "Is that right"? and in no uncertain terms, I stated this was the last time I would be talked to with such disrespect.

Three days later Isaac and Isaiah, moved all of my belongings over to my dads empty house that had been up for sale since he was no longer able to keep it up. I had driven around in circles for three days, depressed at the thought of leaving everything that held any comfort, and finally realized I was being stupid not to simply ask Mom, if she minded if I use the house until it sold! On one hand I was so exhausted from all the moves, and yet on the other, it made sense. "Trust Me" was what I heard, and assuring my sons, that I would not be making any quick moves this time, they walked me through this like the troopers they have always been. "Son's, your dad has to be left totally alone, and I need to get out of the way. I believe God is going to work this out, but you are all getting hurt even if I am in the house, so I might as well, go make a nest and let God have him!"

There!

I had "Let Go"…and letting go…meant just that…

Chapter 60

"The Nest"

I MAY HAVE GONE KICKING and screaming, but I was never more sure of anything in my life! It had taken over a year to completely trust God and myself! Valiantly I fought what I was hearing, to make sure, really sure, that every other alternative had been exhausted. I had invested many prayers, cards, notes, letters, phone calls and more.

A basket sat in the corner of the living room, like an altar of sorts, full of attempts at communication. The basket was physical evidence. A picture of my response to Dennis yelling "divorce." Dennis often wouldn't even open the cards or gifts that I would give him, so off they went into "the basket."

Before the actual moving day, I thought about twice before when I almost "let go". I had moved out once to my fathers empty house for about two weeks, and when Dennis came calling, I instantly moved home. There even had been a time that I had miraculously found a little nest of a studio, literally by a river, that had horses. My husband had no idea I was even looking, and calling a pastor friend we prayed for Gods perfect will. The door mysteriously shut and the next day, Dennis had once again said he wanted to "try to get help." As an enabler I was well trained to go where I believed I was supposed to! The question was always when and where!

All I knew is that truly Dennis and I were being ground to dust and it wasn't very pretty. The hardest most painful part of all was the cost to those I loved! My children, who knew of the mighty works of God, did not understand why we couldn't just get along! They really couldn't conceive that we were right where we were supposed to be! There was so much pain at the holidays, birthdays, any special event where they needed their parents to be supportive and "together." Pain as Dennis was missing moments with my father that could never be regained! Then there were my children assigned from God! My heart was for everyone who had met Dennis and I during this time to know the man who the book "Breaking Chains" was written by. Where was he? How could we tell people about how wonderful Jesus was when we were such a mess? Well if we truly had realized that our message needed to lift up one, and one alone, "Jesus," I wouldn't have cared about how we looked! I know the Bible says don't go by what you see but this was extremely hard!

My empathy for the widows and orphans was growing, and I can honestly say, I went through a total spiritual, mental and emotional divorce. I placed my husband in the hands of God, and I was not going to be fooled again. All my life I had preached Jesus was enough and now He had to be! Dennis would be civil for a few days when he wanted something and then the moment he did or didn't get what he wanted, he was back to the same behavior. It really didn't matter whether he got what he wanted or not! The moment the conquest was over? The other guy surfaced!

My mind was so bent, so bruised, and so weary, I actually welcomed the peacefulness of solitude. God in His infinite wisdom, may have asked me to leave home and all that I loved, but kindly I was placed in a nest, in the very home I grew up in! Mom was wonderful and offered to pay me on top of staying there for free, to do the yard work! The place needed kept up while realtors showed it!

My first night all alone, I looked around the room that I had worked so hard to set up! The overhead pastel gold colored glass shade emitted a warm glow that softly lit my new bedroom. Placing the bed in the corner of the room allowed me to stack up pillows along two sides making the bed look absolutely inviting! Covering the soft king sized bed was a comforter that had been given to me by Dennis' sister Sheri. The feminine cross-stitched comforter had squares of the daintiest little designs that were mostly pinks and purples. The little flowers and lacy parts made one feel like a princess. A fuzzy, brown, stuffed bear that Trish had been given sat proudly in a corner just begging for a hug. A crocheted ivory covered doily sat on the nightstand under a reading lamp and sitting next to the baby blue lamp was an adorable figurine that Trish had left when she moved, the figurine was of a sitting bear dressed in a robe, holding a tea cup. The bears robe was a matching baby-blue, and for some reason that was comforting. Next to that I had placed a hand-tied bunch of lavender to remind myself of a day that Dennis and I had been to the coast.

Walking down the beach a little child was selling beautiful little bunches of fresh lavender and approaching timidly asked if we would like one? To my surprise, my husband barked out harshly that we couldn't afford that, before even knowing the price. The look on the child's face was heart breaking and quickly, I enquired how much? Two dollars was the reply, and buying one, I couldn't help but think what on earth had happened to the man I used to love. He was smashing everything in sight, blind and numb to the results of his actions. Oh he had money to buy a beer, or a bottle of vodka if he wanted, but there was no money for flowers!

The bunch of lavender on the bedside was to remind me of the brokenness that was going to be needed to lead to repentance... true repentance!

Follow Jesus! Focus on Jesus! Get to know Jesus!

The final item on the nightstand was my Bible. Ironically there was an inscription from Dennis, encouraging me to grow as God had greater things for me to learn! Well true, there was nothing said about "sharing" what I was learning. Sinking into the bed, such a peace permeated the room, and I pictured our friend Trish wondering if this is how nurtured she had felt at being in a nest provided by the Lord? Peace, Peace, wonderful peace. I knew that I was in the right place and I slept like a baby for the very first night in my new home!

By the second night, Dennis who was losing all control was banging down the door late at night. Dropping off our little dog,

"Frito Boat" he shoved his way into the house, and declared I was going to keep the dog for my own safety! Right! A three pound old tiny terrier mix who had a cataract, and was toothless! It would have been funny if it wasn't so sick. Ushering him out of the house, I locked the door, and returned the dog in the morning!

Writing yet one more letter I asked Dennis to leave me alone! I will not answer calls! I will not pay your bills! Whether we lost the house or whatever, Dennis was not my problem anymore! The crazy thing, was that he honestly acted like after literally telling me he hated me, get out, and didn't need me, he told me I should continue to pay the bills, and do everything to make his life wonderful! On top of that he was angry telling his family I had "left him," Yikes!

This tormenting spirit was determined to kill both of us, and I had put my foot down. I refused to be part of all of this and told Dennis any further communication would need to be in writing. I tried to explain literally for our health's sake, all the harassment was not okay, but my husband was out of control. Until you have talked with Mama Lori, or Greg, I am not going to even consider coming home. Dennis simply could not believe I was following through with what I said!

School was going along, the horseback riding classes for the third semester were wonderful, and being in the home I was raised in was such a gift of comfort. Continuing to walk through the process of seeing my dad preparing to leave his physical body, I fought and wrestled as we all do trying to somehow make the process far more gracious than I was seeing. Taking Dad for wheel chair rides outside of the convalescent home was emotionally hard, and yet somehow strength came. I never will forget a particular day when I felt led to take dad outside to where the roses were and the Holy Spirit nudged me to sing for Dad! A music teacher who loved to hear his daughters sing, I couldn't believe what I was hearing! Sing?

My Dad was a shadow of his former self, and yet his eyes still twinkled with light and recognition. When he could still communicate he had told me that his favorite song was "Oh how I love Jesus". So praying for divine grace to be the hands of love extended, I softly sang to my Dad, for my "Father". God promises to be a father to the fatherless, and truly my Dad, an orphan who had grown up in an orphanage, was greatly loved during his sojourn on this earth. In my adult years, I grew to respect his strength and joy in new ways, and truly it was a privilege to sing to him. Singing "In the Garden" and several other songs, I was amazed at the strength that I was given to "see" Dad's spirit and not his physical body. Watery eyes and a smile were my reward for the mini concert, and it was wonderful, that knowing here in the stench and indignity of failing bodies, there were moments of love, peace and joy!

Christmas was fast approaching and the dumb devil hated lights huh? When I had the boys move me, I had taken all the Christmas decorations, and decided that since Christmas was about Jesus… NOT DENNIS, I was going to celebrate, and so was our family! Getting out the tallest extended ladder from my dad's shed, I prepared well. Since I was going to the roof top I carefully put all the lights I wanted to use on the roof into a trash bag along with extension cords, a hammer and some tape.

Since my father's house is two stories, it didn't hit me until I was actually on the roof, looking down that I must be crazy. A few days before, I had battled through another bout of headaches and nausea, and even had to take medication to be able to keep anything on my stomach. The doctor simply stated my body was shutting down from all the stress, and even wanted to give me an anti-depressant! Thanking him, I refused that part of the therapy as I truly believed some Godly sorrow was in order. After all, Dennis and I were in the middle of having our hearts torn out, and a major surgery done in our lives, some sorrow seemed appropriate. I was sure that now I was not going to be under attack daily, I would be ok, and I simply needed something for the nausea.

Well here I was on the roof that had a very steep pitch to it, with a bag full of lights and all of a sudden, "super woman" had a fear attack! Laughing, I laid on my back on the roof, and one by one tried to call my children to see if any of my sons might be available. No such luck! No answers anywhere, even from Jake, who had moved back to Visalia, after living up north for seven months! Connecting with Heather Dawn I explained that I was losing my mind but if no one was available I was just going to have to finish the job! Three hours later I had decorated the house with every light that we had ever owned. It seemed fitting. I don't ever remember it ever having so many lights.

All of my children had been invited over for a holiday evening, and somehow we all managed to make the best of the situation! Christmas music filled the house and a beautiful tree with lights glowing like a scene from a Charles Dickens book, greeted the children. My heroes! Asking the kids if they wanted me to invite their father over for Christmas morning, they agreed, and I honestly wanted to make an opportunity for everyone to enjoy the day as best we could!

Calling, I invited Dennis over for Christmas, and shared that we honestly would miss him, and if he could come, and celebrate family, without turning the whole thing into him being the focus, he was welcome! Christmas morning came and went, and the greatest joy that made the day monumental was the good news that our son Isaiah, and his Heather were expecting their first baby! Dennis did come and tried his best to focus on the kids and not us. Our Isaiah pulled out the bubble gum cigars and passed them out with great fervor. Talk about reminders of promise and hope. How on earth could any of us have any peace until our family was restored? Anyone who has lost a loved one will tell you, there is a gaping hole that cannot be filled until restoration happens! It is just so! God can fill it, and make the pain go away, but something is still missing!

Ever wonder how God must feel when someone he loves is missing?

Chapter 61

"Standing"

MAKING IT THROUGH THE holidays, the truth was that Dennis was discovering, not Vodka, no amount of Elvis videos, isolation, not even sitting in the spa for hours could make up for being alone. Months before he had actually admitted, he did not know what he wanted. He didn't like this new Diana. .

Being alone allows someone to have everything their own way and can be quite a comfy place. Both of us were searching and asking questions, and all I knew was that the same God who had delivered my husband in the beginning had promised to see me through one day at a time, one step at a time.

Since my husband had continually blamed everyone and everything for his life, it was quite a mirror to have everyone removed! No one to blame! No one's fault. Dennis, like George Bailey from the movie, "It's a Wonderful Life" was given the gift of seeing what his life would be like without me. Here I had watched as one by one everyone was removed and he was given the ultimate opportunity for selfishness! To say he was not in heaven is an understatement.

After all, he had a pension. I had not taken a dime, when I left. The Lord had told me specifically not to take any money. He wanted Dennis to experience what life would have been like without me. I was specifically told not to give him any extra excuses to have to blame for his unhappiness. Wow! Over the years, our favorite movie was, "It's a Wonderful Life," where a kind man named George Bailey gets to see what the world would have been like if he never had been born!

It seemed that once and for all, God had allowed my precious husband to have what he wanted in his heart and it turned out not quite like he had pictured it! So many movies have been made about men who came to the defining moment of giving up pure selfishness. Jim Carey, in the movie 'Bruce Almighty' discovers at the end of the day that true love is when you honestly want what is best for the other person whether it benefits you or not! Dennis was coming to the end of himself and like God had promised him at the river, my heart was starting to be softened.

Broken was the angry raving man pounding down the door and demanding his own way! Gone was the dishonest enabling wife who now had learned the meaning of the scripture, "Faithful are the wounds of a friend, but deceitful are the kisses of an enemy." Never again hopefully would I say what was expected just to keep peace. All I knew was I was not released from my best friend, I simply was needing to get "out of the way."

The next two months were an ongoing breaking and finally Mamma Lori wrote Dennis a letter! Sharing that the legions of hell had returned, Mamma wrote a letter sharing her love for Dennis! She commanded the demons that had returned to leave, and now that Dennis truly wanted them gone, leave they did! I do not know how to convey the reality gracefully of what we walked through, and yet there is a need for the followers of Jesus to be transparent and real.

Years ago, we thought we did God a favor by acting like there was no battle, never realizing that we were holding up our own works, not the true power of God. Has anyone noticed when a baby is birthed it is messy? Has anyone read the Bible lately with an eye that sees how messy, following Jesus was and is? I am sure when Jesus called the fishermen to follow him, and it says they literally walked away from everything that they were in the middle of, prudence and common sense would dictate that at the least they were irresponsible and rude for walking away from their jobs without more preparation. Men try that on your wives, leave work and say I am following Jesus! Well how are you gonna pay your bills? Oh, He said not to worry, a little fasting would be good for us anyway!

I am not suggesting that you do things you haven't been directed to do, but what I am suggesting is that most of us really care how things look, and appear, and find it very hard to go sometimes where the Spirit of God might lead us!

Remember the story of how Paul was stoned and left for dead when he preached to a city that made its living making pagan statues, that they needed to stop? This becoming a follower of Jesus is not easy, and it will cost you everything, like it or not! That is if you allow it!

Several weeks after getting Mamma's letter, Dennis called and spoke with his spiritual mamma for the first time in years! After that he called his best friend Greg. Dennis actions were finally lining up with his words, and he shared that he was indeed truly sorry for all the choices that had hurt so many.

In February, of 2008, I moved home to a husband that really wanted me there. Dennis personally packed and moved every piece of furniture, everything with tender loving care and together we started the long hard work of healing, restoration, and simply trying to understand what we were supposed to do next.

Continuing to walk my dad through the process of letting go of his earth suit, my sisters and Mom all showed our love in any way we could. Most the time, Dad was non-verbal and yet in rare moments we connected. He would tell me enough how much he loved me. In the Spring I had been chosen to play a part in the local college musical, and whisking into my Dad's room, I started singing songs from "My Fair Lady" one of our favorites that we used to share. Bursting into tears, he wept like a baby, and kept saying how happy he was that I had chosen to pursue using a long-lost talent. He was one of few who deeply appreciated my love for singing, dancing, and acting. When I married, I buried myself totally into the privilege of being Dennis' wife, and the boys' mother! I reassured him the tears were okay, and sometimes he was able to muster some very lucid moments, with loving clear communication. What a gift! My father provided greatness for all of his daughters. Leading by example he touched the world and made it a nicer place to be! A whole book could be written about all the awesome things I have learned from my earthly father.

May first, in the year two thousand and eight, my father's spirit left this physical earth. In his last hours it was very apparent, Dad was already on the "other side" and we were simply waiting for the final breath to escape from his lips. He was at peace, and God had answered a prayer I had breathed many years before. Knowing that Dad went through being orphaned, I had prayed for the privilege of being by his side, to hold his hand, until he was escorted by the angels into the waiting arms of those he so loved.

I read recently that in heaven, only that which we have done, that is fit for the "kingdom of God" remains. I have no doubt that my father's house in heaven is full with treasures from all the lives he truly touched with love. I have no doubt that the wonderful Choral Mass that he wrote in honor of Jesus, has been performed in heaven with great celebration.

It is very few people who literally bring a smile to the face of virtually everyone who knew them.

As a former student, Bruce Halen, so aptly wrote,

"I can't even begin to tell you how influential that your father has been in my life. I love the man and his spirit. But, here is a brief attempt:

- ☐ He taught me how to be a team player
- ☐ He taught me that hard work makes dreams come true.
- ☐ He taught me to respect, respectable authority and how to know the difference
- ☐ He taught me about believing in myself
- ☐ He taught me that life is a long journey with good times and bad times (his own example being my inspiration of this.)
- ☐ He taught me music
- ☐ He taught me the importance of music
- ☐ He taught me how to sing.

Honestly, Ivan Hershey and my father are the two men that I hold the deepest respect for in guiding me to where I am today (a middle school science teacher that sings a lot!). I owe much to Ivan and , although saddened at his passing, I recognize that his legacy lies in the lessons that he left with all the students who had the privilege of spending time with him.

I'll bet that there are a lot of my peers who would say the same.

Sincerely, Bruce Halen"

I can honestly say, yes Bruce, there are so many more with the same love and respect for such a wonderful man who I know is in heaven and is very much alive! In many ways my father truly reflected God's love for the world while on this earth!

Strength that I never knew I had, peace like a river, and growing, ever growing into the person I was created to be.

God is jealous, and if you have not yet had the opportunity to lean on Him and Him alone, you can rest assured, times of testing and trials are coming to reveal what is inside. And yet, even in this, the Spirit of God is polite. I could have bailed at any time, and I am sure I would still be loved, and would be given the opportunity further down the road to learn the same lessons if they were avoided earlier. This is the message of mercy and grace that is so important to a hurting world full of people who have a performance mentality! God knows you after the make-up is off, the shades are drawn, and what is lived in private is recorded in heaven.

Now, both Dennis and I knew much more about ourselves, our weaknesses, and how far grace and mercy will go!

Ivan and his first grandson "Isaac" Mizpah, Daddy

Chapter 62

"Summer Surprises"

ISRAEL AND JAIME HAD moved home in early February, and once again, I could not help but be in awe at how giving Dennis could be. Late January, Dennis and I had visited the kids at the beach, and discovered that they were coming to a turning point in their lives. While going to school at the coast our son had left school to work for a man who owned a coffee company. Offering Israel a "partnership" it seemed like our son's dreams were coming true. His years of experience were paying off and he was offered a real co-ownership if he would help to open a second coffee shop.

Later we all discovered what really happened, is this man used Israel's experience and youth and energy, and by calling him a partner, he didn't pay him for lots and lots of work that our son poured out. Working often seven days a week, he was so excited to have a real shot at success, until he figured out he wasn't being paid for his work. If what we do to others is how we have treated Jesus, lets just say, I had trouble picturing this "business man" paying the Lord, what Israel was paid. Meanwhile Jaime had finished another semester of school and both had discovered that when you work at the beach it seemed like you rarely had time to enjoy it!

During the time that Dennis and I were apart, I had a wonderful time visiting the kids several times and they were always very hospitable.

While we visited the kids together Dennis offered for them to come home. Things had not worked out quite as they thought, and since my husband had figured out that other people were not really the root of his problems, he actually thought it would be nice to have the kids back. As anyone who knows me will attest to, I am normally in my element entertaining others, and whether it is making nachos for the masses at 2:00 A.M., or visiting with our kid's friends, I always looked forward to good fellowship and company. I really looked forward to getting to know the young lady who we all thought was destined to be our daughter in-law. Jamie has a heart as big as they come. Surviving her parent's divorce recent divorce, Jamie had been through some battles in life and thankfully had a "feisty" attribute that would equip her well for dealing with my son's tenacity!

Around the same time, our newest son Jake had confirmed that he had met someone extra special that he knew was "the one." He and his "Esther," just could not stand to be apart, and when Jake told us he was thinking of inviting her to come to our city to live, once again Dennis was the first to offer. Israel, and Jaime were so excited to meet Esther and started saying how wonderful it would be if she could come live with us. Once again, with a house filled with love, things seemed like they were getting back to "normal." Still quite wounded, Dennis and I walked out the restoration, one day at a time.

Esther! Vibrant, a ballerina who loved to dance for the Lord, this young lady we were to meet turned out to be everything Jake had said she was! One Sunday before she moved to Visalia, "Dad" and I went with Jake to Fresno, to go to a meeting where Esther was also going to be. Sitting listening to praise and worship, I was so grateful to be spending time with Dennis focused on the Lord, and thrilled that spiritually, the kids wanted to spend time together focused on Jesus. The next thing I knew, as clear as anything I have ever heard, the Spirit told me that Esther was the one for Jake. "Take off the Mizpah from around your neck; I want you to give it to Esther. I will tell you when you do what to say to her!"

Oh how I struggled with this. What if I wasn't hearing God? What would Jake think? Did he really…really know she was the one? I kept trying to put it out of my head and focus on the worship music, but the message was very clear. After the meeting, when the time was right, The Holy Spirit had quite a message for Jake and Esther, and as I handed her the precious necklace, she wept, and barely could receive it. Like my other precious children, these two have such precious hearts and Dennis and I had an absolute blast that evening. Later when we talked it was agreed, truly as surely as God had sent all the other spouses for our children, this Esther was indeed a gift, sent from God to Jake. Israel, Jaime and Jake went out of their way to prepare Esther's room including painting it one of her favorite colors to make her feel welcome.

Meanwhile our wonderful pregnant "Heathers" were both due soon, one in June, and one in August. Bible studies were happening again in the Nickell house and then, when we least expected it, one more crisis. The summer before I had joined several sons, and their friends when they went to the mountains to have some fun. I was ready to do something, anything, to try not to leave home, anesthetize myself, or self destruct. Hiking up a trail at "Potwisha," the boys explained we were headed for some cliffs that they liked to jump off of, into the water below. The idea sounded perfect. Knowing what a rough time, "mom" was having, they let me tag along and I was lost in the beauty of the mountains, the streams, and absolutely perfect weather.

All I can tell you is that it was a wonderful day. I jumped off of a few cliffs myself and it was exactly what I needed. I felt like I left a giant weight behind, as I simply enjoyed myself and laughed, and hiked and swam. The ultimate end to the perfect day was when we jumped into a water duct that reminded me of the log flume rides at Magic Mountain, but this was the real thing. The sun was hot, and the cool water carried us through the most scenic places most of the way back down the mountain. I remember thinking of how much Dennis had always loved water slides and was really sad he hadn't come.

Now a year later, some of the sons had missed the opportunity to celebrate "Father's Day," and since Dennis had been fishing recently, we decided to take him up to the mountains so he could ride in this water duct. Dennis had heard all about this place and decided it might actually be fun. Walking up the trail, we passed the water duct and headed on up to the rocks and swimming holes that were so fun. Israel, Jaime, Jake, and Esther were with Dennis and I. Jumping off of rocks into the icy cold mountain water was refreshing and Dennis looked like a weight had lifted off of him too, and I was so glad he had come. A little later some kayakers went by and deciding to go to a better vantage point, we all headed back to where we had come from. After watching the kayakers I found myself left behind, and decided to jog to catch up with those ahead! One moment I was running happily, not a care in the world, so full of joy, and the next realized I was airborn. Landing full force on trestles that were across the flume, both ribs and knees smacked really hard. I then fell into the water duct and into the swift icy water. Grabbing onto a board so that I would not drown, I could not breath in, cry out for help, or move any thing. I honestly didn't now if my back was broken, and I remember hearing very clearly, "Don't let go, or you will drown." Clutching the board, I prayed and knew only God could save me, as I honestly didn't think anyone saw the accident and I could not make a peep.

Later I discovered that Jamie had heard the splash and told Israel that she thought that I had fallen in, as she headed towards me. The next thing I knew, I was being hoisted out of the cold water by me precious son Israel, and I was so scared as I didn't know how to tell them something was broken. As I started to black out from the pain, I had help laying down flat to try to catch my breath. Everyone was discussing how best to help, did I need air-lifted out, was I broken etc, and meanwhile I was so mad at myself for costing everyone the rest of the day.

Within a few minutes, I was able to breath without passing out, and had help sitting up. Surrounded by loved ones who literally held my hands to make sure I didn't fall, I walked all the way back one baby step at a time. I knew I was broken on the inside, but honestly was terrified of the "help" that might move me less than gingerly, and since my legs were working it seemed like the right thing to do! Driving back the 40 minutes or so to Visalia, I could not believe how many bumps were in the road. Trying to be brave for everyone, I didn't shed a tear…until…alone with Dennis in the ER at the local hospital.

So proud that I had made it out without a big show, I had held it together for over an hour with some groans and such, and I remember one son saying, that if I had broken ribs, there was no way I could walk all that way! (I was thinking if you only knew. Having kids was nothing compared to this, and I was praying I wasn't bleeding internally).

The ER was a whole other story and after waiting close to twenty minutes on top of the long walk out, and the long ride, a fledgling RN took it upon himself to tell us he needed to stick his fingers into the broken ribs to see if they really were. Twice he insisted on literally sticking his fingers into the worst fracture and straight into the swelling bruised liver. This of course was before pain meds, seeing the doctor, or x-rays. Let's just say, "thank God," I didn't have a spinal injury as I would have been left paralyzed from the "treatment". Screaming from this "exam" I begged Dennis not to let him touch me again.

This RN got personal raising his voice and threatening that, he wasn't going to get the doctor, or give me anything for pain until he examined me further! Watching Dennis physically standing in-between this young man and me, they argued while I continued to "wait" for any kind of relief. I imagined my husband ending up in prison, as this young man continued to reach towards the injured area for a "third" exam, trying to ignore my husband. Sent straight from hell was all I could think. Mumbling that you should never start probing someone who has had the type of trauma my body had incurred, without taking pictures, and calling a specialist, I could not believe I was watching this escalate to almost a physical fight in the emergency room. Here I had made it this far, and then this kid assigned from hell was literally sticking his hands into what later proved to be, a severely bruised liver, several broken ribs, and an injured knee swelling like a baseball.

When this RN discovered he was not going to get to physically touch me, he left. About 10 minutes later as Dennis looked for a doctor this young man returned to the room with a syringe full of a pain killer. Looking right at Dennis he laid it on the tray in front of us and said, "I'm not going to touch her," and walked out of the room for another 15 minutes! "Oh my God," was all I could think as the pain was truly the worst I had ever been in. Whatever he had done when he shoved his fingers into my ribs, had sent off pain that I could not control or ignore. Finally explaining to Dennis that he was going to go ahead and give me the shot finally, please let him do that, the RN returned and gave me the pain killer and told us the doctor had ordered x-rays. Amazing, the doctor, who hadn't even been in to see us was able to order xrays, without sticking his hands into the injury. According to the RN, we could not receive further medical attention, not even see the doctor, unless he got to do three hands on exams.

Hours later, at home, on four different pain meds, I started yet another journey. Flying higher than a kite, I was so over whelmed by the amount of pain I had been in I took the maximum of each type of drug allowed, and then some. My poor, poor family got a tiny glimpse of what "mom" would have been like as a druggie and it wasn't pretty. Meanwhile, within three days, I was back in another ER from falling in the middle of the night from all the pain meds. Hearing a huge thump Dennis hopped out of bed and came running into the bathroom asking If I was all right? Trying not to laugh at his stark naked wife laying upside down in a bathtub, he asked what exactly I thought I was doing? I was simply trying to use the toilet in the middle of the night when nature called and since my balance was so bad, I fell into the shower that was near by. That had to be good for the injuries that were already there.

The second visit to the ER produced prescriptions for two more pills on top of the four and the next two weeks were a blur. I am sure, my family would tell you it was not a dull time. My precious daughter Sarah, came by and lovingly brought food since she knew I wasn't cooking much, and Dennis took over all the household chores. Dennis sister Penny who had been such a wonderful support to him while we were separated, brought the sweetest card, and a bag full of little goodies to comfort me! The meds totally affected my memory, and I will never forget one moment preaching to all my kids, and the next totally missing a baby shower for Isaiah's Heather. I was supposed to be decorating the tables, and one day as I called Zay higher than a kite, I slurred out that I had decided just exactly what to make for the decorations for the baby shower. Without any condemnation Zay calmly said, "Mom, the shower was yesterday!"

Then as if all of this wasn't enough, right in the middle of all of this, we almost lost our other Heather due to complications with her pregnancy. Our precious Isaac had to walk through the biggest trial of his life when after watching Heather give birth to their third beautiful brand new bouncing baby, complications forced her into an ambulance, and without even time to hardly rejoice over the birth of "Natalie Joy," his wife's life was literally on the line.

Arriving at the hospital the ambulance crew saved Heathers life after she had gone into shock, and then again after surgery she went into critical shock, and the staff at the hospital kept her alive and finally she was stabilized enough to stay in the intensive care critical unit. To say this was a summer full of surprises might just be an understatement.

Chapter 63

"Thirty Years"

THE NUMBER 30 BIBLICALLY and beyond is so rich with symbolism, that it doesn't take a great leap of faith to understand, that the maker of the universe, is a God of great detail and design. Think of it, how you would occupy yourself if you were so advanced that the bible says the angels that fly around the throne of Yahweh have never seen the same thing twice in all of eternity. Do you really think it is an accident that just as Jesus fit every prophecy to the smallest detail that described the coming Messiah, so too, the times and seasons in your life are not just random? Is it possible that every hair on your head really has been counted?

As Dennis and my 30th wedding anniversary approached we had no idea the significance of the day. It had been an incredibly hard two years filled with life, passion, and growth for all of our family. While Israel proposed to Jamie one way, Jake proposed to Esther another. Even our Sarah who had been through an awful divorce met a precious man named "Denny" who is one of the kindest people I have ever met. Somehow by God's grace, it seemed our family had survived the worst of an unbelievable process that reminded everyone of us what on earth is important.

As our wedding anniversary approached, Dennis and I had no idea the final surprise in store for such an incredible summer. When Isaiah and Heather found out she was pregnant, they were able to buy my fathers home, the house I grew up in. With help from my mom, they were able to jump through all the hoops, get a great deal, and keep this wonderful home, so full of memories, in the family. Heather…now a licensed RN wanted to have a home birth, and to our great joy, On August 22nd, 2008 just a few moments before midnight, Brock Thompson Nickell entered the world literally born in his great grandfather's house on our thirtieth wedding anniversary. NEW LIFE! Oh I can only imagine that my dad in heaven is rejoicing over such a thing. Like the never ending story, as Arthur so profoundly said in the foreword, "One's walk in life with God is not the absence of struggle. It's not where everything works out as we may desire…As I have found in my life, Jesus is enough; all sufficient, unchanging! The end, the book is not the end-they still go on with their Lord today."

Even my precious husband finally committed to paper so precisely, as only he can his understanding of the last several years trials and tribulations. What I felt led to share in 17 new chapters my husband wrote the following in less than two.

""Dennis you will not abuse me anymore!

What are you talking about?

This was a total shock to me. I knew I've always been kind of controlling, but I always looked at it as being humorous or funny. Well I found out that it was not all that funny to my wife and kids. According to my wife this was labeled as extremely mentally abusive. In my mind I definitely diagnosed the problem as Diana going through the change of life and that I have always loved her and my boys more than life itself. Well now that all these issues have been brought to light, Diana does admit to some major enabling through our 30 years of marriage. With all the years of care providing, which is totally giving of yourself mentally and physically, remember at one point in our lives for seven years, seven days a week, plus raising our sons at the time, there wasn't a whole lot of time for Diana and me, so there might have been some deep down jealousy for more of her attention. This might have caused me to treat her less than kind. There were also my issues from Vietnam and being an ex-drug addict and alcoholic. We are still working out all the reasons why all of our troubles came to a head after so many years. All we both knew was we had to be apart before we damaged each other beyond repair. So Diana left and went to live at my father in-laws, empty house.

Oh my God! Then reality hit. It was probably the most painful time we have both experienced in our lives. But at the same time this is something that had to happen. God knew what He was doing. We gave our whole lives to God in 1978. We did whatever we thought we heard him say to do, and went where we believed he said to go. I personally believe I was so exhausted spiritually and physically that I just let down my guard and said screw all this religion. I am going to drink again, the kids are moved out, my wife has left me, and I'm going to do something for me! The door was wide open for a big pity party all right! ("Not")

Well the devil had me right where he wanted me. But like the Bible says, I always try my best to be honest. It was fun for a season, and then I found out life is not the same when you have beautiful children, a beautiful wife, and you owe Jesus everything for all He has done for you and your family.

For all of you men out there going through the change or for whatever reason feel the need to act out your youth again, I'd just like to say, Be patient with yourself, and your wife and kids and the Lord will help you work things out. He promises to do that. I'm 58 years old. I was sober 25 years. I backslid, so I have the experience to suggest to you trust me it was not even worth it.

The joy in my life still and always will come from the understanding and unconditional love of Jesus Christ, my wife, and my sons, and daughters.

Men out there, I am very blessed to have these people stand by me in my time of darkness. But my darkness didn't have to be if I hadn't been blinded at what was standing right in front of me.

Men and women, I pray right now in the name of Jesus that you do not choose the path of giving up on your marriage. But that you would pray that God would give you the strength to stand up and fight and keep what belongs to you, your family! Your family was given to you by the Lord, so don't let anything take that away from you. If you ever allow this to happen, you don't want to know the pain.

I want to take this time to apologize to all of my family and friends that were hurt through this awful time for all of us, I thank you all for all of your thoughts, prayers and for helping us get through this. Most of all, I'm so sorry for putting my wife through what she had to walk, and I am so grateful she was a warrior and was faithful to me and Jesus. Jesus forgive us, we don't know how evil our hearts can be. I will never judge another again, that is truly your job!"

Our precious friend Linh Vo, who is the personification of love and gratitude, has two incredible sayings, and when I read the first years ago, Dennis and I were amazed. "My life is a Haiku" says Linh and the beauty of this poet, and the healing he brings to our nation and its veterans is truly a "Haiku." When scanning Linh's site to email him for his ongoing permission to be in our book, my eyes rested on the following prayer... that says it all.

"Dear God, I have found peace within for I now know I am empty and meaningless without you. I love you; and in you I trust, always. Prayerfully, Linh D Vo"

So you might ask, why share all of this?

So you can meet the real King of Kings, and Lord of Lords,
Yeshua the Messiah
known by the name "Jesus" to the gentiles
He is alive... He is real...
He lives for the privilege of introducing you to His Father,
Yaweah!
The God of Abraham, Isaac and of Jacob.

&

So that those who know Him
will be encouraged to know
by the word of our testimony
that He is.... and He is a rewarder of those who diligently
seek Him!

Dennis carrying the cross in front of where the journey started after getting off the bus from Seattle, Wa.

Lightning Source UK Ltd.
Milton Keynes UK
UKOW05f0603290617
304289UK00001B/67/P